On the Border of Opportunity

Education, Community, and Language
at the U.S.–Mexico Line

ೞೞ

Sociocultural, Political, and Historical Studies in Education
Joel Spring, Editor

On the Border of Opportunity

Education, Community, and Language at the U.S.–Mexico Line

ℰᴑℂℛ

Marleen C. Pugach
University of Wisconsin–Milwaukee

LEA LAWRENCE ERLBAUM ASSOCIATES, PUBLISHERS
1998 Mahwah, New Jersey   London

Lawrence Erlbaum Associates, Inc., Publishers
10 Industrial Avenue
Mahwah, New Jersey 07430

Cover design by Kathryn Houghtaling Lacey

Library of Congress Cataloging-in-Publication Data

Pugach, Marleen Carol, 1949–
     On the border of opportunity : education, community, and
language at the U.S.–Mexico line / Marleen C. Pugach.
        p.   cm.
     Includes bibliographical references and index.
     ISBN 0-8058-2463-4 (alk. paper). — ISBN 0-8058-2464-2
(pbk. : alk. paper)
     1. Education—Social aspects—Mexican–American
Border Region—Case studies. 2. Mexican-American children—Education—Mexican–American Border Region—Case studies. 3. Educational anthropology—Mexican–American Border Region—Case studies.
I. Title.
LC191.8.M58P84   1998
306.43—dc21
                                                                98-22068
                                                                CIP

Books published by Lawrence Erlbaum Associates are
printed on acid-free paper, and their bindings are chosen for
strength and durability.

Printed in the United States of America
10 9 8 7 6 5 4 3 2 1

Contents

Foreword

Eugene E. Garcia
University of California, Berkeley

Educating children from immigrant and ethnic minority group families is a major concern of school systems across the United States. For many of these children, U.S. education is not a successful experience. Only 10% of non-Hispanic White students leave school without a diploma, whereas 25% of African Americans, 33% of Hispanics, 50% of Native Americans, and 66% of immigrant students drop out of school.

Confronted with this dismal reality, administrators, teachers, parents, and policymakers urge each other to do something different. Changes in standard educational strategies are needed, but will be meaningless unless these students are thought about differently. In order to educate these students, we must discover and rediscover their true identities. Thinking differently involves viewing these students in new ways that may contradict conventional beliefs.

This is particularly the case for educators and communities along the border, an extensive geographical region bordering the United States and Mexico and intellectually and empirically a significant social and economic zone quite distinct from either the United States or Mexico. This volume does much to explore this geographical, social, economic, and intellectual reality.

The U.S./Mexican border has always been a multilingual and multicultural place. Students from border families are often defined by the characteristics they share, such as a lack of English fluency. But such a definition masks their diversity and underestimates the challenge facing schools. Schools serve students who are new immigrants, ignorant of U.S. life beyond what they have seen in movies, as well as Mexican American students whose families have lived here for generations. Along with linguistic diversity comes cultural, religious, and academic diversity. Some students visit their home countries or regions frequently, whereas others are unable to visit at all. Some students have experienced excellent schooling prior to coming to the United States, some have seen their schooling interrupted by migration, while others have never attended school. Some are illiterate in their own language, and some have languages that were only oral until recently; others come from cultures with long literary traditions.

How can schools cope with the diversity presented by their students? Should they hearken back to the model of education developed in the early decades of this century to deal with the large influx of immigrant youngsters? At that time, educators responded to increasing cultural and linguistic diversity among their students by attempting to accelerate the assimilation into the U.S. mainstream. Their mission was to Americanize immigrants by replacing their native languages and cultures with those of the United States. Educators confidently sought to fit newcomers into the U.S. mold by teaching them the English language and literature, a sugar-coated version of U.S. history, and a respect for the U.S. political system and civic life.

Although some recommend a similar approach today, it is no longer possible even to describe U.S. culture with confidence, or decide into what mold educators should seek to fit all children. There is no single definition of U.S. culture; multiple definitions have been informed by ethnic minority voices. This is particularly true along the U.S./Mexican border. There is some evidence that assimilation may actually inhibit academic success. Studies of Mexican immigrants suggest that those who maintain a strong identification with their native language and culture are more likely to succeed in schools than those who readily adapt to U.S. ways.

Yet, these students will change U.S. society. Our society is not the same as it was a century ago, or even a decade ago, partly because of the different peoples who have come to our borders and beyond. The impact of an educator on the life of young people can hardly be overestimated. For children of a different culture and language especially, education has a tremendous impact; schools are their critical links to society. Without the caring guidance of educators, these youth of today will have great difficulty getting into college and becoming engineers, playwrights, or educators themselves and, serving as positive contributors to our social and economic well-being.

This volume touches the many aspects of how education is meeting this challenge at the border. It tells a particular in-depth story worthy of our attention as educators and members of the changing U.S. society. We can learn much from this story and others like it. Together they piece together a mosaic of meaning that is both painful and hopeful, at the same time illuminating and yet begs for further study. It is a worthy contribution to our intellectual and everyday efforts to live with the diversity among us.

Introduction

The *jornada del muerto* is the north–south route in New Mexico that was traversed by the Spanish in the 1600s as they made their way from old Mexico and Mexico City to the new center of activity in the north in Santa Fe. Its name, translated as "journey of the dead man," reflects a desolate and grim region that separates the southern part of the state from the northern. When most people think of New Mexico, they imagine Pueblo culture, silver and turquoise, centers of art, the Spanish heritage, land grant conflicts, the distinctive architecture that blends into the mountains, and the artists of Taos. Yet at the southern end of the *jornada del muerto* are communities that are distinguished chiefly by their proximity to the Mexican border but look more like their counterparts in Texas or Arizona. Their populations are primarily Mexican-American; agriculture and ranching, more than tourism, support the struggling economy; and the geography is less stunning than in the north. It is not the place most people visit when they say they are going to New Mexico. The mountains are not as high nor as green, there are no ski valleys, and the weather is hotter and more extreme. Although it holds its own kind of enchantment, it is not the same enchantment New Mexico boasts through its northern culture and geography.

This is the region in which Havens, New Mexico, the town whose schools and students are at the center of this story, is located. Havens is far from what has become the glamorous view of New Mexico. It does not boast the contested Spanish heritage of the dwellers of small northern villages whose residents often held land grants from the Spanish conquerors. It is a community lodged on the Mexican border; you can be in Mexico within 30 minutes by car. It is in Havens that I spent 7 months living, making lifelong friends as well as passing acquaintances, and working to understand the daily realities of life and education on the border.

Most of us who live beyond the border region know least about the daily realities; what we do know typically has been learned from the popular press in this country, a view that regularly portrays the border as a source of problems for the United States generally and for border communities specifically. Life on the border is clearly more complex; Havens is home to families who struggle on a day-to-day basis with the same things with which most families struggle: raising their children well and making sure they are well educated, finding and keeping jobs, balancing home and work. They also share struggles as a community: questioning who makes decisions and how those decisions benefit or penalize the community or parts of the community, supporting youth in a location that often lacks enough for them to do, fighting the isolation of living in a small rural area. Because the border so often has been misrepresented as a monolithic entity to those outside of the border region, few who live beyond its reach are likely to consider the obvious: It is from these day-to-day realities that life on the border is enacted, and there is a story here, rich in detail and complex in character, far more complex than simply seeing the border as one long, uninterrupted source of social and economic difficulty. Those who live and work in the border region of the two countries have to address concerns stemming from the vast differences in the social and economic conditions in Mexico and those in the United States. These issues must be addressed in the context of the lives people lead and the dreams and goals they have.

On the whole, there is still considerable confusion elsewhere in the United States regarding the political status of the state of New Mexico, so much so that *New Mexico Magazine* runs a monthly column entitled, "One of Our Fifty is Missing," which humorously chronicles stories illustrating how often New Mexico is mistakenly considered to be a foreign country, that is, part of Mexico. Amidst this general confusion and lack of awareness is the specific tendency to view the border generally as distant and strange. Border communities tend to be isolated from centers of activity to the north, not necessarily by an identified physical span of distance like the *jornada del muerto*, but surely by a psychological distance that results in a lack of knowledge and under-standing. They are seen as being worlds apart from mainstream activities in the United States.

In 1993, I set out to gain some understanding about school and community in this one small place, Havens, New Mexico—a place where I had the opportunity to be immersed in border culture, where I could learn how the border figured into everyday life, and where I could pay uninterrupted attention to the issues as they occurred in the personal and professional lives of those who taught in and administered the schools, and in the lives of the students who studied there. I moved to Havens with this singular purpose and with an understanding that no matter how much I was able to learn from those who made their permanent home in Havens, what I could learn—and represent in this book—would reflect my own idiosyncratic interpretation of the community and its schools.

It is this interpretation I offer in *On the Border of Opportunity*, an interpretation that is at once disciplined by the long hours, days, and months I spent in Havens and by the personal stance I, like any other researcher, brought to the study of this place and its people. The dilemma of conducting qualitative studies has festered in the past decade as scholars and activists in education and academia struggle with the question of who should tell which stories and with what degree of authority and credibility they can be told. This struggle is at its most strident when those who come to a place to learn cross cultural, racial, or ethnic boundaries and are placed in the difficult position of telling the story of others whose life experiences are not the same as their own. The question concerns not merely credibility, but the whole realm of societal and institutional privilege when the researcher is, as I am, a White, middle-class academic, and the people in Havens from whom I learned are mostly Mexican-American and often of a lower socioeconomic status. How dare I, the argument goes, attempt to represent the voices of those who are struggling to have their own voices heard, to say for the people of Havens what they are surely capable of saying for themselves? Is this not just another instance of the centuries-old colonial approach to field research?

The question is legitimate and the postmodern times demand, finally (and belatedly), no less than a deep and serious questioning of how studies of other places and people are conducted, what the perspective of the researcher is, and whether a researcher who is not a member of the group being studied should even attempt to engage in such field-work. These are crucial questions that cut right to the heart of a society that cannot seem to solve the problems of racial and ethnic inequity, cannot hear multiple voices clearly, and perpetuates institutional prac-tices that far too often fail to meet the needs of children and adults who are members of minority groups. So for me the question was, "Can I in good conscience conduct this study?"

I responded in the same way I respond to the question of who makes a good teacher in urban schools, which is the work I do at the university where I teach. In that context, the question that is often raised is, "Can anyone other than an African American be a successful teacher of African-American children?" "Can a White teacher be effective in an urban school?" These are really questions about the degree to which we believe that interaction across racial and ethnic groups is worthwhile and can contribute to reducing the inequity and lack of understanding that does exist. If we aim for only group-alike teacher–student relation-ships, we cut off an important source of learning across groups and reduce the likelihood of engaging in the deep dialogue that is needed to build sensitivity on the part of majority teachers. So my answer to the question of who makes a good teacher is, "Anyone who is committed to all the children they teach, to validating them, advocating for them, and creating classroom communities in which their students thrive and learn." It is in the relationship between the teacher and the child where the issue is played out.

In a similar manner, in conducting a field study on the Mexican border I had to ask myself whether I could or should attempt to tell the story that I found. As I thought about it, and continue to think about it when asked, my response is that as long as I had honest relationships with the people of Havens and learned to be more sensitive to border issues and issues in the Mexican-American community in Havens and across the border in Mexico, then my work was worthwhile. Furthermore, as long as I (a) acknowledged the perspectives and biases I brought to the work and the lenses through which I was likely to interpret what I learned, (b) use what I have learned in my own work preparing teachers in Milwaukee, which has a sizable Mexican-American community (and a larger Latino community as well), and (c) portray the issues so others can gain greater understanding of these same issues, then it has been a worthwhile effort. As such, this volume joins others, carried out and authored by Mexican-Americans and non-Mexican-Americans alike in building a body of knowledge about the border and how we might better understand it and act differently in relation to it in the future.

It is important to raise this issue because I have had several conversations with aspiring scholars in various doctoral programs who as European-Americans are hesitant to engage in the study of others, fearful that they will be appropriating someone else's story. They seem apprehensive, unable even to justify pursuing a serious interest. These are students who have broad life experiences, who are committed to building a more just society, and who in their daily lives live sensitively in multicultural worlds. I have been troubled by their hesitation in the same way I am troubled by those who believe that children can only be taught effectively by teachers who belong to the same cultural or racial and ethnic group as their students. There is no doubt that we need to increase the diversity of the teaching force to provide role models for all students and to enable teachers across racial, ethnic, and cultural groups to engage in cross-cultural dialogue; we must also prepare European-American teachers to work sensitively with whomever their students are. Similarly, we must be thirsty for field studies and interpretations conducted and written by those whose world we are interested in (and make sure such studies are supported and carried out), but we must also recognize that others are interested in and committed to understanding these phenomena—and that engaging in field study on site is a deep and life-changing way of coming to such understanding. Proximity, interaction, friendship, being hit in the face with the life and challenges others regularly encounter—this too is a crucial kind of learning.

And it is not just a matter of acknowledging and corralling one's subjectivity if one is studying another place, culture, or people and their dilemmas. Rather, it is a matter of bringing to the work a recognition of one's own place in society, one's own position of privilege, and a serious commitment to understanding the place one is studying—in this case, Havens—from a the broader societal context that emanates *from* the local perspective of Havens' permanent residents. It is a matter of taking nothing for granted, of constantly and consistently reaching inward to question oneself: *"How am I seeing this? How am I interpreting this? What am I failing to take into account? Who am I failing to account for?"* It is a stance of willingness to be taught, to step outside of one's predilections, to take a position of ignorance not in the service of qualitative methodology, but rather as a human endeavor in relation to building a world where the possibility of its being more equitable exists.

* * *

In the debates about privilege and voice, how to name racial and ethnic groups is an important part of the conversation. It is a constantly changing landscape. In describing people whose origin is one of the many countries or islands south of the United States, the term *Latino / Latina* is currently favored, denoting the broad and varied origins of Spanish-speaking people in this hemisphere. In Havens, the population that is not European-American is virtually all of Mexican origin. As I wrote, I found myself using the terms that the people of Havens used to describe themselves and the European-Americans in their community. These terms include *Mexican, Mexican-American, Spanish,* or *Hispanic.* One or two students used the term *American-Mexican* to denote their place of birth or residence and primary identification as the United States. Many times, individuals would move from one term to another in one conversation. I have also included the term *Hispano* to identify northern New Mexicans who, in contrast to origins in Mexico, see their Spanish heritage as dominant.

European-Americans were nearly invariably identified as *Anglo,* and occasionally as *White.* The term *Anglo* does not appropriately identify the origin of the European-American people who have lived in Havens over the years. Most came from Texas and did not talk much about their

European heritage. There were Czechs and Germans and a few individuals of Greek origin. All of these people were called *Anglo* because they were not Mexican. Merchants who had lived in Havens in the past and were Jewish were called Jews, and their national origins were ignored in favor of religious identification.

Rather than impose a different set of descriptors, a different language, I have instead relied on the students and community people to portray how they name themselves and their neighbors on a day-to-day basis. It is the terminology of the people with whom I talked and lived that I have tried to preserve in the interpretive portions of the book—and of course in the direct quotations from interviews. It is through their terminology and their language that I was able to learn about their lives, and it seemed inappropriate to use another set of terms, or use my time in Havens to force a conversation about the terms themselves. It was a conscious choice; this was not my purpose in being there.

* * *

Telling stories—this is what we do as the result of fieldwork. It too is a conscious choice, the telling of a particular story from a particular point of view. *On the Border of Opportunity* tells the story of Havens from the perspective of the present in all of its complexity, as a window, on what might exist in the future in this border community. This window on the future is defined not as an exercise in speculation, but rather stems from the commitments, desires, and concerns of people in Havens who wish to see their community remain stable and bicultural, and who, at the same time, are realistic about the constraints that exist. Telling stories is a matter of what frame one uses, and for me, it has been a matter of portraying Havens not in a singular way from a singular frame, but as a series of frames that coexist in the lives of its citizens and in the school lives of its children and youth. It has been the way I can do the most justice to the varied perspectives that exist in any community and that are complicated and enriched by a community lodged on the border of the United States and Mexico.

Chapter 1 begins with a description of Havens and its inevitable interdependence with its Mexican neighbors. In chapter 2, three "cultural mediators" are introduced, two students and one teacher from Havens High School (HHS). These individuals are highly conscious of their border-bound lives and work actively to mediate between their local and Mexican cultures. Chapter 3 lays out the language landscape in the community and in the schools, focusing on the relation between the use of Spanish and English. This is followed by a specific description of the development of bilingual education programs in the district in chapter 4. Chapter 5 introduces the social structure of the high school and describes the students' interactions across cultural lines. Chapter 6 presents an alternative metaphor for thinking about the border, and identifies markers of opportunity that already exist in Havens as it works toward defining what it means to be a bicultural and binational community.

*   *   *

I was able to learn about Havens chiefly because the people there were willing to talk with me and to accept me and my strange little entourage from the midwest. Barbara Seidl, then a doctoral student at the University of Wisconsin–Milwaukee and currently an assistant professor at The Ohio State University, came along officially as a doctoral assistant. In reality, without Barbara's perspective, intelligence, unfailing curiosity, persistence in asking hard and harder questions, and absolute commitment to equity, this work would have been very different. Unofficially, she became my children's adopted *tía*, their aunt in the absence of their father during our stay in Havens. My son, Lev Rickards, and my daughter, Anna Rickards—displaced from their friends, their schools, their home turf, and their father for several months, and the only Jewish children in Havens—took this temporary move in stride, made new friends, and learned to see the world from a different perspective. Each of their teachers in Havens smoothed the way, but I am especially grateful to Anna's third-grade teacher that year, who appears in this book briefly as Sally Mills, for the special climate of acceptance she established for Anna in her classroom at Jackson Elementary School.

One does not live in a place for 7 months without it making a profound impact on one's life, and my time in Havens was no different. My reference points have changed, my friendships have changed. Given these kinds of changes, it is frustrating to thank people in the absence of their real identities. I struggled with the convention of confidentiality (another methodological dilemma that requires attention) throughout my work in pseudonymous Havens and in the writing of this book precisely because I am beholden to each person who willingly helped me learn. None of their real names appear here. I am left to thank the people in Havens by their titles and by the groups to which they belong. The superintendent, the school board, and the entire administrative staff in the Havens School District opened the door and invited us to come in and learn whatever there was to learn. We did most of our work at HHS, where every door was open to us and each teacher, aide, administrator, and staff member—and of course, the principal—was willing to give us the time to hear his or her perspective and understand their concerns. Teachers and staff at all of the other schools in Havens—and in particular teachers involved in various aspects of bilingual education—made sure we had the full picture of language learning in Havens. Our special friends throughout were the students at HHS—those from Havens and those from Mexico alike—whose forthrightness, energy, and interest constantly challenged our emerging understanding of the school and the community. Their parents, the parents of my children's friends, as well as community members at large always took the time to meet with us, showed forbearance and goodwill in the face of our ever present tape recorders, and made sure we felt welcomed everywhere we went. It is not always the case that a community is as welcoming as Havens was and we were extraordinarily fortunate to be there.

How did that come to be in the first place? I knew that some portion of the sabbatical I would take in 1993–1994 would be devoted to learning about bilingual education. In a casual conversation in 1992, I mentioned this interest to Alan Peshkin. He was working at a site in the northern part of the state at that time and had visited Havens as a possible place for studying the border in New Mexico. But it seemed doubtful, he said, that anyone would be able to move to Havens. So he casually asked, "Want to go down there?" I, of course, was more than ready and began posing the possibility to my family and to Barbara Seidl, and the rest is here for the reading. I am indebted to Alan for introducing me to Havens and smoothing the often rocky path of identifying a place in which one can live and learn so well.

* * *

A book written alone is not written in isolation, and it was the consistent support of my dear friend, Corrine Glesne, and the wonders of e-mail that enabled us to communicate in a literal flash that spared me from total isolation as I wrote. Corrine read chapter drafts as well as the full manuscript. She provided a consistent source of feedback on both the writing and on my thoughts in progress about the study, and pushed me with her insistence that the task was not insurmountable. And when it was possible, we met in Vermont or hiked down to the Rio Grande near Taos or in the mountains above to talk some more about writing, Havens, poetry, and the challenges of doing qualitative research. It is a rich conversation without an end as we continue to puzzle over teaching our students to do qualitative research responsibly and well.

Others outside of Havens I can also thank by name. It must be inevitable that Naomi Silverman, senior editor at Lawrence Erlbaum Associates, befriends each author with whom she works; her track record in this regard is documented in every introduction or acknowledgment I have read where she has been the editor, and my experience is no different. Joel Spring, series editor for Sociocultural, Political, and Historical Studies in Education at Lawrence Erlbaum Associates, and Pamela Bettis of the Oklahoma State University insightfully reviewed the prospectus and the manuscript, and each helped strengthen this volume. At the University of Wisconsin–Milwaukee, Cathy Mae Nelson prepared the manuscript in her usual impeccable way and I am grateful to her for her highly skilled work. Marie Lewandowski in the School of Education kept us connected to the university during the long months of our absence. The study of Havens was possible due to the support of the University of Wisconsin–Milwaukee, which granted my sabbatical, and the Spencer Foundation.

When I proposed moving to New Mexico with our children for my sabbatical, my husband, Bill Rickards, who grew up in the west, said simply without blinking an eye, "Of course you should go," and eased into a life of commuting to Havens each month (getting there a feat in itself). Sometimes you look back incredulously on choices you make at another time in your life and say, "How did I ever manage to do that?" My work in New Mexico was possible because Bill was willing to keep watch over the Milwaukee part of our lives. More importantly, he believed this was important work.

There is a refrain in my thinking now that did not exist before I lived in Havens. It is at once a general refrain about life on the border and a specific refrain about the people I know who live there. Like any refrain, any well-ingrained tune, it can pop into my head unexpectedly, at any time of day. I cannot escape it, nor would I wish to. It is the reason I wanted to go to Havens in the first place—to understand a set of issues through the eyes of the people who live there, to build new understandings about the border in my own work, and to keep those issues central in my thinking and in my work. The refrain is there now because of the generosity of the people in Havens. *Muchas gracias.*

—*Marleen C. Pugach*

1

"But We're Not in Iowa, You Know"

People here like the adventure. They like the fact that they can take a vacation one afternoon and drive just 30 miles and be in a foreign country, *sort of,* and back again.

It's a Friday in mid-October. As usual, the sun is shining and the sky is a clear and striking blue—a jewel-like intensity that occurs only in New Mexico. There is no school today because it is the first weekend of the county fair and long-standing rural tradition, I quickly learned, holds that everyone is expected to participate in the Fair Day Parade. At 9 a.m. the streets are already packed, the temperature is already up, and people are vying for seats under the shade of the awnings fronting the many small shops along the parade route. My daughter, decked out in an old-fashioned dress and straw hat, is riding on her school's "School in the Past and the Future" float. Everyone in town seems to be there; it's a time to strut Havens' stuff. Military veterans are out in full uniform. The high school band plays, accompanied by cheerleaders and dance team members performing their routines. Despite the heat, Future Farmers of America club members march wearing their regulation dark blue cordu-roy jackets, complete with insignias. Miss Teen-Age New Mexico candi-dates, the local chile queen, the adult literacy project, the gymnastics team, church service clubs—whether they are marching or riding, every-one is smiling and waving gaily. In small towns all over America, whether it is for the Fourth of July, Memorial Day, or Fair Day, all the stops are pulled out for such parades and Havens is no exception. Sirens blare from the long and impressive line of official safety and law enforce-ment vehicles as they pass through the town's only traffic signal on the main drag: fire engines, ambulances, the state police, the Havens police, the sheriff, and, as usual, the green and white Border Patrol trucks. It's a real community celebration.

* * *

1

Anglo and Mexican people have lived together in Havens, New Mexico, for more than 100 years. During that time, the border has been mostly inconsequential as the citizens of this community cross back and forth in the conduct of their daily lives. The physical proximity of the political line, regularly represented by the presence of border patrol officers taking their morning breaks in local coffee shops or filling up their trucks at local gas stations, is neither treated nor perceived as something unusual. On the contrary, it is simply part of the landscape. Since the time when the community was founded in the 1880s with the advent of the railroad, its inhabitants have lived a quiet, unassuming binational life.

On a day-to-day basis, people cross the border in Havens exactly like I crossed the street from Englewood to Teaneck, New Jersey, as a child—without much thought and without much complication. They step over the line at the Frontera checkpoint, a short drive away, where in 1990 more than 600,000 northbound crossings were registered and more than 250,000 vehicular crossings were logged.[1] On a monthly basis, individual crossings average about 50,000. Informal local analyses indicate that people cross the border from Frontera to commute to work in the United States, or they make the trip both from Havens and Frontera to shop—either in the United States or in Mexico. Compared with the traffic in a major border area like El Paso, where more than 3 million individual crossings a month are logged, travel here is light.

One of the most common reasons to enter Mexico from the U.S. side is to shop at the local pharmacy. People ride south to get haircuts and go to the dentist or the orthodontist. Although U.S. citizens rarely travel to Mexico for daily employment, the rural agricultural and ranching character of the area means that the border checkpoint is regularly host to cattle crossings and the transportation of agricultural goods. Farmers, ranchers, and merchants in Havens depend on Mexican business for at least a portion of their profits—the figures reported informally hover around 40% to 50%. There is an immediate payoff to good binational relationships.

But crossing for work or commerce is only one part of the story. In reality, like their counterparts all along the southwestern United States from Brownsville–Matamoros to San Diego–Tijuana, people in Havens—and their neighbors in Frontera—live in a perpetual cycle of crossing, going back and forth as need be to see family, to attend social functions, to find entertainment, and to make professional connections. It is an old pattern of behavior for Anglo and Mexican people and one that has existed for as long as anyone can remember. "We knew a lot of people in Frontera then," Lydia Silva began, as she described growing up in Havens in the 1920s. A gracious and talkative silver-haired woman in her 80s, Lydia and her husband, Roberto, had lived nearly their entire lives in Havens. Lydia was born not far from it on the U.S. side and was among the first Mexican students to graduate from HHS. Throughout her marriage she has lived on the "Mexican" side of town in the same pink house on Socorro Street that borders the local barrio in Havens.

> We had family there [in Mexico], and I had a lot of friends there. The Anglos knew a lot of people too. The Oldtimers Club, I bet you didn't know that started in Frontera. There used to be a bar in Frontera and they would go. The big building you see when you enter the gate [at the Mexican port of entry] used to be called La Caracas, and they had a big dance hall. I used to go dancing there when I was 13 or 14 years old with my cousins. They would take us to the dance hall and oh, did we have a ball. Sometimes we would go for the fashion shows that Leticia put on every month. We didn't even think twice about it.

These festive social gatherings were regularly reported in the Havens' *Star*, the local newspaper; in fact, in the 1960s, Leticia herself, who was a Frontera resident, wrote a column that was published weekly—always accompanied by a large, formal photograph of her.

From the U.S. and Mexican sides alike, people cross to and from the United States or Mexico to visit their families, some each weekend and some only for holidays. If the families in Mexico do not live in Frontera, they might live in one of the small farming cooperatives, or *ejidos*, along the east-west road just inside Mexico, or south along the main Mexican highway in a *colonia*,* or in one of the larger cities or ranches 1 or 2 hours away. Some Mexican people come to work each day in the United States but live on large ranches in Mexico; others are day laborers who are poor by any standards and come to the United States chiefly to pick chile and work in the onion sheds—the agricultural mainstays of southern New Mexico that require hand labor. During the harvest, workers are transported on the labor contractors' buses that leave from just inside the U.S. line each morning. Each evening these workers return to their families. Anglos who are Mexican citizens can be found living close by in a Mormon community in Mexico but they have family in Havens. During the winter they often come to town on Tuesday or Saturday nights to attend basketball games in the HHS gymnasium.

If there is a family wedding in Mexico, relatives on the U.S. side will make the trip for the day or for the weekend. Tourists of Anglo and Mexican origin drive south to see archaeological ruins; if they have

---

*Farming community.

family on "the other side," they may combine their visit with a quick meal with relatives. When there is a *quinceañera*[*] in Frontera, students at HHS know about it well in advance and are likely to attend the celebratory dance held on the evening of the ceremony. Frontera's small size means that if you tell the Mexican border guards that you are coming to the *quinceañera*, they know exactly whose it is and ask if they can dance with you there later that evening.

Most of the day-to-day border crossing is done quietly and on a noninstitutionalized basis. No fanfare accompanies its occurrence, you will not read about it in the *Star* and no one much pays attention to it. What does receive regular public notice are charitable, social, cultural, or salutary cross-border events. When a local church helps establish an orphanage in Frontera, it is front page news. When a local dance teacher holds a monthly class for a school 1 hour into Mexico, there is a reporter on the scene. A local Anglo politician receives an international award for decades of work fostering cross-border relations and it is a front page headline for 2 days. The cast of a play is binational and it is also news. The Havens branch of a national service club establishes a private school for children with disabilities in Mexico in collaboration with the local Mexican branch of the same club and it is a lead article accompanied by a page of photographs of the first binational visit to the school:

> Once the handicapped children of this Chihuahuan agricultural city were locked away out of sight. Today, through the collective efforts of service clubs here and in Havens, the children have a school of their own. The Escuela Rotari opened in 1991 after three years of work by members of the Havens and Frontera rotary clubs. It is the city's first special education school.

These charitable efforts tend to be shepherded by individuals or social and service clubs and the public display of interest parallels similar displays in other small communities that rightly view their own local good works as newsworthy. Otherwise, the everyday comings and goings across the border are not recorded formally, nor are they particularly noted by the townspeople.

From the U.S. side, it is precisely because Havens is a small, isolated rural community that traveling to Mexico represents another option, a mild form of entertainment where such diversions are rare, just as it did

---

[*]Chiefly Mexican and Catholic rite of passage for girls on their 15th birthday; usually an extremely formal pull-out-all-the-stops celebration. The classic celebration includes several attendants—males and females—who are peers of the girl whose birthday is being celebrated, as well as a group of younger girls who often distribute small mementos. All are dressed in matching, formal attire.

when Lydia Silva was growing up. If one stays in Havens for the evening, one of the only possibilities is having a meal at one of the restaurants along the main thoroughfare, a road that seems to exist primarily in order to link the interstate exits leading to Havens. The only movie theater in town is small, worn, and poorly attended. There are few cultural events; an occasional concert by a local outside performer might occur once or twice a year. As a result, a real night out means one must take a drive in any direction, and Frontera is one of the closest alternatives by far. In fact, it is closer than most other out-of-town locations. Although there are no longer weekly dances, Mexico is still a draw. "You know," a teacher told me,

> If you want to eat out you can drive to El Paso or Las Cruces, or instead you can just go to Frontera, 30 miles, go down there have a good time, eat, and come back. It's fun, it's a chance for us to get away. There's also a disco there every Sunday night, and I'll bet you there's 50 kids from Havens that go down there every week.

The community theater south of Havens puts on a play at least twice a year, and local people can be found at dinner in Frontera before the theater; some of the actors are from Frontera and their families are avid members of the audience. Although there is general agreement that Frontera has lost its previous glamour, the flow south is unmistakable.

In addition to these comings and goings, and for as long as anyone can remember, students from Mexico have traveled to Havens to attend school. Like frequenting the dances at Leticia's and making visits to relatives, children from Mexico have crossed the border to get an education in Haven for decades. This is a one-way relationship noted as early as 1949 in the minutes of the Havens School Board. Historically, students from Mexico have attended in small numbers and at times they have been required to pay modest tuition. They have come because their parents want them to learn English and thus increase their chances for success. After graduating, many border-crossing students stay in Mexico and make their lives there; others move to the United States permanently and make their mark in Havens and elsewhere. Much is made of former Mexican students who have subsequently made it in the United States, who now contribute their fair share to the U.S. tax base, who are giving back the schools' investment in their education. Similar to other local binational practices, crossing the border for educational purposes has been considered an agreement among neighbors, a family matter rather than a political one. Life is lived on both sides of the border here; binationality is nothing new. It is been practiced for more than a 100 years.

Going to Mexico: An Interlude

Wednesday (during an interview)
Marleen: "Do you or your family go to Frontera often?"
Ricardo: "Nah, we never go."

Thursday (in between classes)
Marleen: "I was down at the bakery in Frontera yesterday after-
noon. I ran into your brother and your mom."
Ricardo: "Oh, yeah, I guess they go down sometimes."

Ricardo Herrera is a senior at HHS, an average student, a star football player, and what his classmates would consider a regular guy. He is polite, on the quiet side, and is always ready to help when you run into him at his job in one of the local supermarkets. He is a first generation native of Havens who lives with his mother and brother. In Ricardo's case, it is not that he is unfamiliar with the lifestyle of his older brother and mother while he is at school; his is a close-knit family. They keep tabs on his schoolwork, watch him play football on Friday nights, cheer for each touchdown he makes, and attend church together each week. Nor did Ricardo seem to be intentionally masking his family's routines. He readily shared stories of driving deeper into Mexico each summer at vacation time to visit with his mother's family. To Ricardo, the lifestyle in Mexico, sitting outside in the evenings, the warm feeling that seeing family brought, the opportunity to compare notes about school and adolescent activities, the jokes about his forgetting too much Spanish, all of these are important parts of his experience there. But going to Frontera just isn't a big enough deal to talk about; whether the *pan de huevos* * or *bolillos* ** come from Lopez's bakery in Havens or Garcia's in Frontera is mostly inconsequential, and definitely less important than making sure they are there for the eating (although obviously it made a difference to Ricardo's mom). If the physical act of crossing the border was fit dinner conversation, in many homes in Havens few other topics would make it to the table.

This is the border as I learned to see and experience it during the months I resided in Havens. I learned that when I was in Mexico, I might run into a principal from one of the schools in Havens having lunch with his wife, or Ricardo's brother and mom, or a teacher's aide who works in the Havens schools but lives in Frontera, or a local Mexican student who attends HHS. In Havens I might see a teacher from the *primaria* *** in

---

*Varieties of sweet rolls or plain rolls.
**Rolls.
***Elementary school.

Frontera or a waiter from the town's newest restaurant. I went to Mexico to shop, to have dinner, to participate in a fledgling cross-border educational program at the local *primaria*, or to accompany a teacher from Havens taking students home.

Certainly it is possible to live on either side and never cross the border; if you are from Mexico but all of your family moved to the United States generations ago, you might not venture south. If you live in one of the towns to the north or the east and commute to Havens, the border might be too out of the way. Or, you might only go when out-of-town guests are visiting to show them the local sights. It is always possible to stay close to home. But every person who does not make the trip regularly himself or herself knows someone who does, and no one goes unaffected by these traffic patterns. On a day-to-day basis, the border is unmistakably what Gloria Anzaldúa calls "an unnatural boundary"[2] dividing politically what in many ways is a contiguous web of personal, filial, and commercial relationships. More pointedly, Sonnichsen's early observation regarding the decades just after the 1848 Treaty of Guadalupe Hidalgo,[3] which finalized most of today's borders, still holds true:

> The people on the left bank of a river were supposed to be American citizens, and their cousins a hundred feet away on the other side of a nonexistent stream were supposed to be Mexicans. Most of them paid no attention. They and their ancestors had passed and repassed the river at their pleasure for ten generations, and the idea of a "boundary" set up by a handful of gringos who had moved in only twenty-five years before was a little comic.[4]

Lydia Silva put it more directly during one of our talks: "We aren't immigrants like other immigrants. We didn't cross an ocean and we didn't leave our land behind. This is our land." The romantic notion of leaving one's home with only a suitcase in hand, never to see one's family again, of crossing the ocean and finding relief and welcome at the sight of the Statue of Liberty, has never been the case here, as others have noted:[5]

> Anglos and Hispanos have fought and quarrelled along the border as only close relatives can quarrel; but they have not faced each other across a fixed boundary with the sullen and undying enmity that the Germans and the French have faced each other across the Rhine. Borderlands unite as well as separate; they make for fusion rather than total acceptance or rejection.

Traveling to Havens from Frontera and back does not involve crossing the Rio Grande; the border literally exists as a line in the sand of the

Chihuahuan desert, a political boundary amidst the borderless miles of tumbleweed, yucca, and mesquite. Daily life attests to this interdependence in Havens, extending well beyond relationships between Mexican people who may find themselves on either side of the line and Anglo people as well. Rather than living on two sides of a line, human behavior and interaction more readily suggest living in a single shared region.

* * *

Its proximity to the border has left an undisputable imprint on Havens. Demographic trends indicate that the population in Havens of Mexican origin is growing and nears the 50% mark; in the schools, the statistics are closer to 70%. The majority of Mexican people have either lived in the region for generations (remember, this part of the country *was* Mexico not long ago) or came up from the south. A much smaller group migrated from the northern part of the state generations ago and have lived and ranched close by "up on the river." These few families count themselves among the old Spanish families of New Mexico who often call themselves "*Hispano*."[6]

Patterns of interaction among Anglo and Mexican people have shifted over the decades. In the 1950s and 1960s, it was almost unheard of for Anglo and Mexican youth who attended the schools to date one another; one of the most popular stories Havens' longtime residents tell is what is heralded as one of the first modern intercultural marriages that took place more than 30 years ago between the daughter of a well to do Anglo rancher and a young Mexican man. The impression of that social milestone remains deeply felt. Today intercultural dating and marriage have become a common occurrence and such unions are routinely announced in the newspaper. As a result, Anglo people, who years ago never gave a second thought to the physical, political, or social limits of their lives have newfound reasons to cross the border: to visit the families of their sons and daughters-in-law or to see their mothers and fathers-in-law. Anglo teachers whose spouses are from local Mexican families might move here to take jobs so they can see their relatives in Mexico. Some Anglo spouses-to-be see learning Spanish as an essential part of their prenuptial commitments. How else would they be able to converse with their in-laws?

When the citizens of Havens talk about their community, few express animosity toward the border. In fact, many are quick to make a distinction between the stereotypical notion of a border town as a wild, seedy, uncontrollable, and crime-ridden place[7] and their own hometown. It was important that we, as outsiders, understood this distinction well: Havens was different. It is a border town by virtue of its location and its interdependence with Mexico, it is a border town because of its population, which is increasingly made up of people of Mexican origin; and it is a border town because of the frequency with which one hears Spanish spoken. Materially, proximity to the border is visible primarily in the prevalence of Mexican restaurants (reputedly among the best in the southwest) and the stock in the aisles of the local supermarkets, which includes buckets of lard for making *frijoles** and *biscochos,*** a rich array of fresh chile when it is in season, and racks and racks of locally made tortillas. Each August during the chile harvest, large steel drums turned makeshift roasters appear on the corners of sidewalks so the local population is assured of being able to roast and freeze enough green chile to last the year. A sole sign on one of the interstate exits notes the access to the port of entry south of town. These constitute some of the external indicators that Havens is not like other American small towns and that the border is close by.

It is undoubtedly a border town of another stripe, however, different from the rest, and the distinction is obvious to Sally Mills, an elementary teacher in her late 50s whose entire career has been played out in Havens:

> One of the things that is unique about us is the closeness to the border. There are lots of other places close to the border, but we've accepted that closeness and we've intermixed with the people in Frontera and they are our friends, they're our relatives there. There is less friction here than in other places. People come and go quite easily. It's a way of life around here. And I think another unique thing might be, although it's not as strong as it used to be, the family aspect is still quite strong, the reaching out and helping the neighbor is strong especially with the people who have grown up here, lived here a long time. So you know, it's a community.

A Mexican counterpart of Sally's from high school, Juan Martinez, a Havens native who planned to retire in the year following our stay, described it this way:

> We're basically a friendly group. We're nestled down in kind of an isolated area close to the Mexican border, and probably we don't consider it to be as bad as, like, El Paso would be. To us El Paso is a *real* border town. But I don't really consider Havens to be a border town because it's not anything like a border town would be as far as corruption or being a big old rat race. It's a nice, quiet little town. People here are not in a big hurry. Driving

---

*Refried beans.
**Cookies.

down the road, they wave and say hi to you. You don't have all those problems that big city people have. You can still trust people around here. And it's easy to go to the mountains, to the big cities, to Mexico.

Repeatedly Havens was billed as the quintessential American rural town and paid the highest form of compliment: It is a good, safe place to raise kids. You can let your children run all over the bleachers in the football stadium on Friday nights and know that someone will look out for them. You can wave hello to drivers who pass you on the way into town and they will always wave back. As soon as it is known that a teacher has a major illness, an enchilada dinner is organized to help pay the bills and it is announced where everyone can see it—on the electronic display outside of one of the town's two banks. It's the kind of place people leave and then often return to, despite the fact that they never thought they would; its down home quality is a draw. On returning to his hometown with his family after several years away, Gary Cardoza, who worked regularly with the juvenile justice system, said, "If I fall short on my parenting in any way, I don't want the city to be the straw that broke the camel's back." Drug use is infrequent, although drug traffic decidedly is not. Havens has certainly not been spared increases in crime and gang-related activity, but by most metropolitan standards it is quieter. People in Havens are good at being neighborly; there is a genuine feeling of care.

Randy Weston, a veteran high school English teacher and the father of two grade school children, came to Havens from the midwest 20 years ago.

> I like Havens. One of the reasons I stay here is because I like the small town atmosphere. And for the most part, it's a pretty trouble free community. We don't have any real major problems where I worry very much about the safety of my children. And I think the school district is a good size in that the students are not just numbers, that you still have the opportunity here through athletics, clubs, organizations and things to really make an impact on what happens in the school. I've been told by lots of people that this is a real small town, that there's nothing to do here. But the town I grew up in Kansas had three hundred people, so Havens seems like it's a pretty big town to me.

Few were shy about uncovering the town's failings, but there was usually a lack of bitterness about them. Nearly everyone complained about the limited shopping opportunities, mothers and retirees complained about the lack of high quality medical care, teenagers spoke of being bored, parents complained about the lack of enough real cultural opportunities. The range of jobs was limited, so young adults were often encouraged to leave so they could pursue better opportunities. The most serious failing was that discrimination continues to exist against people of Mexican origin. But among Mexican-Americans in Havens, its existence is often compared with points east in New Mexico (much of which is called "Little Texas") and Texas itself, where those who might experience overt discrimination on a daily basis in places like Roswell, New Mexico, or El Paso, Texas, do not feel the same kind of pressure in Havens. In Havens it was not as overt; no one would treat you badly in public, in a shop or a restaurant. Things were "getting better," they were improving, but very slowly. The current mayor is Mexican-American, the school superintendent and, several successful shop owners are, and a balance is being sought in the staffs of the schools and in civil service positions. Local people do not so much accept the situation as they are usually patient with it; incremental improvements are considered better than no improvements, and it is best, local practice says, to continue to be neighborly and friendly, and work within the system to make gains, however slow that approach might be. Despite these developments and shifts in family relationships as a result of decades of intermarriage, power in the community continues to rest mostly with the Anglo population.

The territory surrounding Havens is a flat of land that smooths out beyond the mountain ranges rising west of El Paso. The mountains are visible in all directions; sometimes they are sporadic, sometimes they are a whole local range, and all are inhabited by snakes, roadrunners, and toads. The mountains provide a backdrop for the spectacular sunrises and sunsets New Mexico is famous for and that gives any town here a sense of charmed beauty. Most people reach Havens by exiting the interstate highway that connects such solitary towns all along the southwest border region—towns that first became viable when the railroads laid tracks and began to transport goods west on a regular basis near the turn of the century.

Like its small town personality, there is also a small town feel to Havens. Most businesses and the small array of motels are located on the main strip that parallels the interstate; cliques of ranchers, farmers, or businessmen, nearly all in Stetsons and boots, can be found each morning at coffee shops attached to a motel or at one of several freestanding Mexican restaurants. Fast-food places fill the niche for the town's hungry teenagers who are free to leave their school at lunchtime; only Taco Bell seems to be missing from the bright neon displays sealing Havens' membership in the national queue of McDonald's, Dairy Queen, Burger King, Pizza Hut, Long John Silver, and whatever other popular haunt was slated to open as time went on. Next to these busy places one might find an abandoned motel or a closed gas station, or a busy auto supply shop, printing shop, or convenience store. One of the town's three supermarkets is located here, and each weekday at about 5:00 p.m., busloads of day laborers who are contracted to work on the local farms arrive in the parking lot to make small purchases—often a cold beer—before returning to Mexico. Their presence at the market is a source of some conflict.

Businesses not located on the strip are housed on the wearier-looking main street that intersects with it at the town's main traffic light. Three or four large, empty brick buildings speak of a richer time past: an empty department store with the name "Jordan's" carved on top in stone, the old Havens Bank, slated shortly for rehabilitation, a hotel nearby, an old movie theater partly turned dress shop. Today a series of small, family owned stores make their way selling jewelry, greeting cards, clothes, videos, office supplies, books, and fabrics. The two main banks and public services offices are also located here. A small shopping mall to the south includes a supermarket, a variety store, a beauty shop, a video rental store, and a hardware store. Little wealth is evident. Per capita income hovers around $8,000 per year; a quarter of the population lives below the poverty level. It is by no means an affluent community. Few are wealthy by eastern, or for that matter, by northern New Mexican standards.

Conventional beliefs about the southwest, and New Mexico in particular, would suggest that the architectural style might be adobe and wood, natural and flat-roofed. In contrast, in Havens the houses more look like those lining a street in some of the less flashy parts of southern California. In the downtown area, they are small, conventional-looking bungalows—ranch houses—with an occasional large brick home that had once belonged or still belongs to one of the town's "oldtimers." Surrounding the downtown are a series of newer neighborhoods with houses in small developments grouped on streets named after the towns of New Mexico, flowers, or trees. With the exception of some isolated houses and restaurants, few buildings suggest the architecture so prevalent in the northern part of the state. In the two neighborhoods that are primarily Mexican, homes are smaller; trailers and permanent additions extending out from trailers are not uncommon. One of these neighborhoods is the more stable, traditional *barrio* with single-family dwellings; the other has more trailers, more migrant worker families, and in some cases, no running water like many of the *colonias* just inside the U.S. border. In every direction there are active farms and ranches.

Churches dot many street corners, and it is either with pride or pointed, self-deprecating sarcasm that Havens is described by its inhabitants as a town where "there are more churches than bars." All the major Christian denominations are represented. There are two Catholic churches: St. Cecelia's is considered the "Anglo" church and St. Veronica's the "Mexican" church. Although some Mexican families now worship at St. Cecelia's, Anglo families are not often found at St. Veronica's. Fundamentalist and Pentacostal churches are increasingly common; Mormon, Methodist, and Jehovah's Witness congregations have newer and larger buildings than many of their religious counterparts. At nearly all churches one can find both Anglo and Mexican worshipers, although a few of the smaller, newer fundamentalist congregations are sometimes split along ethnic and linguistic lines.

Economically, Havens is a depressed community in a state that is among the poorest in the nation.[8] Traditionally dependent on farming and ranching, it now also boasts a growing retirement community. Some see this as its only hope for the future. There is virtually no industrial base here, although economic and industrial development are high on the agenda of the town's business leaders. Although the North American Free Trade Agreement (NAFTA) was passed during the time I lived in Havens, few were hopeful that it would have a boomtown effect on the local economy; small local business owners believed it would draw jobs to Mexico but of course hoped otherwise. Jobs here generally fall into three major categories: picking the local crops, which is work performed both by local and migrant families; governmental, civil service, and school district positions; and service jobs in the small, independent business sector, fast-food restaurants, or at one of the local supermarkets. Businesses are primarily family affairs and most hire only a few outsiders; the obvious exceptions are the supermarkets and K-Mart. Whether the agricultural and ranching basis of the economy should continue is a topic of some conversation; one cynical observer noted that without agriculture and ranching, as an economic base, there would be no reason for Havens to be here. He hastily added, "There's no reason now."

In this shaky economic environment, a growing number of Mexican-origin families are now moving up into the middle class; a much smaller number have always been there. Historically, wealth in this community has been apportioned by ethnicity—which almost always meant it has been apportioned by class. Bank presidents and vice presidents are Anglo and it is common historical knowledge that Mexican-origin people have had difficulty being supported in their attempts to engage in new business ventures. Successful farmers and ranchers may be of either Anglo or Mexican origin; the first mayor of Mexican descent has been in office for several years. School principals are evenly divided; the current superintendent of schools, Eduardo Rios, hails from one of the oldest and most successful Mexican-origin farming families in the area. Teachers may be of Anglo or Mexican origin, but those who assist teachers as aides are nearly always the latter. The economic extreme is represented by agricultural day laborers and migrant workers, who are virtually always Mexican, and the persistent Mexican and Mexican origin lower class. A good way to move up the class structure is for the husband in a Mexican family to work construction, which means being away from home for weeks at a time. The owners of the companies are invariably Anglo. Another way to move up is to save enough to buy a bus and become an independent labor contractor.

Elementary schools are scattered throughout the community. Due to long-standing housing patterns, some continue to be segregated de facto. The former line of demarcation along Socorro Street separating the Mexican and Anglo populations has ceased to be an inviolate border. Mexican and intercultural families have moved into formerly Anglo neighborhoods. These middle class neighborhoods are increasingly integrated, as are the schools that hold them together. But few Anglo people live in the two neighborhoods informally designated *barrios*. Although there is progress, it exists more along class rather than ethnic lines. In the past, only one or two old-time Anglo families lived in the traditional *barrio* and as a result of this arrangement, some of their children now speak Spanish fluently. Like the story of the first intercultural marriage, the experiences of these families and the fact that Anglo people successfully learned to speak fluent Spanish is another part of Haven's historical lore—told many times over by many different people, most of whom themselves never learned to speak Spanish.

Protected by its diminutive size and its rural flavor, this border region means to distance itself from its troubled counterparts, the ones that are featured prominently—and usually negatively—in the news and that are fodder for anti-immigration and protectionist politicians. Although there are people from Havens of both Anglo and Mexican origin who question U.S. border policy and believe it is too lax, on a day-to-day basis rancor is rare. One rarely hears comments like "Shut down the border," "Build a fence," or "Keep the Mexicans out." In fact, longtime, multi-generational residents make a distinction between those who embrace the town's historical, binational commitments and those who, by virtue of having recently arrived here from "back East," do not. These outsiders, who might hail from anywhere east beginning with New Mexico's neighboring Texas, are chiefly members of the growing local retirement community. Like any other small, isolated town with a set of well-entrenched norms, the norm of binationalism comes with the territory in Havens, and local people expected you to understand it and stand behind it. Your reluctance to do so brands you as an outsider.

There is a certain sense of pride among Havens' natives regarding the apparent strength of their relationships with their Mexican neighbors. But it is undoubtedly binationalism of a casual, neighborly sort, a set of relationships within which regional, family, and community dynamics have existed outside of any political or formal structure.[9] It is a condition of geography that most people readily accept. Havens' secluded location and modest size ultimately mean that few elsewhere have been interested in what goes on here. Local people conduct their lives as they have always done—along the way defining border policy for themselves in private and informal ways that suit their families, businesses, and social lives, and enacting a set of values based on the unremarkable fact that many lives are lived on both sides. In this way, they function much like the "street level bureaucrats" Lipsky[10] described, frontline social service and community workers who set informal policy in their day-to-day actions that may or may not be harmonious with formal policy or policy directions. Although others may have grand ideas about how lives should be lived on the border, in Havens, people are not so much setting policy as they are getting on with their lives.

Were it not located near the border, many aspects of how this community defines itself and what it values might not be dissimilar from life in any other small town. The features that make Havens a good place to live and raise kids do in fact characterize hundreds of small, isolated rural communities across the United States. For many, the relationships and responsibilities that have existed for so many years are a metaphor for living a life of rural civility. It is a genuine feeling of care played out in an array of personal relationships that are lifetime affairs. It exists despite deep economic and political inequities among those who live here. But in Havens these relationships *are* enacted across a political line and within a binational and bicultural context, and most of the qualities that differentiate it from its small town counterparts elsewhere in the country and that make it unusual exist *because* of its location. The border is its defining feature. It is not just a matter of being neighborly; it is specifically a matter of being neighborly across two cultures and an international line. This movement creates meaning and vitality; it makes life more interesting than life in other small rural communities; it broadens Havens' identity. As my friend Richard Logan, an English teacher at HHS, a fluent Spanish speaker, the brother-in-law of a Mexican-American woman, and an Anglo native of Havens, liked to say in our talks about the community, "It would be different if we were living, say, in Iowa. But we're not *in* Iowa, you know. We're 30 miles from the Mexican border." To him, this accounted for not only the difference, but also for the demands, the challenges, and the responsibilities that Havens faces. These stem from a complexity that transcends the fact that the border is unimportantly ever present, that it is crossed and recrossed daily, that it regularly figures into the way lives are lived. It is not *just* a matter of getting along. Instead, it is a matter of getting along across ethnic, language, and socioeconomic lines that exist *in relationship to Havens' proximity to the border*. And as is so often the case, it is in that commonly held institution, the schools, that these challenges, opportunities, and responsibilities are first played out, and where the creativity to address them is most required.

* * *

I came to Havens to study its schools at a time when Havens was in the midst of a transition from being an informal binational community to one seeking to create a more formal educational and cultural framework for local binationalism in the schools. I embarked on this work as a fledgling scholar of bilingual education seeking to understand the local educational and sociocultural dynamics that were governing the district's efforts. With the luxury of a sabbatical from my university post in hand, I moved to Havens in August of 1993 with my daughter and son (then 8 and 12, respectively), I enrolled my daughter in a third-grade class at Jackson Elementary School and my son in seventh grade at Havens Junior High School, and began to learn how the schools were enacting this transition and what it meant to people in Havens, in the schools, across the community, and across the border.

We lived just outside of the city limits proper, in a relatively isolated rural area between a set of railroad tracks and a main north–south artery that led to Mexico in the south and to mountains and mining country in the north. The elementary school my daughter attended included Anglo and Mexican-American children and a staff that was bicultural as well. Historically it had been primarily a school for the children of Anglo farmers and ranchers, one whose attendance area neatly bypassed one of the poorer areas populated almost exclusively by Mexican people and its *barrio* school, a policy that directly favored the larger ranching and farming families north of town. But in the past several years, as housing patterns became more integrated, so did Jackson Elementary. The district's sole junior high where my son attended school was the meeting place for all the children of the county; some had attended elementary school at one of two schools several miles south of town, even closer to the border, and for many students this was their first time coming to Havens proper for school on a daily basis.

Our house was surrounded by yucca and mesquite; our neighbors included two families who lived in three trailers well behind our own scruffy lot. Our neighborhood sported quail, roadrunners, toads, desert centipedes, and an occasional snake. We lived together in Havens from August through January, when Barbara Seidl and my children returned to Milwaukee. I stayed for 2 more months, moving into one of the many small trailers that ringed the town not far from the home we had been renting. Including visits prior to the study and those following my return to Milwaukee, I spent time in Havens over a 2-year span.

Like those who live there permanently, I too found Havens to be an affable place. We arrived as strangers, but were welcomed as warmly as family. Doors were open for conversation in the schools, the stores, the restaurants, the library, and in people's homes. On both sides of the border people were willing to share their food, their recipes, their celebrations, and their perspectives on the local situation. Thus we were invited to *quinceañeras* in Mexico, to First Holy Communion at St. Veronica's, to graduation parties, and to the *posadas*[*] in town and on the border at Christmastime. Toward the end of my stay, when I had finished eating a solitary meal at my favorite Mexican restaurant and was ready to pay the bill, I found that a local businessman who was there with his family had already taken care of it. This kind of generosity was commonplace and was an important reason people born in Havens returned. They were willing to overlook its shortcomings to be in a community where actions like these were the norm.

I was not a stranger to the southwest before I moved to Havens. I had lived in Los Angeles for 8 years in the 1970s and had been an elementary school special education teacher in Culver City, a community that had a growing population of Mexican origin children as well as a long-standing Spanish immersion education program. I had traveled to northern New Mexico periodically and had driven across Arizona and south into Mexico to some of the smaller villages. But I was a total stranger to living in a small, rural community and especially one this close to the border. I did not speak Spanish when I began to think about this fieldwork, so I studied for a year prior to my departure. By the time we moved west, I was comfortable holding basic conversations, and had a good working vocabulary, but was by no means fluent. When I interviewed students from Mexico who had not yet acquired English, student translators often assisted me. When I visited with families of students

---

[*]Procession re-enacting part of the Christmas story.

who attended school in Havens but lived in Mexico, I was fortunate to be able to rely on an instructional aide who lived in Frontera but worked in a Havens elementary school. My Spanish improved significantly during my stay, and I continued studying with Ana, the mother of a junior at HHS and a native of Mexico City.

The fieldwork we conducted centered mostly on HHS, which houses Grades 10, 11, and 12. At this level the students of Havens were together at a time when they were making important decisions about the next phase of their lives; HHS was a microcosm of the community during this transitional time for its students. Although we interviewed teachers, administrators, and parents from throughout the school district, the students we came to know best were all high schoolers. We talked with students in all three grades and interviewed some 50 of them in depth. This group included those who were natives of Havens of several generations—both Mexican and Anglo, new immigrants, and those who crossed into the United States daily to attend school and returned to Mexico each evening. We interviewed nearly every teacher at HHS, its administrators, several former and current central administrative personnel, and nearly every bilingual education teacher in the district. We attended classes, faculty meetings, and extracurricular activities at HHS. We were willingly among the teams' faithful supporters at football, basketball, and volleyball games; we went to dances and pep rallies and club meetings; we attended school board meetings and community meetings that centered on youth and on issues related to the town's sizable migrant population. We participated in all of this with the schizophrenic attachment–detachment that is the special lot of resident field researchers: participating fully yet knowing you are watching and listening to events in a way that only some of the permanent residents themselves might also watch and listen. It was from these resident "watchers" that we probably learned the most about Havens; some were students at HHS, others worked in the schools, and others were community leaders outside of the schools. Because no other educational options exist in town (no parochial or other private schools operate in Havens), at some time past or present, most of the adults we talked with were also parents of children in the schools.

In all communities, the schools are the public crossroads. Like other small towns, the schools are the public measure of Havens' commitments and its values. Schools at the center of the community mean that they are supported wholeheartedly, but that they are scrutinized carefully, fishbowl-style, for how well they represent the community and its values. Historically, Havens' informal style of binationalism has been an important community value—and thus an important school value—one driven not only by economic necessity but by the belief that being neighborly is the appropriate and right thing to do whether one's neighbors live across the street or across the border. Because children from Mexico attend school in Havens, it is the school buildings themselves that are the most visible meeting places for those who live on the U.S. side and those who live down the road in Mexico. Historically, being neighborly in the schools has meant that it was all right for students from Mexico to attend as long as the numbers were small and as long as the existing system met the needs and expectations of all the students, including those who crossed the border. Operating under this limited definition of binationalism, the friendships that developed had long been considered an important measure of its success. For decades there was no deliberate cultivation of extensive programs to accommodate daily border crossers, or for that matter other legal or illegal newcomers.

As the school district moved toward dealing with the question of language and how to serve the whole population of its schools, the simple question of how to do this in a way that preserved the historical value of binational friendship as new resource and value decisions were made in a public and political arena (namely, the schools), dominated. And in Havens, the issue of how the schools serve students who come from Mexico and who in reality are daily "immigrants," is bound up with the question of how they serve students who more formally can be designated immigrants in the conventional sense—those who have come from Mexico to stay.

On the border, the concept of who is an immigrant exists along a continuum. From an historical perspective the Anglo settlers are in actuality immigrants; as a guest speaker at a required district-wide inservice noted, if nonnatives were asked to leave, most Mexican-origin citizens would stay because they were in fact the original inhabitants of the region. Within a contemporary framework, however, on one end are the second or third generation native U.S. children of Mexican families; in school, these are students who may or may not find school to be a means of getting ahead, may belong to the lower or middle class economically, and may speak Spanish, English, or a combination of both at home. The parents of first generation students may have become citizens or may be permanent resident aliens. Their English may be good, or it may not be so good. They may have "made it" economically or may still be struggling to get out of the poverty cycle. Their families may or may not value education; class remains an issue. On the other end are the daily border crossers, who might become legal or illegal immigrants in the future and who may or may not already be U.S. citizens, but who, for the time being, or permanently, are living in Mexico and commuting to school in Havens. A smaller number retain their Mexican citizenship but live with relatives in Havens—eventually to return to Mexico or stay in the United States. They may think the United States is a good place to stay in or may wish to continue to live in Mexico. For the time being, they are "just" neighbors who are attending school in the United States as a friendly gesture under New Mexico statutes. In between are a range of students who were born in Mexico but now live in Havens permanently, or others who roam from community to community in the United States as migrants following the crops.

As a result of this complex picture of who can be considered an immigrant on the border, once the schools publicly begin to deal with the question of what kind of context they wish to create for one set of "immigrant" students, the implications immediately go beyond how either conventionally defined immigrants or students who cross daily are served. Programs—and especially bilingual education programs—that are designed for "new" immigrants may also be appropriate for "old" immigrants whose language needs have never been met, or for daily immigrants whose educational goals may be immediate but may be disengaged largely from the question of citizenship or residence. Students with widely varying motivations for being in school may find themselves in the same classes, seeking the same goal with regard to learning English, on one level, but seeking an entirely different goal with regard to where and for what reasons English is likely to be used. When deliberate programs are enacted, they have the power to make the "immigrant problem" worse or better, to make the transitions immigrants experience easier or more difficult—and so, to impact the eventual success of the immigrants who pass through the classrooms. The implications for second and third generation Mexican origin students and citizens are clear-cut; it is not just the issue of immigrant strangers, but how society encourages or discourages interaction and human understanding. The context in which immigrants find themselves matters, whether it is in the schools, in the community—or both.[11]

As a former special education teacher, I always worried about the trend toward overidentifying students for those programs, and long ago I had learned to be extremely cautious about the marginalizing role any specially identified program can play in the schools. As a result, during my stay in Havens I was in a state of heightened awareness that it was much too easy to confuse language learning needs with disability as well as with socioeconomic class. I also knew that categorical programs in special education and in bilingual education had very different roots and served very different purposes—the first to support learning and behavior problems, and the second to build on the asset of a language other than English—and it was critical not to group the two together. But in Havens I quickly came to understand that when you are talking about special bilingual programs in communities along the border, yet another layer was automatically added to this already entangled situation: Just as language, culture, and class are not separate, in Havens, language, culture, class, and border and immigration policy are not separate. It was not a lesson I needed to look far to see or stay long to learn; once my interest in the schools was publicly noted, it jumped out in nearly every encounter, every interview, every passing conversation I had.

I arrived with my own personal commitments with regard to language. As a parent, there were things I hoped my own children would gain from this community during the time we lived there. These were things I would have wanted should we have lived there in the future. I wanted them to learn about Mexican culture and history and to learn to speak Spanish well. I arranged for private Spanish lessons to supplement my son's fledgling language classes at school and to give my daughter a chance to feel less strange around the language that many of her new friends spoke at home. I believed that the schools in Havens had a responsibility to develop strong bilingual education programs that included learning both Spanish and English. I believed it was important that the schools make no mistake about the value of the dominant American culture and the rich Mexican heritage held by so many of Havens' students. Not everyone I spoke with saw all these things as important. But I often talked with the parents of my children's friends about their own expectations and talked with the teachers as well.

What I learned in Havens I learned as a student of the individuals with whom I spent time—during informal and formal interviews, in the lunchroom, over chile rellenos at the Guadalajara restaurant. But I also absorbed what I was learning as a student of the Spanish language at a relatively tentative point in my ability to converse, as a professional worried about what was appropriate to teach all prospective teachers in preparation for fairly and equitably teaching students whose first language was not English, and also as the resident parent of two children attending the schools. These roles were not neatly exclusive ones. I fit them on at different times and they served as filters for how I understood Havens from the conversations, formal interviews, and observations in which we were immersed throughout our stay.

* * *

In the beginning, it was from the teachers' perspective that I gained understanding. I attended the first inservice in August 1993, a district-wide affair that was the traditional motivational kickoff for the coming year. The introductions of new staff and administrators allowed me an early glimpse into the demographics of the schools: both Anglo and Mexican people worked in all levels of the district. In this meeting we learned about new projects the district was involved in, and greeted the current superintendent, Eduardo Rios, who since the end of the last year had been acting superintendent and was now permanently installed in the position—the first Mexican-American superintendent in the history of the community and a native son of a local successful farming family that had lived in the area for several generations. By chance I sat next to Janet Otero, an Anglo teacher, married to a Mexican-American man, who voluntarily provided me with a running commentary on the changes in the district and the optimism everyone had about the fact that the superintendent's appointment had been made permanent. Eduardo had grown up in the district. He had been a teacher, a coach, and an assistant principal; his insider status was judged to be healthy for the district. He was one of their own made good. Eduardo gave a rousing kickoff speech about the dedication of Havens' teachers and the direct relationship between their work and the quality of the community. "If the teachers do right by the children, the community will be taken care of in the future. If the teachers do their job well, the community will continue to support the schools." The theme of community support dominated. He also reminded everyone about the challenges ahead, mentioning new assessment techniques as one important development. Throughout the speeches, introductions, and commentary, no mention was made of the special challenges associated with culture and language in the Havens schools: children were children, it seemed, and the teachers needed to do a good job with them all. The fact that bilingual education was expanding and that students from Mexico came to school in Havens each day was not on the opening agenda—not so much to hide its existence, because it was obvious, but rather because what actions to take, and what programs to support were still, as I quickly came to understand, contentious issues in the community. The choice at the start of the year was to avoid contentiousness and instead take a stance of unity. At that point, I *could* well have been in Iowa.

Throughout my work I kept returning to this contradiction. As I began to make the hard choices about how to portray what I came to understand about schooling and community in Havens, I struggled continuously with how to talk about what seemed to be on the one hand a public reluctance to acknowledge the challenges that surfaced regularly in conversation and observations, and on the other hand privately held opinions about what the options were as the district moved from informal to more formal binationalism. What story would I tell to honor the good intentions of so welcoming a community—in spite of this public reluctance? What stories would I choose not to tell?

* * *

Two days into 1995, at a time when I was deep into making sense of the interviews, field notes, and conjectures about Havens that had taken over my life, I tuned in to the *MacNeil / Lehrer News Hour*, a luxury that, as a working mother, I am only rarely afforded. On that show a panel of political observers, writers, and journalists were commenting on the issues that faced the country as the year loomed ahead.[12] The conversation inevitably turned to the "immigrant issue." Proposition 187 had passed in California's recent elections and the sting was being felt all over the country. I was angry about its passage in general and specifically about what it meant for the people I had come to know in Havens. "If they ever passed something like that here," my friend Carmina said, "they could begin stopping anyone with brown skin. My family has been here at least four generations. I can't bear the thought of any of us being stopped or anyone at all being stopped." Hers was one of the oldest Mexican-American families in town, her father was one of the first to own a large, successful ranch. During that same news show, Roger Rosenblatt, an observer of political phenomena in American life, commented that in the United States, "life is a continuous test of generosity" and that for the United States, the greatest test of that generosity is our variety. Perhaps nowhere was this town's generosity tested more than it was in the schools.

How a community defines its generosity on a day-to-day basis, when this generosity reaches its limits, and whether we are compelled to find ways to overcome those limits is the story I found in Havens. In many ways, it is a story of generosity not merely tested, but challenged, because daily relationships in Havens mean encountering not only people in the community itself, but people who live in communities on the other side of the border. This is a story about the role of schools in creating a life on the border. What happens when a community with a long history of informal relationships begins acting on them more publicly? How does a community navigate the shift from informal to formal relationships across cultures and language and across the border? What I observed was a community filled with opportunity, one that was honestly trying to figure out how to acknowledge that when the issue of immigrants strained the community, the distance between who was the "problem" and who was the "community" was not always easy to distinguish.

The story of Havens' transition exists against a well-acknowledged backdrop of discrimination toward Mexican and Mexican-origin people related to their long-standing role as laborers on the local farms and ranches. This is a tale all its own. As laborers, Mexican people sometimes arrived to work legally on a seasonal basis through a deal with agricultural interests known as the *bracero* program.[13] Many other times they arrived and worked illegally. The facts tell this particular story in Havens. More Mexican-origin people are in lower SES categories, more do poorly in school, more are victims of prejudicial behavior. It is a story of class discrimination as well as it is one of ethnicity. This story can be told in Havens as it can be told in communities across the southwestern United States, and led an Hispano state government official from the northern part of the state to throw his hands up in disgust one day and complain, "It's this damned plantation mentality." Yet telling the story from this perspective would mean portraying all Mexican and Mexican-American people here as victims, without much agency to change life in Havens. In reality, discrimination in Havens exists side by side with a slowly increasing power base among Mexican-American people in the community and an increase in bicultural families due to marriages between Anglos and Mexican or Mexican-American people. But the story of discrimination is never far from the surface and one that cannot be separated from the tale of the schools and their efforts to broaden their sense of binationalism.

As the country's attention moves more and more toward its southern border, Havens is faced with the opportunity to use its practical, casual version of life across the line and its cross-border rural sensibilities as a departure point for creating a life that is no longer only informally binational, but one that is deeply and insistently so. In the 1990s, the border has taken on a dark persona in the United States. All of the fears periodically or cyclically associated with immigration have surfaced and the choices seem forced by political grandstanding into simplistic, polar alternatives: either support immigrants or ask them to leave. Border towns have always experienced the heavy impact of immigrants, and especially of those who enter the United States illegally and tax the social services system—Havens as well. At the same time, those who live in border towns can readily recount stories of exemplary immigrants who are making it through the classic bootstrap dynamics that worked so well in the 19th and early 20th centuries—options that because of the current economic and labor context are becoming more and more rare.

Between these two extremes stands the question of how a community like Havens can create welcoming situations for its southern neighbors who live in Havens and remain Mexican residents, and those who immigrate permanently, while at the same time create structures that convey the message that being neighborly is more than just being nice. In the next generation, it will take much more than being nice to figure out how to live together. For against a backdrop of economic chaos in Mexico, a resurgence of political conservatism in the United States, the globalization of the economy, and changing economic conditions in Havens itself, it is human beings who are trying to figure out how, on a day-to-day basis, to build a life that comfortably and respectfully crosses the line.

2

Mediating the Boundary

For months we've been filming all over the border, the whole 2,000 mile stretch, and this is the only place I've been where people aren't angry, where everyone is civil and people seem to get along. It's the first time I've seen anything like it since we started this project. [filmmaker from El Paso]

Tradition runs deep in Havens and at HHS in particular. And the tradition is that of a rural American high school. Things have always been done a certain way and change does not come easily. As the demographics have shifted over time and as the border seems closer than ever before, individual students and teachers have begun to figure out how to mediate the cultural, language, and status shifts that are an inevitable part of a sound life on the border. These are personal accomplishments that enable individuals to make sense of the location in which they find themselves and negotiate relationships beyond the confines of their own ethnicity. Although everyone in Havens lives a life that bumps up against cultural and language differences, there is not uniform interest in sorting out what it means to live a binational life; not everyone has been successful in this, nor has everyone attempted to try.

Liliana Sanchez, Maria Cruz, and Richard Logan are among those in Havens who are interested in and who have thought about their lives in the context of biculturalism and binationalism. Their life experiences and their backgrounds differ markedly. Liliana, a senior, is the daughter of an immigrant who married a third-generation Mexican-American. Maria, a sophomore, was born in a small village in Mexico and illegally immigrated with her mother and her siblings at the age of 5 to follow her father to the United States. Richard, an English teacher, is Anglo; his great-grandfather moved to Havens in the 1880s and eventually helped build the first high school building in Havens. They are all bilingual. Liliana grew up speaking both languages, Maria learned

English on her arrival, and Richard learned Spanish in school and from his friends when he was a student at HHS. Although in the future they may not choose to stay in Havens, none is interested in leaving the southwest and all expect to live in this region. Each has given thought to how one might make sense of the relationship between the two cultures and the languages and how, on an individual basis, to mediate between the two.

As people who, on their own terms, have worked toward living a life that comfortably meshes these two worlds together, Liliana, Maria, and Richard are also people who try to bring harmony among the relationships between students at HHS. They have struck a balance between their native culture and their adopted culture in Havens. Although they have very different ways of acting on finding a balance and different levels of motivation for doing so, they have figured out ways to make their lives meaningful in terms of binationalism. They hold in high regard the need to honor both cultures and live in an atmosphere of mutual respect, irrespective of the various borders that others might define or use to separate people. Their understandings have developed naturally out of their lives on the border, and their roles as "mediators" have evolved as a natural consequence of the stance they take toward themselves, their peers, and their community.

They are people who intercede around issues of culture and language, and who—either deliberately or casually—make a point of crossing the interpersonal borders that exist in schools everywhere. In a school this size, and in a community this size, there are many such cultural mediators. Deciding to portray only a few of them means that I have chosen not to portray others who also played a role in forging strong interpersonal relationships across cultures and borders at HHS.[1] Some appear in this book, others will have to be imagined. Many have unrealized potential to be cultural mediators.

Liliana, Maria, and Richard exemplify individuals who, in different ways, actively move between the Anglo and Mexican worlds in Havens, if not physically, then certainly interpersonally. As students, Liliana and Maria have already made some conscious decisions favoring one culture or another, but have not done so at the expense of continuing to be bicultural. As a teacher, Richard has committed himself to providing opportunity and access to students within the realm of his own classroom and has made the issue of language more public in his work with the school newspaper. Perhaps more detail is appropriate.

Liliana was one of my closest friends among the students in Havens. As such, her perspective on life in the school was a constant source of learning for me. She was in the midst of making choices regarding culture, lifestyle, and values, and she was always willing to use our conversations as a sounding board for her own cultural decision-making and dilemmas. Liliana was close to the issue of immigration although she was not close to Mexico. Her active, public sense of pride about her Mexican origin coexisted easily with her self-identification as an American; she seemed to be comfortable and confident in and thoughtful about the choices she was making. And I never doubted that she would continue to protect and nurture her Mexican heritage throughout her life.[2]

Maria, on the other hand, had one major interest and that was the social scene at HHS. Classes seemed incidental to this interest. Despite her overriding social concerns, she had also given some very serious thought to her bicultural role. I was interested in the seeming incongruity, in the fact that all over HHS there were students who were very much aware of the transitions they and their families were making or had made—even if it was not apparent as they waltzed through the school checking on who had done what with whom the previous weekend. The fact that Maria's extended family was in a constant state of immigration and that she had taken on the role of mentoring her newly arrived cousin were serious issues, issues that seemed inconsistent with the more flighty, social self she presented in the hallways, in her classes, and in our conversations.

Teachers, too, have a powerful role to play in building bicultural relationships, in bringing cultural issues to the fore, and in modeling what it means to actively respect culture and language. Richard is one such teacher at HHS. We talked often about issues of equity in teaching, about where the power resides to make changes in a school, and about the day-to-day challenges of creating classrooms that support his students. Mostly I was drawn to the fact that Richard made space in his teaching life for students who were not the highest achievers, students who needed a break, students whose access to the good things in school was often limited. As one of the few Anglo teachers who was bilingual, Richard stood out in his capacity and willingness to communicate with many students and their families.

Liliana, Maria, and Richard are not power brokers; they are not responsible for setting school policies that might support the movement toward a more binational milieu. Instead they are day-to-day players who, by their individual and mostly quiet actions, work on the task of building positive relationships irregardless of national origin or of which side of the line one lives. Their varied stories are not uncommon here but they are also not common enough.

Liliana's Story

I met Liliana early in my visit to HHS. Short and slim with a crop of curly black hair and a shining smile that made you want to stay and talk with her for hours, she was at once thoughtful and energetic, active and introspective. Several teachers suggested she could easily provide perspective on the issues I was trying to understand. I first met her through her English teacher, Janet Otero.

Liliana was a senior who played in the band, was one of two drum majorettes during marching season, played in a musical group at her church, taught catechism at church, and was eager to attend one of the local state universities in the coming fall. She had been contacted by several high stakes Ivy League schools "back east" and talked about the possibility of transferring to one of them for the last 2 years of college—after her mother had gotten used to her being gone. Her teachers thought this was a very realistic plan. Whether she would feel comfortable going so far from home was another issue. Like so many other Mexican-American youth, the conflict between leaving and staying is prominent, not only pitting one generation against another, but also pitting individuals against the culture in which they grew up. This was Liliana's major concern—leaving the area where her family lived. By the time I returned for graduation she had received a full scholarship to the state university only a few hours away. She is the daughter of a immigrant mother and a third generation Mexican American father who was a former U.S. Marine; as such, she fits no uniform description as first or second generation. Her immediate and extended family all live in the barrio east of Socorro Street, in the part of town that historically is Mexican; she and her siblings attended one of the two elementary schools whose population is nearly 100% Mexican.

Liliana sat and talked with me as if we had been old friends for years. We visited often in the halls of the school, I ate lunch with her and her friends from the band, and spent time at her home with her family. We struck up a fast friendship as she explored what it meant to her to live a bicultural existence, and she willingly guided me in understanding her own life vis-á-vis her Mexican heritage, her relationship with students from Mexico, and life at HHS from this perspective as well. Eighteen months after graduation she married a young Anglo man, the son of a teacher in the school district. She interrupted her university education to do so and moved back to Havens as a young married woman. A year later she gave birth to her first child.

Liliana's story, in her own words, follows:

My father went to school in Havens and graduated from Havens High School. My mother was born in Chihuahua. She grew up around Juarez and lived most of her life in Frontera. She only went to school there in the *primaria* until fifth grade. She was raised by her aunt and uncle, and they believed she should go to work. She was living in Frontera and cleaning houses in Havens, and she met my dad when she started cleaning his cousin's house. Before all of this, she worked in the fields picking chile. She was quickly made head of the section she worked in. She learned English here, she got her GED, she got her citizenship, and now she works at City Hall in the planning department. These accomplishments are things everyone in my family is very proud of.

My dad is a construction worker. He is a head oiler, but he's out of town for 2 weeks at a time like all the other construction workers around here. So we all have to help out at home, and as the oldest I often helped out with my brother and sister when my mother was at work. My grandmother and grandfather, his parents, went to the old Wood School here, which is by our house. It's a very old school here in Havens. It was the first school here. The building is near our house, but it isn't a school anymore.

They moved over here from Mexico with their families at the time they were building all of the railroads. My great-grandfather worked on the railroads. We all live down by Page School—my grandma lives on the corner, her sister's down the street, my aunt's there and my dad and his brother and his sister, and the farthest is my Uncle Alejandro, over by the junior high school. One of my aunts is a nun. She doesn't live here in town, but we see her almost every week.

Most of the kids I hang around with at school are in the band, like me. Last year I hung around with Anne, Sharon, and Kim. This year the group I hang out with are mostly Mexican [Mexican-American]. This is the year I really began noticing the differences in me and what I do. Last year I never really noticed how different they [my Anglo friends] were from, you know, from our Mexican friends, but this year I do. Last year I always felt uncomfortable speaking Spanish. I've never been embarrassed because of my Mexican heritage, my culture, and I'm very proud that I speak Spanish, but when someone doesn't understand it, it's weird, you hold back, and I was holding back from them, but I was also holding back in a lot of different parts of my life. This year I use my Spanish more, and then I began taking the Hispanic Writers class and it starts sparking your, you know, your Spanish side, and it really started coming out this year. I'm just thinking in both modes and I'm using both sides of my life, not just one.

When I'm with Maribel [who is Mexican-American] and I go to her house, it's like you just know the etiquette, you know what to say. And it's funny because I always felt uncomfortable going to Sharon or Kim's house. But you don't know when to come into a conversation. We're all still close, but we notice the differences more now. We talk about them. I think we have all grown because of our friendships.

Liliana continues to be close to both her Mexican and Anglo friends. During the time she was at the university she roomed with one of her Anglo friends from Havens. None of this diluted her deep commitment to "use both sides" to enrich her life. She was secure in the combination and intended to continue to explore how they coexisted. The Hispanic Writers class she took during her senior year provided a space for this exploration and was a new offering in the high school's English curriculum the year I arrived—a one semester course designed to fuse literature and cultural issues. It was created and taught by Randy Weston, the English teacher from Kansas. With the exception of traditional Spanish language classes, this was the first time in years a class specifically addressed issues of culture and the first time that institutional space and time had been devoted to such conversation. It came at the right time for Liliana, who was eager to talk about all of the issues the class raised for her.

The only other such opportunity Liliana conceded to discuss issues of culture and language was the dialogue she and I had throughout the fall and winter. As my stay in Havens neared an end, she returned to these two opportunities as the stimuli for her thinking about how these cultural pieces all fit together: the class, and our ongoing explorations.

> I knew Hispanic Writers would be great. I mean, what better thing to learn about than something that has do to with my culture? I haven't been as aware of my culture as I am this year. I have really noticed it—realized what my culture is. You just do it, you just pick it up, but you don't really notice it or put any importance to it. But this year, talking to you and taking that class, I'm really picking it up.

To Liliana, the community's demographics meant that the students at HHS really had no choice but to accept their bicultural school society.

> You never really have run-ins at school here between Mexican and Anglo kids, not really, because I think in Havens you learn how to accept it and there's no possible way to quit it [the difference between the two cultures], and you really stand out if you don't. There's an Anglo culture, there's a Mexican culture, and you learn how to accept that.

Having accepted this herself, Liliana was also attentive to the sometimes complex nature of the lines that are drawn relative to culture and ethnicity, the stereotypes that can be heard in her school. For example, because she is in the highest academic track of classes, Liliana is often one of the few Mexican-American students in them; the achievement gap is wide, although it is narrowing steadily.

The main thing that I have bumped into in most of my classes, these are honors classes, is that it's not really because you're Hispanic or because you're Mexican. It's not that. It's because you're Mexican and you're *smart*. "Mexicans are dumb." That's the stereotype that goes around. "They're not smart" and all of this. I've never seen myself that way. I see my family on both sides and they're very smart people.

The historical record of how Mexican and Anglo people have gotten along in Havens also framed Liliana's understanding of the context in which she lived and studied.

There's a lot of relationships and marriages between Anglo and Mexican people here. Now it's accepted. Before it wasn't heard of, or it was like a taboo—it was something bad. Now I think people finally realize that is is dumb to hold something against someone just because of their race. You see a lot of the prejudice, and it's finally going away. In my family, the one that faced it the most was my grandma. She went to school here and she tells us stories about how she was treated, how they were all treated. Even my little brother would say, "Grandma, you had to use a different water fountain? I thought they only did that to Black people." And she said, "No, that's they way they treated us."

This historical scenario in Havens is not one of its prouder moments. Segregation was a long-standing practice until the 1950s. Sections of the movie theatre were off limits to Mexican people and the swimming pool was open for Mexican families to swim on only one day of the week—the day on which the pool was drained in the evening in preparation for the next week. These practices, reminiscent of the south, were not unusual along the border in the southwest.[3] In Havens, people spoke of them as things that existed long ago, more as a comment on the times than on any individual in town. As Liliana saw it, today the challenges existed more with regard to the students from Mexico, and not with respect to local Mexican-origin students whose families have been in town for some time. But she doesn't make a distinction in terms of how she defines herself—she is Mexican-American, and that means that Mexico figures into her life.

At school, you see this sometimes and a lot of times I see it with the kids from Frontera. Right away kids say "Oh, those Mexicans," or whatever, here at school, about the kids who come from across the border. So you say, "I'm Mexican also." But if something goes wrong, if something is messed-up at school, or you hear someone, you know, talking bad down the hallway, an announcement will call the kids and there will be a lot of Spanish names, and you hear, "Yeah, all the Mexican kids." You hear that and you say, "Excuse me?" Otherwise, it's not prevalent. It has more to do with the crowd you're in. There will be a bunch of Anglo kids and Hispanic kids all together. It think it's more grouped by the band crowd, or the sports crowd. But I do have a lot of friends that are from over there. It's very likely that someone from Havens can have a friend from Frontera, but it's mostly during school. A lot of times you can't build up really close times because after school you're over here and they're over there—unless you travel a lot.

We went to Mexico a lot when I was younger, until about 3 years ago. We have a lot of family there. One of my cousins, they wanted her to learn more English, so she came home with us. It's just like that, you open your doors to your family. That's the way it is. That's how we kept our ties with my Mom's family in Mexico—we always had somebody living with us. We had a girl who wasn't related, too—Gabriela—you know her from school. She lived with us for nearly a year. My mother knew how hard it was to come from Mexico and try to get an education here. She didn't have her education. Gabriela was going to go back to Mexico because she didn't have anyone to live with here, no one to stay with after her aunt moved up north. And we were really good friends and we were talking about it, so my mother said, "You tell her that she has a place to stay," and she stayed at our house. She'll be graduating in December.

Although her intimate group—the band kids—were all from the United States, Liliana made few distinctions between her friends from the states and her friends from Mexico. Gabriela lived in town with Liliana and had the opportunity to participate like one of the "town" kids. Thus, although she was Mexican, and not local, she was able to participate fully in the life of the school. In reality the distinction between who was Mexican and who was not ceased to be an important marker—Gabriela, for example, lived in town and did not cross the border daily. However, Gabriela identified herself with Mexico, a typical occurrence for many new, or in her case, temporary, immigrants.[4]

Because they had to return each day on the school bus that leaves at 3:15 PM sharp, as Liliana noted, for daily border crossers extracurricular activities were a hardship and few could afford to drive a car to school each day. Gabriela, on the contrary, was on the dance team, worked on the school newspaper, and had been in the band until her senior year. Twice Gabriela recounted the story of how she became a band member, which is how she first met Liliana.

When I moved here with my aunt, we came to school so I could register. The counselor wasn't here, so we went outside and were sitting in the car. I saw the band practicing and I said, "Oh my God, it's not like in Mexico." I was telling my aunt about it and she asked me if I wanted to join the band. I said, "I don't know," and she told me, "Yes." And then we saw Mr. Montoya [the band director] and she was telling him that I was in the band in Mexico, and he told me to come the next day. I wasn't registered for school yet. So, OK, he wanted me to come the next day, and I did, and I started practicing. He taught me to read the notes and all of that. I was in the band before I was registered in school.

Liliana helped Gabriela navigate well before Gabriela would ever live at her home. Although Gabriela's intention was to return to Mexico for college and she did this directly after graduating, this was not a distinction that was important to Liliana. Where Mexico fit into Liliana's life was clear—and it was entirely different from how it fit into Gabriela's life. Liliana continued:

> Part of my family comes from Mexico and some of my relatives there can't stand to see that I don't honor the Mexican flag. But that's not my flag; that's my ancestors' flag. I don't have an Hispanic culture and I don't have an American culture. I have a culture of where I'm living and I take in everything around me. Because you can't, you can't be totally Hispanic and you can't be totally American. You have to accept something at some point, and when you accept from both I think it's best. I feel more Hispanic when they start talking about race and when you start talking about tradition and culture. But mostly, you're still an American, but your have your Hispanic background. I can't say I'm totally Mexican, totally Hispanic, because I'm not. I live in America, and I'm very much American, but I'm not totally Americanized.

"But what about Mexico itself?" I asked during one of our conversations. "Where does that fit in?"

> Well, my relatives talk about how wonderful Mexico is and all of that. I love being there. It feels like you're in the old days. It's a time to get away from all the running around we do here. It's like going from the city to the country. But overall, I personally do not think Mexico is such a wonderful place. Look at all the problems, all of the poverty, the unpaved roads. I've only seen the outskirts, though. I've never seen the really beautiful parts of Mexico.

"So you extract the culture and separate it from the country," I said. "But do you ever feel that by being respectful about being an American and living in the bicultural way you describe yourself, you give up anything in your own culture to do that, anything important?"

> I don't think so. I've never had to give up anything. There are a lot of people who probably don't agree with me. I think you stick to your own ideas, but at the same time you're open to the ideas of others. There are a lot of cultures where you just follow the tradition and you never have your own individuality come out. I think we do have enough room for our individuality, but at the same time you follow the regular, you know, the traditional

guidelines. But you have your own way of thinking, and you're independent, too. Look, you have all the American traditions, but you still have the Hispanic traditions, just like at Christmas you have the *tamales* and the *menudo*. That's one thing I still have to learn—how to make *tamales*. I've got the *menudo* part under control. But, you have Fourth of July and Veteran's Day and you also have *Cinco de Mayo*.

We spent time at Liliana's home during the Christmas vacation and had dinner there with her family. The house, which had started as a small trailer, now had several small additions, including a new bay window that housed the Christmas tree. Liliana, her sister, and her mother, Paloma, cooked the *flautas,** rice, and beans, and served platters of Christmas *biscochos* for dessert. It was easy to see where Liliana got her energy; she and her mother, Paloma, shared the same looks and personality—open, animated, focused, and engaging. This seemed to be a family where the issues were out on the table and where friendly disagreements were invited. Paloma and I talked about her work at the church where the whole family was active, her son's upcoming First Communion, and her life as a young girl in Mexico. Her own independence, now mirrored in Liliana, was about to be a problem as she talked about her fears as Liliana considered the possibility of leaving the area to go to school. Liliana seemed to be the pivotal energy point, the stabilizer.

For Liliana, striking a balance was the only reasonable way to make sense of her two sides. Under no personal or family pressure to choose, but the product of a strong value system based on Mexican concepts of family and a close tie to the Catholic religion, she chooses instead to cross back and forth each day at school—socially, culturally, and linguistically. She has all the resources to do this skillfully: the knowledge, the strong belief in her own way of defining herself, solid values that tell her being Mexican is an asset, and the capacity to communicate in two languages. Her home is unmistakably characterized by the Mexican side. She sees her extended family daily, the church plays a central and important role in her life and the life of her family, and the customs and traditions and foods in the house are Mexican. She had a textbook celebration for her *quinceañera*, complete with a panoply of formally outfitted male and female friends as attendants, 15 young girls bearing trinkets commemorating the occasion, and a lavish party and dance afterward. It was as traditional a *quinceañera* as the one I attended in the small stone church in Frontera during the winter of our stay in Havens—formal, each part of the tradition honored, and no expense spared. Her high school graduation party featured a small band playing the well-known Mexican celebratory song, the "Mañanitas." But America was her reference point, to be sure.

---

*Rolled, fried meat-filled tortilla.

Look, she continued, I'm very Americanized. There are conflicts at home. For example, this weekend we had a big old conflict because I wanted to go out with my friends. It's funny—in the Anglo culture it's a lot easier for everyone to go out, and all the four of us were getting together and all four of us are Hispanic, we're Mexican, and it's just like, well, you know, after a certain point your parents say, "Well, it's time for you to spend time with the family. You need to stay home."

"So what did you do?" I asked.

I stayed home. But it wasn't what I wanted to do. You just do it, because it's expected. But you also push.

Regarding language, Liliana was not the one to push boundaries; language was an area that for her was uncontested—Spanish was simply important.

At home we speak Spanish. We all understand and speak Spanish, but my little sister has some trouble because at home you can speak either way [English or Spanish] and you know everyone understands you. My brother speaks pretty well. I'm the most fluent in the Spanish language. My grandmother and aunts all speak mostly Spanish. At school in class you don't really use it, but with your friends you do. A lot of the personal things, like down-home things that have to do with things that are really close to me, it's mostly in Spanish. But when we talk about school and classes, it's English. A lot of times you notice that at school you don't tend to talk in Spanish because there's a lot of people who don't understand what you're saying. But that's just out of common courtesy.

Both Liliana and her best friend, Maribel, had the same view regarding the use of Spanish in school. They were wary of excluding others from their conversation, but had developed a personal, shared sense of when it was more natural for them to use Spanish. Maribel's Spanish was still quite shaky; she spoke mostly English at home, but her parents were supporting her efforts to regain the language—as was Liliana herself. Also, they talked about this with each other, and encouraged their Mexican-American friends—those in their social group who they were very close to—to learn Spanish and purposely cultivate this part of their heritage. This was done quietly, as a function of their friendships, and they helped each other with words and phrases. Our conversation continued:

"But are kids who speak Spanish in this school put down?"

Not really. It depends when you speak it. If you speak it and there's a bunch of kids around that don't understand you, they'll say "Oh, you show-off," or "You're talking about me." I wish there wasn't the automatic assumption that you're talking about someone if they can't speak the language.

Sometimes the decision to use Spanish was a conscious choice to provide an opportunity for someone whose Spanish was weak to practice it. Liliana helped Maribel, and both of them prodded and helped their friend Colin, who until recently chose not to act on the fact that his mother is Mexican-American and that Spanish is part of his heritage.

Liliana continued:

In my French class, there are a lot of girls whose first language is Spanish who live on the other side. And they were very surprised when I—they were making jokes and I joined in—and I just felt comfortable joining in and they all stopped laughing and turned and looked at me, and I felt like, "Oh, God, I said something wrong," and they all were like "You speak Spanish." They were so surprised, and it's funny because they assume I didn't speak Spanish because of the crowd that I sit with in that class. I was trying to tell the kids in that class that we're all Mexican, whether you come from Havens or Frontera, and there's no difference. There shouldn't be, but yet there's that barrier there, and it's very prevalent in that class. It's not really the Anglo and the Mexican, it's the United States and not the United States.

The fact of the border, then, for Liliana, was the point of demarcation in terms of social relationships in school. She recognized the powerful division the political concept of the border exerted—although she herself did not see the border as an important day-to-day issue and it did not dictate her choices. She understood that life was more difficult economically across the line, but also that in many ways the lifestyle there was quieter and less complicated. While Mexico did not figure strongly in her life, being Mexican did and it conferred a certain sense of relationship with people from Mexico that she honored. Her roots there were both recent and distant, reflecting her parents' varying origins. Amidst peers at school who seemed to make marked distinctions between those who lived in the United States and those who lived in Mexico, she recognized that instead of a dichotomy, people could be arrayed more along a continuum in their relationship to Mexico. Combined with the ability to communicate in both languages, this realization enabled her to make judgments according to the more natural divisions that occur in high schools—interest groups, activities, and the classes she took—rather than who was identified in which category.

Liliana mediates the boundaries of her life easily. She does not so much identify with Mexico as she does value what that part of her family history has brought to her life. Her own lack of ambivalence is precisely her strength. Maria Cruz, equally unambivalent, mediates out of an entirely different set of experiences.

Maria's Story

I wandered into the drafting class early in my classroom visits. It was a good size classroom with drafting tables filling one third of the space. The teacher's desk was at the front of the room, but no formal teaching took place from it during the times I was there; instead students left their spots to walk up and talk with the teacher, a Mexican-American native of Havens, or he circulated to comment on their work. At the back of the room, directly opposite the door, two students were working on the only computers in the room; the teacher told me that each of the students should have computers, but two is as many as the school could afford.

There was a relaxed give and take among these students. They worked on their own projects, walked around the room talking to one another, planned activities, and talked comfortably with the teacher. It was an easy setting in which to get to know students: the teacher was welcoming, the students worked alone, and it was not disruptive to walk around the room and chat with individual students as they completed their drawings. And so, I returned here often. About 70% of the students in the class were Mexican-American; these were students in 10th and 11th grade. Many were active in the vocational clubs at the school, one for each of the major vocational programs. In general, the school took this organization seriously with students participating and often winning at the state level competitions each year, and typically advancing to national levels as well. Among the group in this particular class was a junior who came from Mexico each day, a Mexican-American sophomore who was one of the heavy-hitting academic stars on the school's Academic Decathalon team, a rising star on the football team who was a sophomore, and Maria Cruz, who, by virtue of her accentless English, her assertive personality, and her easy interaction with everyone in the room, I first mistook for a second- or third-generation Mexican-American. Early on in my visits we talked only in passing.

As the fall progressed, I got used to seeing her at the boys' basketball games, where she was the team manager. She was a social magnet; seemed to get along with everyone and that year was crowned queen of the winter dance for the sophomore class. She "hung around" with several cheerleaders and with some of the more popular boys from her class. Unlike Liliana, Maria was not part of the academic or band crowd; we rarely talked about her classes. Instead, she was part of the active social life of her sophomore class. As she strolled through the halls, she greeted nearly everyone she saw. She was always engaged in conversation, and

nearly always with a group of girls—mostly Mexican-American, mostly
cheerleaders, but with one of the Anglo cheerleaders among them. This
was a group of conventionally popular girls. Maria, with her long, light,
straight brown hair and green eyes, did not fit the conventional stereotype
of a "Mexican" girl.

We lived in Mexico before we came to school here. My parents only reached
the third grade because it's not a big deal over there. They reached the
third grade and that was it. We lived in a village farther down, it's just a
little place, Las Hermanas, and it's mostly just my family there. My
grandparents have always lived there. Everyone raises cattle, and that's
about it. My parents met there. My dad left us for about 4 years and came
over here to work for us and then he moved us over. We crossed the border
illegally—people call this wetbacks. I was 5 when we crossed and my
parents started us in school real quick.

In Mexico, you wouldn't believe it, we lived in a two-room house. It was
just the kitchen and the bedroom. There were four beds and that's where
my parents and my brothers and sisters and I slept. It's so different over
there, it's so old-fashioned. Our irons were metal that you had to heat
whenever they cooled off. We had a woodstove and you had to heat your
water on it, for baths, too. You had to pump for water and carry it back
home. The floors are hard-packed mud and you have to wet them or you'll
get a lot of dust everywhere. There was a river by where we lived so it was
really pretty. I mean, none of my friends believe that's how I lived.

My dad decided to leave because he wanted us to learn English, to make
something of ourselves, so he moved here and started working. He started
off working in a restaurant and he was there for about 13 years and
became the manager. Then he applied for the amnesty[5] program and
became a [legal] resident. When he moved us over here we applied for it,
too. I started [the process] when I was in second grade and got it when I
was in fourth grade. I'm a resident right now—I'm not a citizen. I still have
to go through all that to become a citizen. My parents are still residents,
too, but they are applying for citizenship. Just yesterday I met a lady who
gives citizenship classes over at Page School.[6]

My dad is, I guess you could say, old-fashioned. He still believes that
everything should be done the way it was back then. He is a Mexican
cowboy. He wears a black sombrero all the time and boots. But some of the
things you have to let go of. You don't want to forget certain things, like
the religion and respect for elders. But I'm 15 now and he expects me to
be working and handing over my money to him to help out the family. It's
kind of hard because in Mexico that's what they do. But here, at that age
you're involved in sports at school and you have a lot of things going for
you there. He expects us to finish high school, but I think to them
education really doesn't mean a lot. He doesn't quite understand that you
need to get a good job. He expects us just to be helping the family all the

time, but we have to do things for ourselves. He has a problem dealing with school because he only reached the third grade over there. He figures that if you're smart you're going to get a good job no matter what.

Here you need an education. Right now I'm living in town because of my job managing the basketball team and I know my dad was upset with me at first. It's hard for him to understand. I've always told people that I wish my parents would be more involved in what goes on at school, especially my dad. I remember when I was in sixth grade and I thought high school wasn't important. I didn't know what high school really was and I figured I only needed to go to junior high. In junior high I met my friends and they started talking about college and I would say "What's college? What are you talking about?" So it was my friends who really influenced me, and my teachers, too. Ever since then it's been important to me.

It's important to my parents that we don't forget where we come from. It's important to them, but then I think it has a lot to do with us, too, because you really don't want to forget all that. But there's some things you kind of have to let go of, you know, from my father's traditional beliefs. Some of the things he believes in, it's kind of like "Hey dad, it's modern times."

The need to distance herself from her family to make good as a high school student has not cut Maria off from her roots.

I still think of myself as a Mexican-American teenager. There are times when I think of myself more as a Mexican, like when an Anglo will start talking disrespectfully about the Mexican culture. That's when I step in and tell them I was born in Mexico, I'm full-blooded Mexican and you have no right to be talking that way. And there are also times when I consider myself more of an American, like when my cousins will have disrespect for Americans, they'll be mad at the Americans for no reason. I think it's because their friends have told them that the Americans want to keep them in Mexico. I guess by just setting an example yourself, you show that you don't hold a grudge against the Americans. Then people will learn from you.

I try to make it known to people that I'm Hispanic and there's nothing that anyone can do or say that's going to make me feel different about my culture. I'm always going to stick up for my culture and no one is going to make me feel like it's lower than anyone else's. I need to show other people that yes, I'm Hispanic, and I'm doing what anyone else could be doing.

Like Liliana, Maria knows about where she prefers to live. Mexico is a family reference point, her ties largely due to family that comes as a stream of relatives on both sides of the border. So Mexico is not only physically close by, but there is a close family link as well. Her language is also an important link, as is the general need to remind her school peers where she comes from and what her background is.

When we first moved here we had to live with my aunt and her husband for a while, my father's brother. My aunt is an Anglo, but being married to my uncle she learned Spanish too, and so talking to us she would teach us English. I remember at home every night she would set us down and teach us words, like refrigerator, in English. We were always listening to her talk and we just picked it up from her mostly. When I started school I just had a little bit of English, but my kindergarten teacher helped me because she knew Spanish, too, and my cousin is in the same grade as me so, him knowing Spanish and English, he would talk to me in Spanish and I would talk to him in English. I remember being frustrated when I first heard the teacher speaking English, like "I'm never going to learn this," but here I am. It's like nothing now. Now I'm comfortable with both languages. My parents understand both, of course. They speak Spanish more to themselves, but around anyone else they can speak good English. Where my parents are we have a lot of family out there and they're all Spanish-speaking. We tend to stick together and so around them I speak a lot of Spanish; I speak more Spanish than I do in town. But they understand English really well. So at home we talk to them in English and they respond to us in Spanish so either way, they're learning more English and we're not forgetting our Spanish. Now my English is better than my Spanish. I use my Spanish on a daily basis just talking to my friends. My guardian speaks Spanish, too, and I sometimes I speak to her in Spanish.

It's hard for my friends to believe that I went through that, living in Mexico, and no one even knows that I'm Hispanic or that I was born in Mexico. I'll be walking down the hallway and people will be talking about me in Spanish, but not bad things, but they'll be talking and if I respond to them they get shocked because they don't know I speak Spanish. Only a few of my friends from Havens speak it, so I teach them, or at least I try to. I get all aggravated because I don't want to forget it because it's a part of me, and so I try to speak it. I have a lot of friends who are from Frontera and I'll ask them the complicated words I forget, like the word for tonsils. I talk to my mom all the time about this and she tells me it's important that you don't forget Spanish. "It's where you came from and it's a part of you and if you lose the language then what are you going to have? Just the fact that you're born in Mexico. Now, that's nothing, you know."

Maria's mother may be exaggerating the degree to which culture itself is unimportant, but the link between culture and language seems unmistakable in her mind.

I've been able to meet some kids from Frontera because I know Spanish and I just talk to them. Unless you know the language it's hard to make friends with those kids, but I'm friends with a lot of them. Of my friends who live in Havens, three are Hispanic but only one speaks Spanish really well—the others understand. The other one who is really good is Cathy

Roberts. She's an Anglo and she understands it more than some of my Hispanic friends do. Her dad is a rancher and he's a fluent Spanish speaker. It's really neat.

A lot of my family is here, but most of it, the greater percentage, is still in Mexico. We still go over there to visit. When we go back to Las Hermanas, we speak English around each other and my relatives get mad because they say we're in Mexico and English isn't the language we speak here. Sometimes they think we're better than they are because we live on this side and it could be a problem, but you know, you kind of just put that off. You tell them that knowing English is an advantage. You have greater opportunities on this side of the border, and knowing English and getting to know everyone over here is important. I have also been down to Frontera. Basically we know where everything is down there and I'm familiar with it, but I don't go down a lot. My friends want to get me down there Sunday, this Sunday, to the disco. But I don't usually have time.

The family I have here are mostly Spanish-speaking. I have two cousins who go to school here. They're what everyone else considers "Mexicans," I mean, you know, you can really tell that they are Mexicans. They're here in school and I can see them, and it's neat.

So I asked, "But what do you mean when you say that they're 'really' Mexican?"

Well, they're categorized. People can be cruel and call them "fronteristas" and all this. But there are people who by looking at them you know right away that they're Mexican, that they come from the other side. That's the way that people categorize here. If you're Hispanic—like I'd be considered Hispanic in most people's eyes because, you know, I'm middle class or whatever. They would be considered low-class Mexican. I don't know, sometimes it's really annoying because people are so ignorant.

Around here the difference is between Hispanics and Mexicans. There are still some people who, even to Hispanics, say things like "What are you doing here?" They can still talk about you. But this doesn't happen a whole lot. It's mostly the Mexican students that people have a problem with. It was hard for my cousins, I know it was. Sometimes they tell me, "You know, your friends sometimes look at me," and I'm saying "No, I'm sure they're not thinking anything, it's just cause they don't know you." My cousin Carlos, he's a really good athlete and the only reason he doesn't want to get involved in sports is because he thinks the Hispanics are going to be looking at him. I think he's wrong. He's a very fast runner, he's a good basketball player. He's strong and so I encourage him and I think as soon as he learns more English he'll be wanting to play. Right now it's because he's scared. It has to do with the language. If he could at least make an attempt to go up to the Hispanics and start talking with them, he could do it, but he's afraid of the rejection. I don't think anyone's going to reject him. You just don't do that to a person.

To Maria, the term *Hispanic* signifies location and social class level, and she uses it where others might use the term *Mexican-American*. You can be an immigrant but be classified as "Hispanic " if you are in the process of learning English and raising your class status, or you can be a first or second or third generation Mexican-American from Havens. You are "Mexican" if you live in Mexico or if you still carry yourself as a native Mexican in terms of your dress, your actions, your friends, and your language. So her cousins, who live in the United States, in the same farming area south of town that Maria herself moved to when she immigrated as a much younger child, are still considered Mexican—whereas she considers herself Hispanic. It is a question of her primary reference point, which for Maria is clearly the United States. She is not divorced from Mexico because of her relationship with her family, who are in the United States, who are still arriving, and who also still remain in Mexico.

Maria's link with her culture exists primarily in relationship to language. She did not have a *quinceañera* and although she sees religion as an important link, she does not talk much about going to church herself. In making a distinction between what she sees as necessary to retain and what she can give up, she has opted for language as the key. Her mother's distinction that if you lose your language all you have left is the fact that you are from Mexico seems to have left a serious impression on Maria. The proximity of her extended, Spanish-speaking family also places Maria in a position where having two languages is necessary and where interaction with students who identify primarily with Mexico (e.g., her cousin Carlos) is a daily occurrence. In many ways, Maria is moving toward an identity that is more American than Mexican. With her family still in a state of migration, she has a defined role to play in terms of helping family members manage the transition to life in the United States. To do so effectively, she has no choice but to be a cultural mediator. In contrast to Liliana, Maria seems more practical in her mediating role.

Richard's Story

Richard teaches English at HHS and has done so for 7 years. Prior to that he taught in various districts across New Mexico, both in the north and the south. By reputation he is considered one of Havens' best; he is a local native, his father taught English in the high school before him, and he leads some of the extracurricular activities that few teachers might want to take on—the newspaper and the yearbook. He also coaches boys' tennis. His is a classroom door around which students regularly congregate between classes, chatting—usually in English, sometimes in Spanish. He always has time to say hello to the students, to other teachers, to whoever passes by—flashing a warm smile from his bearded face. A devout Christian, but not a political fundamentalist, he is active in his church, his children attend school in Havens, and his wife is in the process of getting a teaching license. He regularly attends all school activities—usually with his camera so the event can be captured for the next high school yearbook. Because he is bilingual he taught in the original program for Teaching English as a Second Language several years earlier. Today his assignment includes primarily the basic, lower track English classes and journalism.

We really didn't intend to live here, but we came back to be with my mother when she got sick. And we just decided that this was a better place to raise our kids than lots of other places. So we've stayed here and we're glad and unless something major happens, we'll probably stay here most of the rest of our lives.

I learned to speak Spanish in junior high school and high school. I took Spanish classes from Mrs. Manning [now the HHS librarian]. And then I talked in Spanish with my friends. And I had a very, very Anglo-looking suitemate in college who came from Havens and he spoke Spanish, so we used to have fun walking down the street at college speaking Spanish. They could have expected it from me, but not from him. He was a real *huero.*[*]

In high school the group I hung around with was mainly Mexican. Once I got sent to the office because a Black student, a Mexican student, and me were standing around a trash can that was on fire and the teacher thought we had set it. So they sent us to the office, and Mr. Carson, the counselor, of course he knew me because my dad taught here and he asked, "What are you guys doing?" And I said, "We were trying to put out the fire." He said, "How?" And I answered, "We were spitting into the trash can." And so he looked at the three of us and I'm sure if it had been just the other two guys he would probably have tried to bust them, but instead he sent us back to the patio with some water to put it out.

I don't know. It was polarized when I was a student here, but it seems that it is a little more polarized now. There are some kids who don't know that there is a barrier or a border, and they cross over it both ways. But there are also some who, well, it's funny because the sons and daughter of the "elite" just walk past me right down the hall. There's a lot of prejudice

[*]Light-complected.

from this group, but it's really only about those 50 families in town and no one else, so there's really not that much of a problem. But those kids, I can say "Hi" and they will just walk right past. But some of these kids from Frontera always just have a very nice smile and a "Hi, Mr. Logan! How are you?" I teach lower level kids, so a lot of the higher level kids don't know me that well.

In general I think Havens is capable of a lot more than it is doing right now. I just think that all these people have their own image of Havens and are trying to make Havens in that image rather than accepting it for what it is. So some people see it as a retirement place and they're trying to make it that. Some see it as a farming and ranching area, but they're unwilling to see that without the Mexican workers we would be down the tubes. If we didn't have the workers from Mexico picking our crops they'd have to cut so far back in their crops they wouldn't be able to make any money. We have a high teenage pregnancy rate. We had a chance to write grants that included a program to educate single teenage mothers. But a small group opposed it. The students I talked to, even the ones out of school, said, "That would be great. That's the reason I can't come to school, I don't have any way to take care of my daughter or my son." That's just some of the vision I feel is lacking in the community.[7] Some people say, "We should shut the border." But we're so close to Frontera, and with NAFTA the growth will start off slowly, but I think it will build up to where we have a very high percentage of communication across the border. This is where we live. These are the people who are going to produce some of our food, some of our livestock, they just live 30 miles away, and I think if we coexist we'll have a lot more going for us than if we say, "You guys don't exist, we don't need you."

Some people here feel that there should be a difference between White and Hispanic people, you know, you should stay within your own race. There are some people here, a small group, who see that line and see it very distinctly and would never make that crossover. But just that 10%. I think a lot of those people are holding the community back. A lot of the kids here at HHS, the majority, go right across the line. Outside of that 10%, the kids pretty much mesh together. Now, there's still the Mexican group, which is still an outside group. I don't if anybody else has told you that the Mexican kids in town don't like the Mexican kids from Frontera. But they're starting to make inroads into various things and they're starting to become a little bit more part of the school each year. The majority of the kids who are problems are the Hispanic kids who live here. I think I have only known a couple of kids from Mexico who were a problem. They are grateful to be here to have a chance to learn, to go to school, that the majority of those students work really hard.

For me, I like to know I'm making a difference. In my classes, the basic English classes, the kids have to read the first 10 minutes of every class period. So I had one parent come in and say, "What are you doing with my daughter? She never used to read, and now she's picking up magazines and newspapers." I imagine that 75% to 80% of the kids in my classes have never read a complete book and in this class they do. It sort of amazes them that there is something else they can do. The whole community, the whole school is capable of doing this. We've got good kids here; I just think there's too little reaching out to the kids. I've got kids who work all night in the chile plant to support their families, so I just try to be as supportive as I can be, and you can find a kid like that graduating as a member of honor society a year later. We've got lots of intelligent kids who need to be recognized as intelligent by more of the people here.

If you ever come in during second period, I have Jaime Gutierrez; he can be the biggest jerk. Sometimes I just want to take him and send him to the office when he walks in the door. Yesterday he wanted to go to the nurse. I said, "Well, we'll see. This is reading period and you're supposed to be reading. And then after that we're going to be discussing the story and if you behave well enough you can go." Hey, he was the one leading the discussion. He had read the story and he knew what it was about and so as soon as the story was over he got up and before he even got up I started writing out the pass. If I could get that from him, he could lead this class. And the other teachers say, "Jaime Guiterrez! Aw, no way. He's too much of a troublemaker." But he can do it. I just think there's too little of that, too little reaching out to the kids. And nobody else really wants to teach the classes I teach. They all want to teach the AP [Advanced Placement] and high level classes. The kids I teach are kids who know something about the real world. If I told them I wanted to teach AP, I don't know whether they would be able to find anybody to teach these classes.

Richard has worked with students at the margins of the school in two groups: the local Mexican-American students who are not high achievers and students who are just learning English. In both cases, he believes the school can be more strategic in how it addresses these students.

When I work with the kids whose English is limited, I can understand where they're coming from and what they are saying. Some people might look at the kids from Mexico and say, "You can't even speak English," but they forget that they are speaking Spanish. When I taught in the TESOL [Teachers of English to Speakers of Other Languages] program what I really worked on with the kids was getting them to the point where they could think in English. I kept saying, "This border is going to open up and there are going to be good-paying jobs for people who can go south of the border and negotiate and come back up here and do the same thing." For 2 years I've been saying, "If you have some business sense and some common sense and you can speak both languages, you're going to be able to make some money. If you can go down into the interior of Mexico and stay with a field of chile until it gets through [the border], you know, and make sure that everything is taken care of and then bring it back up here, you're going to be worth money."

When I taught in the TESOL program, sometimes the kids would laugh at my Spanish and I'd say, "I would never laugh at your English. I'm trying to help you. You should do the same with my Spanish, you should have the same respect for me as I have for you." They'll still come up and talk to me in Spanish, and I'll say, "Talk to me in English." And they say, "Why? You speak Spanish." And I'll say, "Yeah, but where else can you practice your English, who else can you practice on and not be embarrassed? So practice it on me." They feel comfortable in Spanish, and they feel uncomfortable in English. They are just trying to learn English, and sometimes they don't want to talk in class because, well, even sometimes the teachers have done it, have corrected them in front of everybody. They don't always allow the kids to have their dignity, I guess. They take it away from them. Most of the kids are doing fine. If they have questions, they usually ask me in English and I answer them in English. I tell them at the start of the year that I do speak Spanish, but that this is an English class so unless there's a real problem, they need to use English.

My wife is working on her teaching degree and she wants to know enough Spanish so she'll be able to handle herself in the classroom. Ideally, most teachers should know Spanish, not so much to be able to use all the time; I think the classes ought to be taught in English. But 5 years ago, before we had any type of TESOL program, we went to a high school in Sierra, Texas and interviewed some of their third- and fourth-year students. We asked them what was most important to them. "Teachers who can teach the class in English, but can explain it to us in Spanish if we have things we don't understand." They said, "The teachers who teach us in Spanish are not helping us because that's not what we need. We already speak Spanish. We want them to teach us in English, and when we don't understand something—the shades of meaning—that they'd be able to explain it in Spanish." I think ideally that's the way to do it. I think it's important for the teachers at least to have an understanding of their subject in Spanish. You know, if you're teaching math, you don't have to know all the terms, but it would be good if you could be able to explain the basic math terms in Spanish. We have lots of teachers who don't speak any Spanish, and I, I don't know, I think they lose something in the translation of the cultures.

Richard's view on the proximity of Mexico and the responsibility it engenders resounded in each of our conversations.

You know, if we were living in Iowa I wouldn't feel so strongly about this. But we're 30 miles from Mexico. And I think it is important to be able to speak Spanish. My Spanish isn't as good as I would like it to be. I'll have some parents come in today who, even when I use the wrong tense or something, they'll understand what I'm saying.

The parents he is talking about may be local parents who have never learned English, who themselves are new immigrants, or who live in Mexico. He continued,

> Just to be able to understand the culture, to be able to understand the kids and the parents, Spanish is important. Because, you know, you lose something when you have a parent come in and she only talks in Spanish and you only talk in English and have to bring in another teacher to translate. I would imagine that the parents who talk in Spanish with me go home saying, "Hmm, there is someone who is trying to do something." Because I can converse with them. I know I make mistakes, but they can usually understand what I'm saying. I think it would be really good if most of the teachers could do that.

For the students who commute from Mexico, "most of the time," according to Richard,

> The family is hoping the child will go to school and learn English. A lot of the motivation is the language. But it seems to me it's the self-motivated ones who do it. I have lots of kids whose English is really getting better. But a few of the kids are not putting out like they could be. Some of these kids could really be leaders if they would just choose to do so. I have two or three kids from Mexico now and I think their problem is more or less not wanting to do it. So I don't have a lot of patience with them. Most of the rest are doing fine. If they have questions, they usually ask them in English and I answer them in English. There are a few who are trying but who will not speak in class. Some of them are very good, but they are afraid that they will make a mistake and say something wrong, and people will laugh at them. And that happens. Teachers and students will laugh at them sometimes when they mispronounce words. And then there are students like Gabriela, who will speak and who don't care what other people say.

> In general the school welcomes the kids. But there's still lots of room for improvement. I think that is the real key. If you could get some of these kids involved in these other things [extracurricular activities], if you could get a few interested in sports—well, there already are plenty who are interested—if you could figure out a way to send a late bus, it would help. If they ever do get a late bus for athletics that'll be a big part because the students from Mexico will have a reason to stay here and watch. And once that happens, that is the real key. If kids from Mexico know some of the players, then if they come to the game it isn't just 10 players walking down the court. They know a couple of them, they have played with them since they were kids. I think the kids on the basketball team last year, the Anglo kids, their Spanish improved working with the kids from Mexico. The kid from Mexico who is on the team, if he gets graded, he's going to work on

getting his grades up, he's going to work on learning English so when the coach tells him, "I want you to be number two presser," he's going to understand what to do and where to go.

A different set of needs exists as well, according to Richard.

I'd say that 85% of the kids in school aren't getting touched in terms of planning for after high school. A lot of the kids don't have a view of doing anything besides working at the supermarket or on their farm with dad. I'm not putting those things down. But there are some students who are very well-qualified, very capable of doing many other things and they just never really have a chance. I think you need to really dig in with those freshmen and 10th graders and say, "Now look, what would you like to do?" We need to show them the options.

In many ways Richard is a far more strident activist and cultural mediator, and is less patient with those who do not cross cultural lines, than either Liliana or Maria. His orientation is located both in the school and the community. He is in a position to make an immediate difference in the lives of the students he teaches and within the classes and activities under his direct influence he does so consistently. For example, it is Richard who inaugurated the bilingual columns in the school newspaper and asked the Spanish teacher to use the columns in her teaching. Like Liliana and Maria, he is forthright in his opinions and is not afraid to take a public stand on issues of equity for students. It is a sense of personal responsibility, an individual role that each of these mediators has chosen to take on in a slightly different way.

*   *   *

As I was making choices about which individuals I might present as cultural mediators, I kept hitting up against the reality that it was so much more difficult for those who cross the border each day to take on this role. For those who had not yet mastered English, it was difficult to move back and forth between cultures; language was a barrier to the role. Many had strong desires to interact more, but did not yet have the language confidence or capacity to do so. Even for those who are becoming fluent, although they may have Anglo or local Mexican-American friends, as a group, students who are daily visitors still feel distanced.

Acceptance is always accompanied by a bit of self-doubt, a sense of being a guest. Although there are certainly students from Mexico at HHS who have mastered English and who are beginning to become involved in the life of the school, they typically are not involved enough to actively foster the kinds of relationships that Liliana, Maria, and Richard do.

One of the most well-adjusted students from Mexico, a sophomore named Yolanda Muñoz, was active in the vocational clubs and went with them to state and national competitions, had a very close Anglo girl-friend who was in the mainstream of the school, was enrolled in honors English classes, and regularly appeared on the honor roll. She had exited classes in bilingual education on entering high school. Yolanda sensed the hesitation, the distance, the difficulty in being fully a part of the school even if no one said it to her. "You know," she told me, "you're not directly told, 'You're not welcome here,' but you know, you feel it. It's mainly from other students." Although there may be students from Mexico who are popular, who are known for a certain activity (basketball or music are the most recent examples), and who, like Yolanda, are academic achievers, and although they may have close friends on both sides of the border, these students do not traverse the expanses of the school in the same way that local students do.

As I thought about what it meant to be a cultural mediator, the distinction I kept making centered around the interpersonal practice of actively bringing people together through one's individual interactions, paired with a commitment to personal cultural understanding across the two cultures. Being bilingual was key, because it provided the capital to move between the student groups and subgroups that often were divided by language. It was this broad interpersonal commitment, this more conscious day-to-day work of moving between cultures deliber-ately, which defined the role for me in the end. Some students may work to bring Mexican culture into the school; others may by example show that Mexican or Mexican-American students can make major contribu-tions to the school. But cultural mediators saw the relationship between the cultures and individuals as primary, and did this work unbidden—as their personal responsibility.

3

Crossing the Psychological Border:
Language in Havens

Actually we've got all the advantages as far as culture and languages and we don't have to study it from books. I mean, it's right here and we're not taking advantage of it. And it's not just the school, it's the whole community.

It was a clear night; delighted, expectant parents and families filled the stadium. In the stands, the sounds of Spanish and English flew; sitting next to us was a family from Frontera, dressed to the nines, and who, like many other families, did not speak English. The grass, where a few months earlier a well-integrated squad of football players—all English speakers, some bilingual—tried unsuccessfully to clinch a few wins, and where the homecoming kings and queens were crowned, held a platform for the distinguished guests, which included school board members and district administrators. Chairs for the graduates were set up on the gravel track. As if to make sure everyone knew in what kind of community this graduation was taking place, one of the newer school board members, a Mexican-American farmer, wore his best black cowboy hat. An occasion for finery, Havens' style. The whole town seemed to be here; no other social event of the early summer would match this one.

The graduates entered; they were mostly brown-skinned, mostly Mexican-American, all grinning, while at the same time trying to accord the ceremony the solemnity it deserved. Statistics project that for most of the students, this is the last academic graduation they will participate in, and they meant to make the most of it. In the formal commencement address, they were reminded by their superintendent of the struggle of coming from a small town and the inevitability of needing to leave to eventually be able to come back and be successful. "Come back, but come back on your own terms," he told them. He also admonished them never to use their minority status as an excuse for not making it. To underscore the challenges he believed students from Havens would face and to offer sage advice, interspersed in his comments were a few Spanish dichos—proverbs—learned from his grandmother. Like their tearful peers across the country, students who made presentations spoke of what HHS had given them, of what they would miss about the school, and of their dreams for the future. The four foreign exchange students from Europe were given the opportunity to thank the community and their host families publicly for their hospitality.

Those who crossed the border daily from Mexico to attend HHS were not represented as a group. They had no host families and, at graduation, no designated spokesperson. Their status still uncertain, their presence best left unheralded, their language absent from the festivities, they blended easily into the mostly brown-skinned crowd. Those who had mastered English could participate as well as anyone else; their families, many of whom were unlikely to speak English well or at all, would not be able to understand the speeches, although they certainly understood the occasion's significance.

As the ceremony proceeded and diplomas were distributed, the near universality of Spanish names was unmistakable. Some were not pronounced correctly; the most startling error was the mispronunciation of the name of perhaps the most politically active Mexican-American student, Luis Estrada, a highly motivated, college-bound young man who had organized a local chapter of an institute to encourage high achieving Mexican and Mexican-American students to attend college. On the program he was slated to speak during a segment that included three Anglo girls. Fluent in both languages, he stood apart from them, creating his own space, then corrected the pronunciation of his name, and made his remarks in English.

*   *   *

In Havens, a formal occasion like graduation is not thought of as a place for Spanish to be used. Graduation represents a politically sanctioned activity, and it is in these official settings in the schools and in the community at large that Spanish seems to be most taboo. One does not hear it at faculty or school board meetings, at the beginning-of-the year all-district staff meeting, or at most other school-wide functions. Spanish is not discernible at community forums, like the one held in the fall to broach the subject of housing for migrant laborers. When the community met for a discussion on prevention and intervention in growing gang-related activities, no Spanish was heard as part of the formal presentation. Although gang activity in Havens seemed to be dominated by the majority Mexican-American population of youth in the community, the impression that was created was that officials might sooner think of having a sign language interpreter than one in Spanish at this meeting. Except for the names and accents, most meetings like these could have been taking place in Wilcox, Nebraska. And although it might seem perfectly acceptable to begin a district-wide teachers' breakfast at the beginning of the year with a denominational Christian prayer, no such partisanship yet extended to issues of language.

Similarly, except for Spanish names, which are always prominent, it is rare to find evidence of the Spanish language anywhere in Haven's daily newspaper. In the newspaper's large city counterparts close by, such acknowledgments exist in the form of the greeting *Buenas Días* located prominently on the front page each morning, and in the El Paso paper, which was regularly read by people in Havens, a standing op-ed column on Hispanic issues appeared twice a week, once in English and Spanish. Typical exceptions in Havens were official notices buried in the back of the paper, which were by law required to be printed bilingually—for example, election announcements. The Havens Public Library sported only a small shelf of Spanish books, mostly for adults. The official position in Havens—unspoken—but a norm obviously well-known, well-understood, and not to be tampered with was, "This is official, public business. It is not a place for Spanish."

But in the day-to-day life of Havens, Spanish is an unquestionable and often welcomed part of the auditory landscape. In certain places, it is the landscape, like at my favorite restaurant, Guadalajara, where the owners were immigrants from Mexico City and spoke only Spanish. English is rare there, but everyone is good natured about those who are attempting to learn either new language, be it English or Spanish. This tiny restaurant is where I sat with my friend and adopted Spanish tutor, Ana, while she made me listen to her fast-paced, native Mexican Spanish—me working hard to get it all while I ate the *chilaquiles* that she later taught me to cook at her home. Here I could practice with impunity. The children, nieces, and nephews of the owners who worked there were all learning English at school, and one of the cafe's regulars, a retired Mexican-American police officer from the midwest and a fluent Spanish speaker, was teaching English to the owners. In places like this, there is a sense that either language is acceptable; everyone believed you were better off speaking both, and this was a place you could safely try if you wished.

Whatever norm existed about when it was and was not appropriate to use Spanish officially did not extend in any way to personal exchanges

---

*Good morning.

and did not seem to affect how widespread the use of Spanish actually is in Havens. At the "Mexican" church in the *barrio* on the east side of town, the 7:30 a.m. mass on Sunday is conducted in Spanish and among some of the smaller, Pentecostal and fundamentalist churches that are springing up all over Havens services might take place in either language or in a combination of both. At businesses in town, transactions might be conducted in either language. In the local clothing shop, at the supermarkets, in the banks, or in the central office of the schools, one is as likely to hear Spanish as English, and employees who can speak both languages fluently are clearly in demand. Wherever there are employees who speak Spanish, one is likely to hear it spoken.

It is not always easy to figure out how individuals decide when and with whom to use Spanish, but one teacher who grew up straddling the border south of Havens said she believed the rule to be, "If you look Mexican, the cashier might assume that you wish to be spoken to in Spanish." To her, this was evidence of a stereotypical attitude toward all brown-skinned people; that an individual who is Mexican-American or Mexican might choose to speak English over Spanish at any given time did not always seem to be a consideration. Not surprisingly, the guesses on the part of the cashiers are not always correct. Such mistaken assumptions were also pointed out by students like Maria Cruz, about whom incorrect assumptions are often made regarding her native language because of her light complexion and hair (my own early interactions with her included). This a priori decision making about who does and does not speak Spanish seems to be most obvious in the supermarkets where daily migrant laborers come to shop—often by busloads on the many *enganchista*[*] buses that drive to and from surrounding fields each day. On the other hand, much of the Spanish language landscape reflects personal relationships that are regularly conducted in Spanish—whether publicly or privately—and it is also on this personal basis that cashiers often choose who to address in which tongue.

Other groups in Havens who are likely to have at least a working knowledge of Spanish include farmers and ranchers and they are predominantly Anglo. For the farmers, Spanish has always been the language of their workers. For the ranchers, it has been common practice to do business trading and buying cattle in Spanish on both sides of the border for decades.

Well, my grandad, he speaks Spanish real fluently, and I just started picking it up when he was talking to Mexicans and stuff, said Chris Lofton,

---

[*]Labor contractor.

a high school junior who was active in Student Council, but whose real love was riding in rodeos. My grandad lived in Horton, that's where he was born and raised, and then there was a cattle disease in Mexico, and he went down there and stopped it before it came up here, so he was in Mexico for 2, 3 years. So that helped a lot.

Chris had great tolerance for others' use of Spanish but saw no immediate need to learn it himself. If your work demanded it, then you found a way to learn Spanish as an adult, but in the case of the farmers and ranchers, it was most often learned so the owners could communicate with their hired help, and the language of social class hierarchy characterized these discussions.

The main head worker on our farm, the manager, didn't speak English except for a couple of words. So my dad had to talk to him. I think he had learned [Spanish] when he was little, because he lived on a farm all of his life.

Knowing Spanish is helpful as a practical matter; you can conduct your business more readily. But for many its usefulness ends there.

Among the rest of the community's Anglo residents, real bilingualism is the exception.

I was one of probably a handful of Anglos who could be considered fluent when I came back [to Havens] in my early 20s, recounted Susan Hartman, now a district administrator in the schools. And it was sort of unusual. People here were always surprised and would say, *"La gringa habla español."** There weren't a great number of us. Jack Russell, a leader in our community for many years, is very proud of his fluency and I remember when I was in high school he was held up as an example of what you could do if you really cared about language. In my Spanish IV class in high school, for example, it was predominantly Hispanic.

When Anglo members of the community have achieved bilingualism, they are bestowed a lore-like status among their peers in the community; everyone knows who they are and how they learned two languages, and their stories are recounted repeatedly. Those who are bilingual in the largest numbers in the community are the native Spanish speakers who over the years have learned English both as a means of surviving and of prospering economically—or who grew up in bilingual households where their parents did so to get ahead. Their language accomplishments are mostly taken for granted; their bilingualism is appreciated

---

*That White girl speaks Spanish.

when it is needed but it does not hold lore-like status. They are also occasionally held up as models of individual effort—of what you can accomplish if you are really motivated to learn English—in the same way that Susan Hartman and Jack Russell are held up reverentially for having learned Spanish.

At HHS, it is Spanish, not English, that fills the hallways. The sound of the Spanish language is what distinguishes HHS to former graduates and to outsiders as a Mexican-American high school. Wherever informal talk goes on at HHS, Spanish can be heard: between classes, in classrooms before the bell rings, in the cafeteria, in the school library, at the bus pickup points in the parking lot, in the early morning or at lunchtime or after school—wherever students congregate. Mexican music, not long ago considered an anomaly here, fills the hallways as well as the airwaves during lunch, when students turn on their radios and drive their cars and flashy pickup trucks off campus for a quick meal at McDonald's or Burger King. In these informal settings, teachers and students can also be heard conversing in Spanish. Between the teachers themselves, it is less frequent; only about 25% of the teachers count themselves as fluent Spanish speakers, and of these, eight are Mexican-American. But it was definitely heard. One of the most likely individuals to use it was the principal.

Like countless other small, isolated rural towns, in Havens sports are the focal point of the school's activities. On the courts or the football field, English is used and it is a point of sometimes fervent discussion whether or not the coaches are trying hard enough to include students who are not yet fluent in English. But whether Spanish is heard in the stands and bleachers depends on who is playing and the crowd the players draw. Girls' volleyball seems to be dominated by English, but at the football stadium on those gently warm Friday nights throughout the fall, Spanish governs the informal banter in the stands. The football announcer, who also hosts the modest amount of Spanish radio programming in town, is careful to enunciate the Spanish names as if it is a point of pride, but speaks only in English.

But for all of its informal use, I went to only one organized meeting conducted in Spanish. It was a meeting of a fledgling club of new immigrant women, and women who had lived in town for a while but had never mastered English. The club had grown out of the literacy classes that were offered at the Methodist church; these women had organized to try and bring Mexican culture to the community and to constitute a service club for the community, specifically for new immigrants. A Spanish speakers' Alcoholics Anonymous (AA) group meets periodically; these meetings are announced in the local paper in English.

A billboard south of town warns parents, in Spanish, to have their young children vaccinated. One of the only other places Spanish is officially, publicly recognized is at occasional elementary school functions. At holiday programs for schools in town at Christmastime, Spanish might appear in presentation by a bilingual class, but rarely by any others. Only at Jefferson Elementary, the school closest to the border, a formal, a school-wide *posada* is an annual tradition, followed by a bilingual program of class presentations. At a few of the elementary schools, usually those with greater numbers of children whose first language is Spanish, it is possible to hear the Pledge of Allegiance and the Pledge to the New Mexican flag recited in both Spanish and English.[1] But at HHS, there is no evidence of Spanish at any formal school event or occasion, for instance, in daily announcements or during pep rallies or sports events. Its only sanctioned appearances, besides the bilingual classes themselves, are periodic articles in the HHS school newspaper—still a relatively new addition to the paper when I arrived in town, courtesy of Richard Logan. In the Fall 1991 edition, the announcement of the new Spanish-language column appeared with some fanfare:

> *Esto es algo nuevo! Vamos a empezar a imprimir temas en español. Es para todos los estudiantes de Havens High. No es solo para los que vienen de México, sino tambien para los que estan estudiando español para una clase. Es la primer vez que habrá una sección en español. Será un cambio total. La realización de ésta sección fue porque mucho estudiantes nos dieron sus opiniones diciendo, "Por qué no poniamos una column en español." Tomamos opiniones y decidimos poner ésta sección en el periódico de las escuela.*[*]

In this same issue, an article about a student from Cuauhtémoc, Chihuahua who was new to the school appeared. The column is also used to introduce students from Mexico to the whole school. For the most part, these articles are usually published only in Spanish with topics ranging from biographies of some of the bilingual education teachers to the benefits and dangers of gossip to descriptions of events occurring in Frontera to commentary on popular Mexican musical groups to mini-surveys among the students from Mexico and new immigrants regarding current topics. Sometimes the column is published in both

---

[*]This is something new! We are beginning to print stories in Spanish. This is for all the students in Havens High. It isn't just for students who come from Mexico, but also for those who are taking Spanish classes. This is the first time there will be a section in Spanish. It will be a total change. This section appears because many students voiced their opinions, asking why we didn't have a column in Spanish. We asked their opinions and decided to put this section in the school paper.

languages. Because the school paper appears only infrequently and because it is primarily a student responsibility, this public debut of Spanish at HHS did not seem to violate the tacit agreement that governed its overall use in the community and in the school.

The other chink in the "No Spanish" norm was beginning to take place in official documents sent home from the schools. For the first time, in 1994–1995 the school calendar was to be printed in both languages; all handbooks were to go home in Spanish, and a bilingual report card was also beginning to be used. Notices to parents were beginning to appear in both languages. By 1997, well after I had returned home, one could find the announcement of the schools' upcoming kindergarten registration printed fully in the local newspaper in both English and Spanish. This development took place quietly, with no fanfare. It was as if calling attention to the slowly increasing use of Spanish might undermine precisely the progress it represented toward any real, substantive public recognition of both languages. When asked what would be considered going too far with respect to the use of Spanish, the high school principal, Daniel Martinez, replied, "Making the announcements on the PA system. That would be crossing the line." A coach at the high school recounted a story of wanting to have baseball caps printed with the name of the school's mascot in Spanish, only to be told this was not permissible—it too seemed to be going too far. The difference between the passive use of Spanish in printed materials and its active, visible use on a day-to-day basis is what seemed to constitute an impassable language use border.

* * *

Although Spanish had been present as the lingua franca of the Mexican-American community as far back as anyone could remember, the language landscape did not always include as much audible Spanish in public places as it does today. Traditionally Spanish was rarely heard on the streets. "You kind of just had to know where, where the place was to speak English. You just had to know," Daniel Martinez told me. And these norms were well engrained. Those who were monolingual Spanish speakers "sort of stuck out like sore thumbs" in the larger grocery stores, where there were always a few people who could speak Spanish. Outside of the home you were really only likely to hear Spanish spoken in town on Saturdays according to Martinez, because of the large number of agricultural workers from Mexico. "On Saturdays there was Spanish because the *braceros* came to town!"[2]

This historical distinction about the degree to which Spanish was used in the community was perhaps best reflected in comments about life in the high school. Mexican-American men and women who had graduated in the 1970s observed: "When we were going to school we were called *Chicanos* because we talked English and Spanish. Now everybody speaks Spanish and everybody speaks English." In the 1940s, when the proportion of Mexican-American students was still low, most Mexican or Mexican-American students who did attend HHS—whether from town or as daily border crossers—also spoke both English and Spanish. Daniel Martinez taught in Havens before he was the principal. He put it this way:

> If I took a microphone down the halls in 1978, it would be predominantly English. Now it's predominantly Spanish. Kids today don't feel uncomfortable using both languages like they used to. People are realizing that it's good to have two languages. Spanish is a piece of who they are.

An article in the October 1992 edition of the school newspaper also echoed the increasing contrast:

> HHS has always had some students talking both English and Spanish. Now, more than ever, while walking around the halls you can hear people who know English speaking Spanish and people coming to school from Mexico speaking English. So, I think I can safely say that HHS is bilingual.

By the time we arrived in Havens, the tide had already shifted; a home language survey of Grades 9 to 12 conducted in October 1993 indicated that of the approximately 1,000 students enrolled, about 400 reported speaking English only, 200 spoke English more than Spanish, 200 spoke both equally, 100 spoke Spanish more than English, and only spoke 100 Spanish only. Nevertheless, officially Spanish was not often recognized. And not everyone speaks both languages.

* * *

Where it was once possible to ignore how prevalent Spanish actually was, its growing prominence has already begun to force an emerging consideration of its value. Citizens of Havens are not, on the whole, proponents of a hard-core English-only position (although some are in small numbers, to be sure), and there is no hint of organized activism against the use of Spanish as there is in other parts of the southwest and across the country. Although we often heard, "This is America; if I went to Mexico I would be expected to speak Spanish, and 'they' should learn English," nearly everyone—even those who made such statements regularly—also believed that it was better to know two languages than one. On a purely practical level, in Havens it was simply a good idea to be able to speak both Spanish and English. Susan Hartman observed:

> It has definitely changed. You know, we have the retired community, the teachers, the business people and they're all signing up for the Spanish classes and wanting to take them. They're finding the need to know the language. And they're getting brave and practicing it. I think it's really as much a part of our community now as English in many ways. There may be more people still speaking only one language, but there's this whole growing vortex; it's real active.

But despite this shift, still missing was the sense that, on a grand scale, things might be done otherwise—that an alternative might exist that not only included, but endorsed, both languages, that it might be possible to conduct official business bilingually and to create a bilingual community. Although a few individuals, primarily school district teachers and admininstrators, believed in such a vision, in reality Spanish was still accorded a much lower place than English in the official hierarchy of Havens—despite its incremental acceptance.

This general devaluing of Spanish is an old legacy in the southwest, that is, Spanish existing nearly everywhere but failing to find a legitimate or secure place commensurate with its presence or use. In this way, Havens and its surroundings had more in common with its neighboring states of Arizona and Texas than they did with most of New Mexico, where Spanish has been assigned status and where officially the constitution of the state has explicitly recognized its existence and requires that children of Spanish descent "shall forever enjoy perfect equality with other children."[3] Nevertheless, the tacit sanctions against the use of Spanish that were enforced in official community exchanges in Havens in no way approached the divisive and rancorous language policies that had previously characterized schools along the United States–Mexico border.

In prior generations, it was common for the speaking of Spanish in the public schools to be forbidden entirely; people remembered the prohibitions against it as if they had occurred yesterday—some bitterly, some simply as a matter-of-fact part of their past history. It is a matter of historical record in schools along the border stretching from Brownsville to San Diego that Spanish was regularly banned.[4] And it is perhaps one of the most well-known tales as well. If you talk with a person of Mexican origin who grew up in the southwest anytime prior to the 1970s (and sometimes after that), you will inevitably be talking with someone who came into contact with the "No Spanish" rule in school as a child. It has become part of the annals of the regional immigrant culture along the border, an experience common to nearly every Mexican-American, and few who speak about their early education in the southwest recount their stories without reference to it.

Spanish was repressed for a variety of reasons, including: the desire for a homogeneous culture based on a single language, the most rapid assimilation possible, the supposedly substandard form of Spanish used along the border, the problems created for teachers when they did not speak Spanish,[5] and "moral and patriotic self-righteousness."[6] Whichever of these reasons was invoked, it inevitably had the same result: Children who spoke Spanish were denied their language as a means of communication, as a form of cultural knowledge, and as a basis for their identity and for their own educational progress. The barrier, of course, was real. But instead of viewing this conflict as a practical problem of language instruction, it was instead often viewed as an instance of the larger goal at hand, namely, Americanizing students whose first language was not English.[7]

Although scholars of the Mexican-American experience agree on the range of reasons leading to the "No Spanish" rule, they weigh in differently on what they believe the real explanation is, including the threat speaking Spanish poses for those in authority (a concern some teachers in Havens raised as well) or mass xenophobia in the context of a "national drive toward cultural and linguistic homogeneity."[8] All seem to agree that conditions were at their worst in Texas, where schools practiced punishments like "Spanish Detention" even into the 1970s.[9] Mexican culture and the Spanish language were often seen as identical and inappropriate for learning;[10] this provided teachers and administrators alike with the motivation to enact and sustain the prohibitions against Spanish.

The "No Spanish" rule served as a general form of cultural exclusion. The Havens version of what took place during this era went something like this. A general policy existed that Spanish was not to be spoken anywhere on the school grounds. Like other mandates, it was enforced to the degree that each principal or teacher wished to enforce it; most created an environment where it was clear to everyone that speaking Spanish was not acceptable. Others stretched the limits, but only slightly. One longtime elementary school principal said that she enforced the rule in the classrooms, but not on the playground. "I enforced it the way I enforced the rule that all little girls had to wear dresses. I looked the other way." Because for decades there were clear demarcations between Anglo and Mexican neighborhoods, it was rare for an

Anglo child in the elementary grades in Havens even to realize that such a prohibition existed. But for the two or three Anglo families who did live in the *barrio*, their children learned Spanish despite the ban—and usually it was on the playground. These same few Anglo students, now grown and prominent members of the community, also recounted teaching their friends some English to prevent the spankings that occurred when Spanish was spoken in school.

Most children whose first language was Spanish had grown up in a Spanish speaking world, so the "No Spanish" rule shattered their sense of reality. Eva Ortiz is a special education teacher at HHS. She was raised in Havens and graduated from its schools during the 1970s.

> I went to one school where for every Spanish word you said, you counted up from the bottom and that's where you put your nose in the crack on the wall. And you had to wear a placard that said "I speak English, I need to speak English. We speak English here." And to me it didn't make any sense, because everywhere I'd ever gone they'd spoken Spanish.

A teacher who grew up in a neighboring school district recalled it this way.

> We only spoke Spanish at home so when I went to school I didn't know English. The teachers would whip the kids across the hands with sticks if we spoke any Spanish, or slap us across the head. I couldn't communicate with anybody. I knew a little English and I would try to converse but then I would run out of English and need to use Spanish and I would get beaten. I would go outside during recess and lean against the wall with my hands folded because I couldn't talk to anybody. I was so lonely. I remember thinking, "School is supposed to be wonderful. What is this?"

For others, the rule was simply accepted and they tried to abide by it. If their parents spoke some English at home, the transition was eased a bit. Carmen Mendoza, who eventually became one of the district's first bilingual education teachers, simply did what she was told. "And then I went to school, and the teacher told me I had to speak English, so I started speaking English that day," she explained. "We were forced to speak English." Compliance seemed to be the appropriate action on the part of a then 5-year-old whose family respected whatever rules the school set out. Carmen continued,

> The time that I was going to school it was forbidden for us to talk Spanish. They wanted us to just talk plain English and that was it, and we were forbidden. We really didn't think too much about it. We just complied with the rules. You had to comply with the rules at school. If you didn't, not only did you get it at school, but you got it at home. That's the way it was.

The children did not necessarily understand or experience this rule immediately as a form of bias.

> As a child I spoke Spanish without questioning whether we should or we shouldn't. We just did. But in school we're not allowed to do it. That's what we were told. "It's bad manners to speak Spanish in front of somebody else." At least that's what I felt. I never felt that it was discrimination or anything, it was just that it was bad manners.

This same woman, now one of the district's most active proponents of bilingual education, went on to teach her own children English first to make sure they wouldn't suffer the same problems in school, and now she regrets that they have lost their Spanish. Others found ways to get around the prohibition.

> Well, thinking back, there wasn't any other way, so it didn't bother me back then. But now I look back and I think, well, you know, they were forcing us to do something that we were not used to. They were trying to force us to talk in English when I didn't even have an English background. I couldn't converse in English. I mean, if I was to do it their way, I would have probably said nothing. I would have just sat there. 'Cause there was no other way of doing it. But we still chanced it when we played outside. We wouldn't yell that much when we talked a lot in Spanish. If I remember right, we would be in groups. That way they couldn't pick on one individual and say, "you."

Only in retrospect, in an era when it was possible to see the situation from another, more long-term perspective, did the meaning of this linguistic exclusion become absolutely clear, as one paraprofessional in the HHS bilingual program explained.

> You know, now you see it and you say, "Oh my gosh, we were really discriminated against." To me, I think we didn't think that we were discriminated against. It was just like a rule. That feeling is really ugly, to feel that you can't even express yourself. If our culture would have been accepted, we would have been proud of our culture. But it was not acceptable, our culture.

* * *

A few days before I left Havens to return to Milwaukee, I was up late at night packing and watching a late-night TV show featuring a comedy troupe called "Culture Clash." As a take-off on Central and South American military torture practices, the skit portrayed an American prisoner who was told that he would learn Spanish quickly. A "general" began, "We know how to make people talk. You are going to be bilingual. You are going to learn Spanish the right way, the right wing way." And in rote fashion, the prisoner rattled off the words he was forced to learn under the watchful eye of the uniformed general. It was such a clever piece of satire, and as only good satire can, struck a raw nerve with respect to what I had been learning about Spanish in schools in the southwest in the old days. Bereft of the capacity to use their first language, children were expected to become English speakers as if by osmosis. No one who recounted this story—and it was a story I heard over and over again from my Mexican-American friends—did so lightly. The stories of language prohibitions were nearly always accompanied by other tales of cultural discrimination—most often the story of being laughed at for bringing burritos rather than sandwiches for lunch or for saying that you had eaten chorizo rather than bacon with your eggs that morning. Although I got the impression that things were not quite as bad in Havens as they might have been, say, in Texas itself, or even in other communities nearby to Havens, accounts of the language bans were easily among the most difficult stories people told. Not quite torture, but painful, very painful, nevertheless.

The great irony regarding language, of course, is that even during the era when Spanish was prohibited in schools everywhere along the border, those students who did know both languages were regularly called on to translate in class. Their teachers, who were nearly always Anglo, depended on it. So at the same time speaking Spanish was forbidden, it was also a fixture of classroom life for teachers who recognized they could not teach school effectively without it. Eduardo Rios, the superintendent, who as a child in the early 1950s, entered kindergarten speaking both English and Spanish, was quickly moved to first grade where he translated for the teacher; the double standard was institutionalized nearly as much as the prohibition itself. A great deal of friendly, informal translating still goes on in the community and in the schools alike and in reality the need for such translation is commonly recognized. Once they let their teachers know their capacity, bilingual students in the high school are asked to translate as a matter of routine, or readily volunteer, unasked, to do so. At one supermarket, if the baggers, usually high school boys for whom this is considered a plum job, are bilingual, they are regularly called upon to translate for customers who do not speak English. "You can hear Spanish all over town now." said a prominent Anglo woman. "Even our church [a fundamentalist Christian church] is bilingual. I mean, the sermon is in English but there are interpreters. I think it's like this everywhere you go in Havens, whereas a few years ago it might not have been so pronounced." The increase in monolingual Spanish speakers has also created new job opportunities in the community; a bilingual court interpreter, herself an immigrant during her teenage years, would not have had such a position 5 years ago—the need simply was not there. In advertisement after advertisement, bilingual employees were regularly being sought to fill positions from receptionist to fast-food worker. Relative to the informal, decades-old practice of neighborly, friendly translating, its institutionalization marks a demographic turning point for the community.

No one I came to know—Anglo or Mexican—had any illusions about the importance of learning English; it was valued as an essential skill.[11] For those whose first language was Spanish, if one wanted to get ahead, if one wanted a better chance at a better job, if one believed in the future of NAFTA as any kind of opportunity, English was a necessity. In the schools, the formal structures for learning English were the bilingual education programs and it was clear that for many of the students who came across the border on a daily basis, learning English was not only their—but also their parents'—primary motivation for border crossing. Outside of the schools, in the community, only a small number of options for newcomers to learn English existed—and all were well used.

The most formalized of these opportunities was the Literacy Volunteers of America (LVA) program funded through the New Mexico Coalition of Literacy. An annual grant supported one administrator, the costs of training the tutors, and a small amount for materials. LVA classes met at the Methodist church, a facility with an annex of bright Sunday School classrooms that the LVA borrowed on weekdays. The director, an older Anglo woman named Mary Crowley, specifically chose Havens as a place to retire because "it was a quiet, friendly place where people sat on the steps of the post office and talked to you and wanted to know how you were." She believes that LVA attracts a serious, highly motivated cadre of students who "want to learn and work hard at it" rather than just put in their time in class—referring to a previous and relatively unsuccessful program specifically designed to enable applicants for citizenship to meet the English language requirement.[12] According to Ana, one of the tutors and my own Spanish teacher, the main motivation for the students—who were mostly women with families—was the desire to understand what their school-aged children were talking about. During their formal classes, these women sat on small chairs in a classroom that was meant for 15 six-year-olds and held simple conversations with Ana in English. The local LVA also sponsors a GED program, a satellite class located directly on the border, and an on-site workplace program providing tutoring for specific workplace language needs.

A second opportunity to learn English was to enroll in night classes held at HHS as part of the night school program. These classes use one of the high school's computer labs to provide individualized instruction, followed by conversational practice. The women in this class also are primarily mothers of students in the schools. The third formal opportunity was a combination of ESL and citizenship classes held at night at one of the elementary schools in the predominantly Mexican east side of town. In each of these three situations, the teachers I observed were all either Mexican or Mexican-American; some were native born citizens of the United States, others were naturalized citizens, and at least one was a permanent resident alien. Ana, the LVA tutor, was born in Mexico City but had lived in the United States for decades. The night school teachers, Monica and Carmen, both worked for the school district, one as a teacher and one as a teacher's aide; Carmen was a permanent resident (alien). Olga Suarez and Juan Garcia, the ESL/citizenship teachers, were among the few Mexican-American people in Havens who were actively involved in trying to improve life for new immigrants in the community. Juan, in particular, had a long-standing commitment to assist those Mexican families who applied for amnesty under the 1986 Simpson–Rodino bill in meeting the English language requirements and also ran the labor office in town (which, given the agricultural economy, was a magnet for migrant workers).

One of the big problems with learning English in Havens, Ana believed, was that not enough of the teachers are native English speakers. Another was the absence of organized opportunities for the community to deal with the newcomers on a variety of issues. Ana said:

> I think there should be a program, something similar to a workshop, a meeting in the community once a month for people who are aliens or whatever we want to call them, to tell them and answer some questions they might have or make them aware of the programs in the community. The people who are going to night classes, who are really taking advantage of English as a Second Language, they are the people who are already here, they already feel comfortable. But a lot of the men and ladies who just get here are ashamed.

But few beyond those who were already involved either in teaching English or translating seemed to be troubled by the limited number of organized opportunities that existed in the community for newcomers to learn English.

Not only are opportunities to learn English in the community limited, but opportunities to learn Spanish are sparse as well. Outside of formal bilingual education programs in the schools, a limited number of night school and informal classes are offered. Local teachers from the bilingual and Spanish language program teach night classes through a satellite branch of one of the state university campuses and for several years free classes sponsored by the school district have been offered once a week to school district employees. A previous superintendent had mandated that all of Havens' teachers would become bilingual and the free classes had their origin in this mandate, which no longer exists under the current superintendent.

In need of a Spanish tutor for my own children during our stay in Havens, I sought advice from people in the school district, but no ready network of Spanish tutors existed. In fact, one of the most ardent proponents of bilingual education in the school district, on learning of my search, asked my advice in locating a tutor for her own granddaughter, to whom she felt she was doing a disservice by not yet having made sure that she could speak Spanish. We finally made arrangements with my friend Ana, who in addition to teaching English for the LVA project tutored my own children twice a week, and regularly helped me with my own language learning.

Because our relationship was anchored in issues of language, Ana and I often talked about the curious absence of a stronger structure for learning Spanish in Havens. Ultimately, there was no sense of urgency with respect to providing opportunities for local, native English speakers to learn Spanish or for newcomers to learn English. Intentionally structuring the intensive learning of language in the community was not a priority—and only in the schools was the discussion of the need for a more bilingual community a fledgling public conversation. This absence of a deliberate means for the learning of second languages is commonplace in the United States, so it is in no way surprising that such a limitation also exists in Havens as well. Despite the immigration surge, concepts like the Ulpan in Israel, an intensive Hebrew immersion experience to meet the immediate, short-term needs, have not transferred to this country. Beyond programs in the schools, developing a community-wide organized response to what could be considered a language crisis in Havens—or at least an immediate, pressing, and increasing need—did not much seem to be on people's minds as a community issue.

The justification for learning English is typically an economic one recognized by Anglo and Mexican people alike. But the motivation for learning—or keeping—Spanish is not at all so one-dimensional. If you already speak Spanish and are learning English, you are on your way to making it, to becoming a full-fledged member of Havens' society. Community members recognize your accomplishments and teachers single you out as being among a select group that really has *ganas.*[*] But if you are learning English and losing your Spanish—whether you are an immigrant or a first or second generation Mexican-American—you are making it at the cost of something that many believe it is too important to lose. "I get all aggravated because I don't want to forget my Spanish," Maria Cruz told me. "It's something that I don't want to forget because it's a part of me and so I try to speak it. Knowing English is an advantage because you have greater opportunities over here." But recall that Maria also carries around her mother's admonition that if she loses her Spanish, all she will have left is the fact that she was born in Mexico and this, to her mother, was not enough of a link.

Many Spanish-speaking parents in Havens work exceedingly hard to help their school-age children retain their first language. Although loss of native language is commonplace for first generation children of immigrants, its loss can also signal the breaking of a cultural connection, often breaking the hearts of parents along the way. But elsewhere in the country, and with languages other than Spanish, the economic consequences may not be as great. In the case of Spanish along the border, the potential for cultural and economic loss occurs simultaneously as more and more jobs require both languages. Nonetheless, as is often the case at least with first generation children of immigrants, for decades many parents in Havens shielded their children from speaking Spanish to secure their achievement in school in English and their sense of belonging—only to find later on that they need Spanish as an economic boost—as well as a cultural connection. Eva, an aide in the bilingual program at HHS, grew up in Havens and suffered through the shame of her Spanish being denigrated and denied in school. Like so many others, at home she taught her children to speak English.

> When I started having kids I was not going to let them speak Spanish. I felt like if they grow up learning the English, they'd be so proud of themselves when they went to school that they would not have to worry about their accent. Then my daughter moved to Albuquerque to go to college and I think the first week that she was there she called me and said, "Mom, why didn't you teach me Spanish? Every job I'm applying for asks for a bilingual person. So now I have to learn because I lied on the application. I have to learn because there are no jobs out there."

The press to learn Spanish seemed greatest among young Mexican American adults who grew up hearing Spanish but not speaking it; as the need for bilingual employees grew, the loss of language was a definite liability.

---

[*]Deep-seated desire.

Those who were learning Spanish anew, for purposes of job enhancement or otherwise, did so in a variety of ways. Some forced themselves to make active what was passive knowledge from a childhood of listening, but not speaking. Like Eva's daughter, another mother described the situation in their home.

> They grew up knowing some Spanish; they took it in junior high. But because of their jobs in the clothing stores they had to relearn it. They'd be coming home and asking, "Mom, how do you say this?" and "Mom, they told me this. What does that mean?" And then, well, Teresa's gone on to work at the cycle shop, and she still does and she's had to learn a different Spanish vocabulary.

Others returned to it by formal study at the university, rediscovering their cultural roots along the way. This was the case with Tony, a highly successful secondary bilingual education teacher who as a child and adolescent rejected his family's Spanish language and heritage. "He was a cowboy and that's all he did in high school," his father told me. "But now my son speaks beautiful Spanish, the Spanish that they speak down in Mexico, and I learn from my son!" Yet others, like Liliana Sanchez's friend Colin, learned from their bilingual friends in school, who felt a certain responsibility toward fellow Mexican or Mexican-American friends who were letting their Spanish go or who were not in touch with the Spanish part of their lives.

There is often an air of confidence about this last group of students as they play the role of informal teachers for their friends who they see as being in danger of losing the little Spanish they have. They seem quite aware of how easy it is to forget one's first language in an environment like HHS, where it is not required although it is ever present. Tony Valenzuela, the child of migrant workers who, as a sophomore, had already been noticed by recruiters for college because of his high achievement, explained his role in his best friend's language learning this way.

> I am afraid of losing it. Eduardo, he almost lost it and I don't want to lose my Spanish. When I have children I don't want them to lose Spanish because I think, "It's from our ancestors, from our background," and we shouldn't lose it. There are a lot of people that don't teach it to their children and I feel sad for them. When Eduardo was born his mom wasn't used to talking Spanish and she would talk to him in English. She was forgetting her Spanish and she wasn't teaching it to him, but he knew a little. Now he started hanging out with me and I have been teaching him. Since I talk to him in Spanish, he talks to me in Spanish, too.

Others model their lack of self-consciousness about being able to speak Spanish as well as about their Mexican background. The mother of Colin Young, Liliana Sanchez's friend, is Mexican, but he had never acknowledged the Mexican side of his family. He didn't look the stereotypical part, nor did his name reveal his heritage. In Havens, no one assumed he might have Mexican ancestry. Liliana said:

> I'm very proud of Colin. He accepts his Mexican heritage a lot more now. Last year he would always make comments like, "You're in America, speak English," and that irritated me. I told him, "If I don't speak Spanish in front of you, it's out of common courtesy because I know you don't understand. It's not because I'm ashamed of it and I never will be." And that's something, we laid down the way, you know, and between us it was okay, *and now he even tries to learn Spanish from his mom.*

Gloria, another member of the band and a friend in Liliana and Colin's circle, began her life speaking Spanish, went to bilingual kindergarten and learned English, and only now is coming back to her Spanish—largely because of other friends in school.

> I'm learning my Spanish again. I have trouble writing some of the words that I don't know. But I have a friend, his name is Alberto, he graduated last year. He's the one who got me to speak more Spanish, because I used to speak pure English. At first I felt weird talking in Spanish. Weird as in maybe I sound funny and what if I don't pronounce this right, and all that. And I have my friend Cristina, she talks in, like, pure Spanish, and she gets me to talk again.

For many of these students, there is a clear distinction between the absolute value of keeping or learning Spanish and deciding when it is appropriate or comfortable to use it. It is not a distinction that is talked about much. Some had crafted a specific position based on their sense of what it meant to be "polite" when you have the advantage of two languages. Liliana's persistence with Colin represents the most common position. She would not use Spanish because he did not understand it; this was a matter of interpersonal respect. Interestingly, this is the same rationale that was often used to explain the earlier, institutionalized ban on Spanish in the schools: "It is not polite and not everyone understands it." But the conclusion about politeness in the 1990s represents an individual choice made by Mexican-American or Mexican students themselves; it is not one leveraged bureaucratically and inequitably by the schools.

The tacit sanctions against the use of Spanish that exist in official community exchanges do not in any way approach a prohibition or de jure policy like those that had previously characterized schools in Havens or across the southwest. But among Anglos who were uncomfortable with Mexican-American or Mexican people in general, the language of "politeness" about when to use which language could also have an edge of anger to it and stand in for more overt discrimination. The timeworn issue of believing someone must be talking about you if they are not speaking in English is often invoked.

> One thing I resent about the Spanish speaking [people]. They're here to learn English but they continue, I resent the fact that when they don't want you to know what they're saying they immediately converse in Spanish. I think it's rude. Of course, you can't say anything to them because you're discriminating against their language. Well, I don't think you are. I think they should have more respect and they should speak English.

Other bilingual students were not proactive Spanish teachers and although many Mexican-American students at HHS are fully bilingual, as the 1993 language survey shows, not everyone advertises their capacity. Instead, they keep Spanish but mostly as private knowledge, drawing on it only as they need. Often even their teachers did not know that certain local Havens students spoke Spanish fluently. Popular students might obscure their Spanish language skills, opting instead to belong to the formal school culture. Other Mexican-Americans students who might be first, second, or third generation, simply never learned their parents' Spanish, sometimes to the dismay of some of their bilingual friends. At the market where he is a bagger, Ricardo Herrera, the football player whose mother buys bread and rolls at the bakery in Frontera, is one of a handful of bilingual employees. The other high school boys who work there, Ricardo observed:

> These are all guys who, they're Spanish. They have the last name Rodriguez, Dominguez, whatever you want to call it, and they just can't speak Spanish. They don't understand it—and some girls, too. They're always calling me saying, "What is he saying, what does he want, how much is it going to be in food stamps, and he wants this and he wants that."

The inconvenience was less important than the loss; according to Ricardo and others who held a similar set of beliefs about the importance of Spanish, it was inappropriate just to let your language go, even if retaining it entailed some difficulty. Those who chose not to learn it had a variety of explanations that sometimes focused on whether or not they really considered themselves Hispanic or Mexican in identity. "I don't really feel like an Hispanic," said a young woman whose mother is Mexican but whose father is not. "We're not Mexicans per se. I mean I'm not Mexican, I'm American. I was born in America," is the way she put it.

* * *

Communities make choices about how to acknowledge and enact their bilingualism. In America, current reality is that these choices are usually made in the form of inaction, and in general second language use remains a low expectation and an unimportant goal. Despite its growing Mexican and Mexican-American population and the majority status of Mexican-American students in the district, Havens is still an American town, albeit one located on the Mexican border. Few models for how a community might in fact be bilingual exist in this country and in many ways it is no different in Havens. At an official, institutional level the two languages coexist only passively; it is individuals who have the responsibility of deciding whether they will integrate English and Spanish into their own lives.

Such individual effort takes great mettle and the sociocultural implications of this incidental, personal decision making with regard to language within the community are evident: Without the force of economic necessity behind them or a structure in which both languages are purposefully valued, Mexican people have learned English in much greater proportions than Anglo people have learned Spanish. This imbalance still is not recognized as a credit to Mexican and Mexican-origin people in Havens. Rather, the expectation for language learning is couched in the long-standing belief that the only real way a community can operate is with one dominant language. As much as Havens is, de facto, a bilingual community, it is in many ways a bifurcated language community.

In the context of an American community, this is the norm. In the context of the border as a binational region, it is a norm that has delayed the potential for border communities to distinguish themselves as places where two languages can purposefully coexist. In Havens, having two languages is finally becoming a recognizable asset on a community-wide basis, if not in the official dynamics of Havens, then clearly in its business world. The world of day-to-day transactions that take place off the official stage and that, in many ways, is the life of the community, differs from the official, formal, and ceremonial world of community meetings, public rites of passage like graduation, or the recognized media in the community. Businesses are quickly becoming places where it is essential to use Spanish as an active part of the work that is done and the interactions that occur. The need for and use of two languages is apparent nearly everywhere *except* in most official interactions that are public.

The purposeful use of two languages is a necessity that is already valued by individuals like Liliana, Maria, and Richard. Their unwillingness to see language use as a monolingual choice and their insistence on seeing dual language knowledge as an asset and a necessity is not the norm in Havens. But the possibility, the conversation, is at least on the table. And the place it is most on the table is in the schools.

4

*Quien Sabe Dos Lenguas Vale por Dos**

If your kids come home speaking Spanish, you're going to have more respect for Mexicans the next time.

Just yesterday, Juan Dominguez, who I knew was Hispanic but I didn't know spoke Spanish, was standing up right near my desk while I was doing something and he was talking to Carlos Rojas and they were speaking Spanish. Eduardo's Spanish is real, I mean, it really flows. He speaks Spanish all the time. For Juan, it was much more pedantic, it was much slower, but he was doing it, more formal, slower, accent wasn't there, but he was carrying on a conversation in Spanish with this kid and it dawned on me for the first time that Juan was bilingual.

Language education on the border is at least as complex as life itself on the border. In the most immediate sense there is a need to provide education for students who simply do not speak the language of instruction; without English, their chances for access to life opportunities in Havens, New Mexico, and throughout the United States, are limited. Socioculturally, language divides; the extent to which Anglo people are willing to learn another language and the extent to which knowing two languages is valued also characterizes the language challenge and struggle that faces students, teachers, and administrators in Havens' schools. Those who are already bilingual, like Juan Dominguez, are a critical part of the language landscape—but are often taken for granted or go unrecognized in the realm of language in their school.

Officially, as we have seen, Havens remains a monolingual community. In neighborly, unofficial terms, it has always been a community where Spanish and English have coexisted and where knowledge of both languages has always been, but is at the same time becoming, increas-

---

*A traditional Spanish proverb: "He who knows two languages is worth two persons."

ingly important. It is really no different in the schools. Cultural mediators like Liliana, Maria, and Richard are successful in their work
because they can communicate on both sides of the line. In varying
degrees of skill and confidence they speak both Spanish and English,
translate regularly in school, and are successful in negotiating in both
the Mexican and American communities—whether "Mexican" means
the Mexican-American community in Havens, or in Mexico, or both. In
the language survey taken in Fall 1993, recall that about 100 students
at HHS reported speaking Spanish only, with another 100 speaking
Spanish more than English. Two hundred speak English more than
Spanish; combined with the 400 who speak English only, this is slightly
more than 50% of the school. The 200 students who are already fully
bilingual—one fifth of the school and a group equal in size to those for
whom Spanish is dominant—are nearly all Mexican or Mexican-American. Liliana and Maria are among this group. When it comes to language, it is rare that Anglos, due to their lack of bilingualism, are able
to broker, or mediate, between people.[1] Such brokering, on the other
hand, is a regular feature of life for many Mexican-American students.
Richard Logan is among the few exceptions.

In contrast to the community at large, schools in Havens do have a
long, if erratic, history of providing at least some kind of support for
individuals whose first language is Spanish. Ironically, this has existed
alongside the conventional southwestern history prohibiting its use.
Historically this has been a curious inconsistency, one that for years
mirrored the informal, neighborly acts that enabled Mexican students
to attend schools in Havens in the first place. Only recently has the
school district begun to provide language programming in a more
systematic way. Teachers and administrators are thinking more about
the role of bilingual education in moving the district toward a more
fruitful practice of binationalism. In the realm of language, this means
supporting the learning of both Spanish and English, and thus, going
far beyond a concern with teaching English to Mexican students who
cross into Havens each day.

"We have always treated language as an important issue in this
district," Susan Hartman, the bilingual district administrator who grew
up in Havens, recounted. "But there have been long periods of time
where little was done in terms of language instruction." Susan is among
that handful of Anglo natives who learned to speak Spanish attending
one of the *barrio* elementary schools and then followed through on her
studies as a high school and college student, also spending summers
with a family in Mexico. She continued:

> One of my personal goals when I began to work at the district level was to decentralize language teaching to all of the elementary schools, to get rid of the idea that bilingual education is only for the schools that have high populations of Mexican students.

This is the district's goal as defined by the central administration. It is an ambitious goal, to be sure, because it sets out to overcome a long-standing tradition that language learning is only a means to "fix" the language shortcomings of Mexican children. It is also a goal with a shifting purpose. Demographic trends suggest that all schools in the community are becoming places that have increasing proportions of Mexican and Mexican-American students—not all of whom have Spanish as their first language. Ethnicity is not the sole factor that distinguishes between students who can and cannot benefit from language instruction; Anglo and Mexican-American students alike may not know Spanish. However, it is Mexican and Mexican-American students alone who may not know English. It is, fundamentally, a more complex issue than it appears.

The origins of language instruction in the district are periodically mentioned in a local book that was compiled to chronicle of the history of Sonora County—a coveted possession among Havens' "old-timers." Biographical sketches, family histories, and community milestones are marked here with pride, and photographs of many of the community's citizens, and of course, its teachers, appear. Often these entries were prepared by family members who saw the book as an opportunity to commemorate their family's early life in Havens. As this history book documents, informal language learning occurred in many of the earliest outlying county elementary schools. "About 1914," one passage reads, "the county built a little red schoolhouse where we drove three miles by horse and buggy. We three Wilson kids and Dora Hunter were the only Anglos among the Spanish-speaking peers, so we became nearly bilingual." And about Alice Edgar, a much beloved elementary school teacher, this entry appears:

> Alice graduated in the first graduating class of the new Havens High School in 1912. Her teaching career started in Astrid, New Mexico. She came to the Havens schools is 1914 as a pre-primary teacher at Wood School [the same school Liliana Sanchez's grandparents attended]. Her area of specialization was teaching Mexican-American children to speak English to prepare them for first grade. Alice taught three generations of Sonora County residents during her half-century teaching career. She was always aware of others' needs and was able to put her vast knowledge,

understanding and deep compassion to excellent use. The welfare of children was always foremost in her mind.

This entry is accompanied by a photograph of Alice—a gray-haired lady in her 80s with a warm smile, wearing a double strand of pearls. Alice herself was not bilingual and a specific record of her teaching techniques is not available.

This historical volume often became the starting point for discussions on many of my visits with Lydia Silva, who in 1935 was one of the first Mexican students to graduate from HHS. Lydia's school experience was unusual in that she was bilingual from her earliest years. Her stepfather, with whom she grew up, was Anglo, and her mother was Mexican. Her dual language skills did not shield her from the discrimination that so commonly existed within the schools and the community as she was growing up. Nevertheless, she placed great importance on learning both languages—English to get along, and Spanish to be sure one's culture and connection to the past were not lost. She connected difficulty in getting ahead economically with language capacity. "A lot of these old-timers," she told me, "the old Hispanics, so many, many of them came from Mexico and they had the language barrier to begin with." Lydia equally regretted that so many of her Mexican peers early on did not have the opportunity to learn English, and that today the children of her friends (and her own children's children) were squandering the opportunity to learn Spanish. Language was often on her mind, but more as a means of achieving equity on the part of Mexican immigrants. As a founding member of the local chapter of the Pan American Club, she pressed for good relationships between the Anglo and Mexican communities in Havens and between Havens and Frontera.

Shortly after Lydia graduated from HHS, beginning in 1941, an act of the New Mexico legislature mandated the teaching of Spanish in New Mexico's grade schools. Havens schools were among the first to comply, and it was Ana Herrera, the only teacher of Mexican descent in Havens at the time, who took up the charge. Lydia remembered Ana and her family well. During one of my visits with her, as we sipped Coca-Colas on a hot afternoon in the living room of her pink stuccoed home on the east side, the border of the traditional Mexican side of town, she plied me with fresh pecans from her husband's trees and with the help of the history book filled in some of the gaps about Ana Herrera's early years as a teacher in Havens.

Ana began teaching in the local schools in 1928, at the age of 22. Her status as a teacher who was Mexican made her quite an anomaly among the teachers, the students, and the community. Lydia recollected it like this, both reading from the written history and adding her own comments:

> Ana came from Mexico with her family. They came by covered wagon from Chihuahua, farther down south. In Mexico her family owned a small carpenter shop and a grocery store. They decided to leave their beloved country after 21 years of marriage and emigrate to the United States because General Pershing extended a kind and generous invitation to the people of Mexico. She taught forever in the schools. She taught Spanish, from what I remember. She graduated in '26. I still wonder how she got into high school or college or whatever so she could become a teacher.

The details of Ana's college admission and attendance, so unusual for an individual of Mexican origin in those days, are not available, but she attended the university in Albuquerque, eventually graduating from a nearby state college with a degree in Spanish and education, which she was determined to put to good use. Her photograph, too, was included with her family's history. She has glasses, her hair is pulled back in a bun, and, like Alice Edgar, she was wearing a strand of pearls.

A generation after Lydia Silva completed her high school education, one of only a handful of Mexican students to do so, Ana's story is picked up in the recollections of Carmen Mendoza, who eventually became one of the district's first certified bilingual education/ESL teachers in the late 1960s.

> When I was a little girl there was one Hispanic teacher in Havens and her name was Ana Herrera. And of course, we viewed this Herrera as some kind of god or saint or something. We couldn't conceive ... "Well, she must be something, because she's a teacher and she's so distinct." It was the strangest thing. It made such an impression on us, that she was a teacher and so she must be very intelligent and very smart. It had to be that. This was the only Spanish [Mexican] teacher we had ever seen.
>
> In fourth or fifth grade she would come to our room or we would go to her class and she would give us a little Spanish lesson and took the whole class, Anglos and Hispanics and everybody. But it was all very, very basic stuff, like the colors, which I guess for the little Anglos was okay, but for us, we just sat there and kind of knew it.
>
> And the next time you got a dose of Spanish was in junior high or high school—they were combined in one building. That Spanish teacher was a fluent Spanish speaker, but she was not Hispanic. Nothing much happened. Now I feel like if somebody had just insisted that they expand our knowledge that we came with—maybe not cater to us in teaching this class, but at least to have worked with the vocabulary to where we would come out reading really good Spanish and learning to at least write with the accent.

Ana Herrera's Spanish classes spanned 17½ years, at which time they were inexplicably discontinued. She went on to work in the district for a total of 41 years as an elementary school teacher.

Alice Edgar's pre-first grade approach and Ana Herrera's fledgling Spanish classes were the first recorded attempts to introduce language and address in at least a perfunctory way the issue of bilingualism—in both directions. The Board of Education minutes also tell of a presentation in 1952 by a first- and second-grade teacher who "gave an effective demonstration of her use of vocabulary charts in teaching Spanish speaking first and second graders." But this was not the only way language was accommodated. The pre-first concept Alice introduced continued for quite some time in various forms. A former district administrator whose tenure began in the 1960s and who served during the rocky transition from informal to formal programs of bilingual education recollected it this way:

> Well, in New Mexico schools the Hispanic children were kept back the first year. We were not permitted to start them early. We had to wait until they were 6. So, we had what we called Pre-First for the Hispanic children who did not pass different types of tests. The Pre-First was designed to acquaint them with the world they did not know. And then they went into a regular first and proceeded on. They were generally a year late. Now, this, of course, was not a common thing, because many Hispanic children already were acquainted with the world around them, I mean, the world out in the marketplace, not just their home. But we had this Pre-First in New Mexico. When Title I came along in the 1960s, we had to work out a plan, so we developed a kindergarten program for 5-year-old Hispanic children to provide them with the experiences and they could be prepared for first grade when they arrived at the age of 6. At that time, kindergartens were illegal in the state of New Mexico.
>
> We had all types of programs, which we felt were helpful. The so-called bilingual education wasn't really known at that time. We were using the immersion concept, and we had ESL people running around loose. We had another concept which never was fully accomplished, and that was that all of our first-grade teachers, at least, had to be fairly well versed in the Spanish language. We had that concept. That doesn't mean that all of the first-grade teachers were Hispanic. It meant that they were, the term that we called them here is *simpático*. They understood the Spanish culture, they had lived with it, they were familiar with it, and they visited the homes and things like that. We always had an aide who was native Hispanic. And we thought we had a pretty good system.

This kind of early support for students who entered the school system with limited English skills was, more than anything else, a program to teach English to Mexican students. With these few primary level supports in place, Susan Hartman noted that most of Havens' teachers still fended for themselves, using practices like buddies, peer partners, or clustering students for translation purposes. One Spanish language teacher at the junior high level divided the class in half, teaching Spanish to the Anglo students and English to the Mexican students. For a period of time the high school English department offered a course called "Living English" for students whose English language skills were weak. And, like all high schools, there was a traditional Spanish foreign language program, which for many years featured an annual trip to Mexico. These activities and classes all preceded formal bilingual programs that were finally developed under the press of federal regulations.

But this array of homegrown efforts, with its inherent good intentions, had obvious flaws as well. Students who did not speak English—at all or well—still ran the risk of being seen only as children in need of help, and not as children who brought with them the power of another language and the richness of another culture. At the same time, attempts to teach Spanish were structured more to familiarize students with basic vocabulary and less, if at all, to support in-depth, conversational language learning. When bilingual education finally became a federal requirement through the Lau Remedies in 1975,[2] the district did move to develop other options.

In the early 1970s, a formal bilingual kindergarten program began at Morgan Elementary School east of town—one of three outlying county schools. This program was designed to teach English to students whose first language was Spanish, that is, for Mexican children. After completing kindergarten at Morgan, the children would then follow their teacher into one of the schools in town for first grade. Carmen Mendoza recalled:

> We had one problem when I was working at Morgan. There were a lot of Anglo parents upset because they'd come and they'd want their children in the bilingual program, and I would have to say, "No, it's strictly for the kids who can't speak English." And they would be very upset, and tell me, "That's not fair. I want my child living in the southwest to be bilingual." It was just not correct that we did not have the facilities and the personnel. Nobody else was allowed in the program and people who wanted to couldn't buy in. That's the way the history of this community has been, that type of bilingual program—to teach the limited English speakers in the bilingual setting English as fast as they can and then just mainstream them. In the beginning, it was more of a remedial program.

Learning Spanish was not part of the arrangement. Eventually, the Morgan program was closed and bilingual education at the elementary level was centralized in town at one of the two *barrio* elementary schools, Brighton, in the town's poorest neighborhood. Arguing that there was a limited number of students who wished bilingual education programs, district personnel designated a "bilingual education" school in an area whose residents were nearly 100% Mexican or of Mexican origin. Parents from anywhere in the district could send their children to this school; likewise, people living near this school could opt to send their children to other schools in Havens. Its location, however, virtually assured that Anglo parents would be less than likely to send their children to the school, even if they wanted their children to learn Spanish.

Despite the beginning of bilingual education as a remedial program only, parents of some children whose first language was English understood the importance of having them learn Spanish and asked for what today commonly is known as two way bilingual education, an approach that is gaining support in the United States but which is still fairly uncommon.[3] So the belief that bilingual education was for everyone, whether their first language was Spanish or English, was not an abstract concept at least to some parents in Havens. The choice to locate the permanent, transitional bilingual program at one of the *barrio* schools removed the eventuality of a two-way program because it automatically confounded the issue of language learning with socioeconomic and class issues, as well as residential patterns, and thus, issues of culture and ethnicity. This undoubtedly is what led Susan Hartman to identify decentralization as a critical personal goal for the district's language programs. But the legacy of those early decisions about language learning was powerful in defining the kind of language instruction that followed. Only slowly, tentatively, is a renewed understanding of the potential of two-way bilingual education beginning to emerge. Carmen Mendoza continues:

> Now people are starting to view it [bilingual education] perhaps as an enrichment program. I think that more and more people are getting ready to accept, or even demand, that bilingual education would be a main instructional program, where everybody can belong and everybody can benefit from it. From the beginning it was more of a remedial program, and people now are starting to view it perhaps as an enrichment program. Also, now among the Spanish kids their Spanish language is receiving more value and it is starting to be seen as an asset more than a deficit.

At the same time, daily, immediate pressure in the schools comes in the form of local immigrant students who cannot speak English, a situation that often masks the larger binational question of providing bidirectional language instruction. This reality check reveals an unmistakable situation. "In Sonora County, here in Havens," according to the former superintendent who oversaw the emergence of those first formal programs, "there is a clear and definite need for an intensive bilingual education program because of the people who are moving in." Nevertheless, redefining bilingual education as a two-way enterprise has steadily become a more common point of conversation among students, parents, teachers, administrators, business people, and community leaders. Programmatically, this is not yet the case.

*   *   *

"There really are no bilingual programs here," said Barbara Montrose, an English teacher at the high school. "The district wants to provide ESL and wants to make every Spanish speaker an English speaker. There is no program to make sure Anglo kids learn Spanish. The students from Mexico are here to learn English, and that is what we provide." Barbara has studied Spanish and can speak at a very simple level; she is by no means fluent and works primarily with advanced level students in the college preparatory track at HHS. The 1 hour a day that she teaches an introductory English class populated mostly by students whose English is still limited, she gingerly invokes some of her Spanish—but it does not go far. Like so many other teachers in Havens, she relies on students to translate and support their peers. This kind of accommodation is so common an aspect of teaching in Havens that an outsider finally assumes that all teachers do this as a matter of coursein the same way they ask students to take the attendance lists to the office.

As it exists today, then, the meaning of "bilingual education" at HHS is a one-way program to encourage bilingualism for students who need to learn English—that is, for Mexican resident students who commute to school and for newly arrived Mexican students who live in Havens but cannot yet speak English well, or at all. This language learning goal is commonly understood by Anglo and Mexican-origin teachers, by community and business people (Anglo and Mexican), and by the students. It is seen as a question of being "fair" to newly arrived or daily immigrant students: Do not mainstream too soon, teach students to speak English so they can be successful in the United States, help them gain the advantage they will need should they return to Mexico. These are not unreasonable, empty, or rhetorical rationales. The most caring teachers at HHS, who form the majority, those least inclined to invoke an anti-immigration rhetoric ("This is America, learn to speak English"), recognize what the Mexican and new local students and their parents already understand and value—that learning English is a lifelong asset not only on the border, but everywhere in the UnitedStates. Language learning is the underlying motivation for most high school students who live in Mexico to come to Havens in the first place. *Lo único es aprender ingles, no álgebra,* [*] is how Laura Aguilar put it in an intense interview. The only places Laura speaks English are in school and when she visits her sister, who lives in Albuquerque. Her goal is to be a bilingual education teacher, in Mexico or perhaps someday in the states. But her primary allegiance is clear: *Yo soy mexicana! No es mi tierra,* [**] was the first thing she told me when we sat down to talk. More than any other student who crossed daily from Mexico, Laura animatedly and clearly described her expectations for language learning as a student at HHS. She depends on her time each day at HHS to provide her with the practice she needs to eventually become fluent in English. Her motivation is related to her job aspirations and her simple, forthright observation about her native land: *México necessito muchas.* [***]

Few in Havens would dispute the goal of helping to make sure students who come with little or no English language skills are prepared for the school, community, and work environments in which they will be functioning. The anti-immigration myth that newly arriving Mexican people (or any other immigrant people) are not interested in learning English and are not learning it is not evident in Havens nor is it evident elsewhere in the United States.[4] But what *is* the case is that in Havens, bilingual education has been structured specifically to meet the needs of the one fifth of the population who are Spanish-dominant as well as those whose English is still not proficient enough to do in-depth academic work well. The two teachers for the Grade 10, 11, and 12 TESOL classes do not speak Spanish, although their counterparts for the Grades 7, 8, and 9 in another building, do. Special classes associated with the program were populated by daily crossers from Mexico like Laura Aguilar, by temporary residents like Gabriela, Liliana Sanchez's friend, and by new immigrant students from Mexico whose families had moved permanently to Havens—legally or illegally—to live and work, like Maria Cruz's cousin Carlos. These residential distinctions were often lost in the conversation about providing language support to the students "from Mexico" and verified the social distinctions in school that Maria and Liliana described so clearly.

---

[*]"The most important thing is learning English, not algebra."
[**]"I am Mexican. This isn't my land." The implication here was that her nationality was not up for discussion.
[***]"Mexico has many needs."

In Havens, bilingual education classes are clearly labeled in their purpose; they are known as TESOL classes, or Teaching English as a Second Language, denoting their explicit purpose of teaching English alone. In addition, special sections of certain academic classes were designated sheltered English classes in which students learn academic content in English to advance their academic progress with what is commonly called "comprehensible input."[5] One science teacher, one English teacher, one social studies teacher, and one mathematics teacher are responsible for these classes; these teachers, who see the students for perhaps one period a day, are all bilingual. Two are Mexican-American and grew up in small communities adjacent to Havens. The other two are Anglo and grew up in Havens; of these, one was Richard Logan. So a student like Carlos Cruz, Maria's newly arrived cousin and a legal U.S. resident, would likely be placed in several periods of TESOL, a few sheltered classes, and perhaps a vocational education class. Vocational education classes are a common choice because either the teacher speaks Spanish or their status as activity-oriented classes readily makes them a logical alternative in terms of scheduling. The old local and limited concept of *simpático* used to describe that early wave of first-grade teachers who worked with Mexican-American children to ease their transition into school also seems an appropriate designation for the sheltered content teachers and for many of the vocational education teachers, although in contrast to Alice Edgar, many of the vocational education teachers are bilingual and Mexican-American. Their personal commitment to supporting students whose English language skills are limited is evident in their classrooms where animated and friendly interactions are the norm and where students seem to feel very comfortable at school. In other vocational classes, for example, in the health occupations, a sympathetic Anglo teacher who is not bilingual insists on English but also provides for an informal support system made up of hand-picked and trustworthy students to act as language guides. Her students work at the local hospital as part of their coursework and quickly realize how important their English language skills are in terms of eventual work.

In addition to sheltered classes and vocational education, several other teachers also welcome students whose English skills are only first developing. Notably, the business education teachers, who preside over courses like computer education or keyboarding, easily accommodate students with limited English skills. Of the three business education teachers at HHS, one is Mexican-American and a fluent Spanish speaker. Academic teachers who instruct introductory, lower level classes are more likely to have students with limited English skills enrolled; teachers of advanced classes, which are few in number, may have little contact with them. Depending on the teacher, the use of Spanish or English varies tremendously. If the teacher is bilingual, it may be the case that very little Spanish is spoken—only to clarify a conceptual misunderstanding or as a light touch to build rapport between the teacher and the students. In others, the language reins are not so tightly held and the use of Spanish is quite dominant. The same thing occurs in English language classes; some of the TESOL teachers are more adamant than others about language use and control the language environment to support the structured use of English, however tentative it might be on the part of the students. The language learning pressures are massed and to some extent unevenly distributed among teachers, but the common concern is how to insure that students do not spend 3 years at Havens High and leave not being able to speak English—which is sometimes now the case.

Providing appropriate instruction to temporary or permanent newcomers from Mexico is complicated by the need for teachers to have a good grasp of the content level achievement students possess when they arrive. Most of the students who come to Havens have at least completed *primaria* in Mexico, and many have also attended some *secundaria* as well. The conversation about prior schooling and achievement is rare among the teachers at HHS, however, and usually occurs only in the field of mathematics, where one bilingual teacher, who is Mexican-American, is sensitive to the high level of mathematics achievement students from Mexico bring and pushes his students into higher level mathematics classes as soon as they can handle it; often they excel. She also encourages them, once they are eligible, to join the school's chapter of the National Honor Society (NHS), something students from Mexico are generally uncomfortable doing without this kind of direct teacher encouragement.

The general lack of knowledge about prior schooling of immigrants is common in receiving immigrant communities in the United States[6] and places newly arriving students in an even more precarious situation. They cannot speak English well or at all, but they may have high levels of academic achievement on which to build. Creating a reasonable balance between the academic content levels students arrive with as a result of their education in Mexico and teaching the English language is an area that, in Havens, requires attention. The 200 students at HHS who have limited English skills are caught in the limbo of realizing that many of their teachers do not understand or attribute to them the academic skills they bring, but these same teachers must unlock students' capacities to communicate what they know in their second language, English. Most Mexican students who come to HHS have had previous schooling and have a well-developed sense of what school is supposed to be like. Most often they are surprised at the loose structure of the American school in comparison with their educational experiences in Mexico. Only a handful of daily commuters and newcomers arrive with little or no formal schooling, but this is clearly the exception. Students who have spent years in school and those who have not are placed together in TESOL classes.

The maintenance of Spanish for Spanish-dominant students is another aspect of language learning in Havens, but one that seems to be far less of a concern for district administrators and teachers as it is for immigrant Spanish-speaking communities north of the border area where there may not be continuous interaction with Spanish. The wisdom is that "these kids are not going to lose their Spanish. They're around it every day." It is true that in Havens students are living in an environment where Spanish is regularly used and that losing Spanish is not so much an issue for the students who cross the border daily, because proximity to the border may reduce the likelihood of that occurring. Students go back and forth regularly, whether they cross for a day or go home only for the weekends. Because so many are grouped together for classes, they continue to speak Spanish to one another.

But the kind of Spanish that is spoken along the border and a deep knowledge of formal Spanish are not necessarily the same thing. Mexican-American people in Havens are quick to discount their own version of Spanish, defining it as "kitchen" Spanish or "border" Spanish, denoting that, to them, it was not up to par. Students who enroll in advanced Spanish language classes at HHS might be working at improving their first language skills. These classes are part of the formal, traditional high school language education program in which Spanish and French are the only options. In advanced Spanish classes, it is not unusual to find primarily native Spanish speakers—often students from Mexico—in the highest class levels. These are the classmates with whom Liliana Sanchez has been building bridges. In these classes, students read literature and learn to write correctly with accents, a skill that remained unmastered for many and seemed to be an important measure of being well educated in the Spanish language. In fact, writing correctly with accents seemed to be the demarcation point between those who "really" knew Spanish and those who did not. It also seemed to be one of the things that kept some local teachers from successfully passing New Mexico's Spanish language examination for bilingual teacher certification.

So at the same time that students from Mexico, or their new immigrant counterparts, might be taking intermediate or advanced level

Spanish, students who are learning English might also be enrolled in ESL or sheltered English classes. A local Havens student like Liliana might be enrolled in advanced Spanish classes with her peers who were just learning English, but for Liliana this was part of a series of advanced academic classes that made up her whole senior year program. This was not the case for students who were first learning English, who might move back and forth between high content classes in Spanish, low content classes in ESL, and sheltered English classes in some of the basic high school subjects like history or science. This configuration of classes meets only some criteria that typically make up a strong program of bilingual education: comprehensible input in English, subject matter knowledge in the first language, and continued literacy development in the first language.[7]

* * *

Although the actual number of students whose English is limited is not that large, and although some teachers come into contact with fewer students whose English language skills are limited than others, the impact is felt widely across the school and the conversation about language learning often dominates teacher talk. The resources that are expended today—resources that are garnered largely from federal funds—support Mexican students who may be citizens, residents, or daily crossers. But as we have seen, it is often difficult to distinguish among the three. Of the students who do not speak English well, some are daily students from Mexico and some are new immigrants. Some are temporary visitors and some are here to stay. But the aura that exists around TESOL classes at the high school is that they exist only to serve daily crossers, which immediately invokes the inflated rhetoric of immigration.

The division at HHS, as both Liliana and Maria explained, is between the "Mexican" students and everyone else. In this way, all of the students who are or have been enrolled in TESOL classes are at one time or another at risk of the stigma of immigration that surrounds everyone who lives on the border. As principal, Daniel Martinez, himself bilingual and Mexican American, reminded his staff in a meeting early on in the year in which this issue came up, "Remember people, we only have 200 kids who are Spanish dominant. That's hardly the whole school." But in a national political climate that is increasingly anti-immigration, and in a local political climate in Havens which, like other border communities, has to deal realistically with finite resources to meet infinite needs, programs of bilingual education can become easy targets.[8]

In reality, as students at HHS gain English skills and move out into regular classes in the curriculum, teachers readily and proudly identify the ones who, by dint of hard work and *ganas*, have managed to learn English well and are among the higher achieving students. Nearly every teacher has a story about a recent student who was a border crosser, initially or permanently, who worked hard to learn English and made it. "He just worked really hard." "She really had *ganas*." "He's a great student—not everyone is like that." There is genuine pride on the part of teachers when students begin to make it. At the same time, few teachers talk about the bilingual program itself as being wildly success-ful. They appreciate its existence, and many teachers take advantage of the support services the bilingual paraprofessionals associated with TESOL classes provide for other classes, services like translating tests or lists of safety measures for welding classes into Spanish. But it is individual effort that is seen as making the difference between a student who has learned English and one who has not. This merito-cratic, "by the bootstraps" perspective is what one hears when learning English is discussed. As a result, the conversation bypasses what can be done more strategically and programmatically school-wide to cap-ture the natural motivation for learning English that students in the TESOL program possess. One recurring suggestion, made by teachers, parents, and students I spoke with was the creation of an intensive, 1-year program for new immigrants to learn English. This was seen as a preferable alternative to the current approach, which is spread out over the 4 high school years and a possible way of increasing students' success.[9]

Not all students are successful learning English by their bootstraps. Not everyone has the confidence of Gabriela or Maria. Nearly every teacher also knows about that small group of students from Mexico who are not serious students, who earn a poor reputation and whose behavior can fuel the inaccurate generalized belief that as a whole the students from Mexico are taking unfair advantage of the generosity Havens' schools offer. As part of the cross border lore, disproportionate attention seems to be given—at least in conversation—to this group, which is actually quite small. In between are the majority—those students who are eager to learn English and who are anxious to become a real part of the school, but whose communication skills still disallow that from occurring. Laura Aguilar, who arrived at HHS so committed to learning English, was disappointed that her conversational skills did not seem to be progressing. At her request, our own conversations were conducted in both languages, with me asking questions in English and she respond-ing in Spanish. In the midst of our last interview, Laura stopped the conversation, raised her voice, and questioned pleadingly in Spanish, "Why? Why? Why can I sit here and understand nearly everything you say, but I can't speak to you in English?" Her frustration was pushing her to the limit, it seemed, and she wanted an answer that I could not provide. She had already devised her own solution to the problem: If she were the principal of the school, she would make sure that all teachers spoke both Spanish and English. She also would not have so many classes in Spanish because she believes the students have little opportunity to practice English if everyone speaks Spanish. If they know they can speak Spanish, they will speak it; it is easier.

When students begin to leave the safety of the TESOL classrooms, their world is less secure. Janice Otero lamented:

> What happens sometimes in the classroom with three or four Mexican kids, is that when they're communicating with the American kids, they're at a certain point, and the language becomes a problem, and then somebody has to step in and translate, and then the whole relationship seems to break down.

This is less an example of placing students in regular classes before they are ready for the academic work in English than it is an indication that conversational levels may not be matching the basic social needs adolescents have to connect with one another in schools. For instance, Laura Aguilar believed that she was not yet ready to participate in the life of the school. In terms of extra-curricular activities, she believed she could not participate because of her English. "I can't speak English. When I feel sure of myself in English, I would like to participate, but in the meantime, no." At first she said she was not interested in any activities, but when I reviewed what was available, she perked up visibly (particularly when I mentioned basketball); it was obvious that she did not know a lot about what was available, nor did she feel she had the ability to gain access to the options. In the programs, which are not well grounded in an understanding of what students bring from their prior educational experience in Mexico, conversational English is subordinate to written and read English—the academic tools. It is reading and writing that enables students to participate in the academic routine of the school, but it is conversation that would most readily enable students to take part in the community of the school. Laura observed that for a Mexican student to be accepted quickly, "In the first place, you have to have the language. To be popular, a student would have to have good grades and would have to know how to talk with the Americans, how to communicate with them." One of the most outspoken students who cross daily, Laura seemed to understand that an imbalance existed that disfavored conversation, which to her—and her family—was the real reason she came to HHS in the first place.

As Laura's situation indicates, the purpose of bilingual education programs in Havens continues to be defined as helping students whose first language is Spanish gain a knowledge of English that would enable them to achieve academic success in the distinctly American schools of the community. At HHS specifically, the acquisition of conversational skills still seems wanting. District-wide, all of the elementary schools have some level of support, ranging from school-wide programs where all students are taught in both languages to itinerant ESL teachers who provide only part-time instruction to small groups of students. School-wide programs exist in the three schools whose populations are chiefly students of Mexican origin; this includes Jefferson, the outlying elementary school right on the border, and the two "Mexican" schools in what are still considered the town's *barrios*, Brighton and Page. In the schools in the increasingly bicultural middle class residential areas, services are offered in relationship to the needs of the students who attend; students might be pulled out for ESL lessons or they might be placed in a special bilingual class. At the secondary levels, a variety of language services ranged from ESL, bilingual, and Spanish as a Second Language classes in the junior high to the existing array at the high school. Capturing a political concern with the impact of increased immigration in the community rather than the more complex reality of the residency situation, where some Mexican people are legal residents and citizens and others (who may also be U.S. citizens) commute daily to school from across the border, the perception still exists that were it not for the children from Mexico who cross each day, bilingual programs would not be needed in Havens. At the same time, many people already want their children to know both languages and are creating a different rhetoric, another set of motivations and understandings as the backdrop for a new, two-way conception of bilingual education that can include all students, no matter what their residence or origin.

Regarding the goal of two-way bilingual education, Jack Sullivan, an administrator at the high school, reminded me of how far the district had already come:

> At least we're halfway there, we're teaching kids to speak English. A few years ago, we didn't even *have* a bilingual education program. It's still growing and it still has lots of things it could use, and we certainly could use more funding. And so, I think we've got to get that perfected before we can start with the other side of the house. It's very important for Anglo kids here to know Spanish, especially if they're going to stay here, if they're going to live in this area. That's one of the reasons why I kept trying to

learn Spanish in high school. It's just part of the area, part of the culture, it's something they ought to know. I would like to see my own kids have at least some understanding of Spanish. Maybe they can learn it better than I did. But as a district we're not at that point yet. We're a lot farther than we were. At least we now have the Spanish-speaking kids learning English, but we haven't gotten the reverse in place yet. We may, it may be a matter of time until we do, but that side of it isn't there yet. So I think we need to do a lot of educating on the part of the English speaking student of the necessity for learning Spanish.

* * *

This "other side" of bilingual education that Jack Sullivan describes is the side that will enable students who do not speak Spanish to learn it. The power of bilingualism was the only near universal point of agreement I heard in conversations about language. Politically conservative businessmen and their wives understood it, wanting their sons and daughters to have the same opportunities as Mexican-origin individuals who were bilingual. "Because this is America everyone should speak English," Pat Wright, the wife of a prominent rancher, began. Pat moved to Havens shortly after her marriage, genuinely loves the community, but believes it can do more.

But if they started in kindergarten with 30 minutes of Spanish a day, all of the students would know Spanish by the time they're in the sixth grade. This would be a real benefit, especially in regards to getting jobs. If you read the job ads, many of them ask for bilingual people. So the Mexican people have a real advantage when it comes to getting jobs. With 30 minutes a day, the kids could practice with the Spanish speaking kids.

Likewise, Anglo school board members and bank presidents knew the economic consequences of being bilingual in a tight job market and valued it. A Mexican-American school board member was equally supportive of the dual language goal, but for another reason. "What the schools in Havens need to be doing is to teach the Anglo kids Spanish, to improve communication and the relationship between the two communities, and to help the Anglo kids respect the Mexican ones."

When teaching Spanish is discussed as a possible extension of bilingual education in Havens, it usually refers to providing Spanish language instruction for Anglo students. In actuality, were it fully implemented, the student audience would include Anglo students as well as those Mexican-origin students who might have grown up around Spanish but who never learned to speak it, or to speak it well. This group of students can be thought of as a "third" side of bilingual education in relationship to the two sides mentioned by Jack Sullivan. Talking about students from local Mexican families, Lydia Silva commented with great sadness about the state of language learning. "It's a shame that kids who were born and raised here, 30 miles from the Mexican border, can't speak a word of Spanish. Actually, most of them know several words in Spanish, but they shouldn't be saying them on the street."

Who would benefit from being bilingual in Havens? The sheer force of economic reality dictates that every student could derive some benefit. In the same way that no one in Havens disputed the importance of learning English, I also never came across anyone in Havens who disputed the advantage of being bilingual; the world along the border is getting smaller and smaller, and those who know both languages will be at a clear advantage in terms of employment opportunities. People uniformly weighed in on the side of needing English to get along; they also knew that being bilingual in Havens was nothing less than a lifelong opportunity. A small number hedged on Spanish itself, citing instead the principle that knowing any foreign language was important and the mark of an educated person. But competition for jobs—a plain and simple economic rationale, was one kind of motivation. A small number of Anglo individuals were motivated by anger that language-related financial resources were not evenly distributed in a two-way program and that Mexican students were getting something their Anglo children were not—the legacy of the region's discrimination. Most were not so negatively motivated, however, and merely wanted their children to be as well suited as possible for life in Havens, and on the border. Mexican-American parents whose children had not learned to speak Spanish often regretted the choice they had made to withhold using Spanish exclusively at home and would welcome the support of the schools in getting it back. Their motivation is part of the position of people of Mexican origin in Havens who consider it important to retain Spanish because it is part of your heritage, it defines you culturally, and it is, not coincidentally, also an economic advantage. If you are Anglo, learning Spanish also has the potential to build bridges of friendship based on extended cultural understanding. If you are Mexican-American, you might learn it to recapture something culturally.

Given these varying sources of interest—and self-interest—in two-way bilingual education, it is very much on people's minds. The range of motivations for creating opportunities to achieve bilingual competency exists within and across cultural backgrounds. Border politics is not going to go away, and wholesale immigration reform is not going to take place tomorrow in Havens. But creating a community of students who are more likely to get along because the language divide has been breached and who, as a by-product, may be more likely to get jobs seems to be within reach. Forging an educational coalition based on these varying motivations is, perhaps, the most practical local means of building a more enduring binationalism. But to do so will take a systematic effort on the part of the schools. Bill Williams, an outspoken mathematics teacher convinced of the economic importance of bilingualism, placed the responsibility squarely in the lap of the schools.

Students are losing an opportunity if they don't speak Spanish. The world is getting so tiny, in particular here on the border. I mean, practically anywhere in the United States there are so many Spanish speakers and we're going to be doing some tremendous amount of trading with the Latin American countries. It would be a terrible shame if we had the same trouble with Latin American trading that we have with Japan. We should have a huge amount of people who are bilingual, who can speak the same language and do trade. There are several folks now who have graduated from Havens High School and they've been working with Mexico and they're totally bilingual and they speak the language without any accent or anything. But that's not due to the training they had from the school.

Enter the Students...

The library, a large room off the school's central corridor, was one of the sunniest and airiest in the school. It was a place I often went between interviews, or after spending time in a classroom, a quiet place to collect my thoughts. In a small room at the back of the library I was often able to conduct interviews with students. During these many visits, Mrs. Manning, the librarian, and Richard Logan's former Spanish teacher, could often be found talking with a few students whose English was limited. Often they were students who came daily from Mexico; at other times, they were local students whose English was still weak. One day I watched as Teresa Allen, an Anglo student and a junior, sat down with Graciela Chavez, a girl who came to HHS each day on the bus from Mexico. I knew these young women were not friends and did not roam around in the same social crowd. They were talking animatedly, as high school girls will, and then Teresa took out a tape recorder and some papers, turned on the tape recorder, and began what seemed to be a formal interview with Graciela, which she conducted in Spanish. That afternoon I caught up with her and asked her what she had been doing.

It was an assignment for my Spanish class. We had to interview a student whose native language is Spanish. I thought I could get to know Graciela better, so I asked her if she would let me interview her. She seemed real glad that I asked her.

I learned a lot from doing the interview. You know, before, when I first moved here last year, I didn't think that learning another language was that important, before I started working in town at Burger King. But now I think it is important, especially living in this region. It's helped me a lot. I understand a lot more now. I understand Spanish when I hear it. I can't really speak it well, but I understand a lot more, just listening.

I think it should be just as important for English-speaking kids to learn Spanish because we should have mutual relations. We always say, I hear people saying "If you're going to be in America, learn to speak English." But then we go to Mexico, I know my family goes to Mexico to buy medicine during the winter months for coughs and that kind of thing and it should be just as important for us to speak Spanish when we go over to the other side. And I know that a lot of the jobs you always see advertised ask for bilingual people, too.

I've never really had a close friend in school who was bilingual. I mean, I know people who speak Spanish because that's what they were taught first in their home, but they don't really consider themselves *Mexican* Mexican, and they only speak Spanish when they're talking to people who can't speak English. If I had spoken Spanish when I got here, I could probably converse with the kids who come up from Frontera and ask them how they feel about school here and what their life is like over there, and that kind of thing. It would have been different, because throughout high school I haven't really had many Mexican friends. When I first came here it was very uncomfortable because whenever I heard Spanish I thought they were talking behind my back. I didn't know. But if someone can't understand our language, I'm sure they wonder the same things about us speaking in English. It's just mutual, I guess.

Teresa was planning to go to one of the state universities to study teaching after high school. She is a quiet student, a hard worker, and on the shy side; just over 5 feet tall, with light brown hair, a healthy wash of freckles, and a pleasant smile, she moves through the school with a serious demeanor dressed in decidedly unflashy jeans and sweatshirts. She moved to Havens during the first year of high school. Her parents do not agree with her position on learning Spanish; they also have made their position clear that she should not date "Mexican boys." Nevertheless, Teresa is trying to work out her own identity on the border, and language is one of the ways she is trying to accomplish this. If her Spanish was fluent, she might surely emerge as a cultural mediator, one of the few among the Anglo student crowd. The potential is there and she is willing to consider her friendships from a bicultural and also from a binational perspective. But the actual capacity to broker in this way is yet undeveloped for Teresa. Instead, this capacity exists nearly exclusively for those Mexican and Mexican-American students who are already bilingual.

The interview I watched Teresa conduct with Gabriela was a required assignment given by the school's Spanish teacher. Along with the Spanish column in the school newspaper, this was one of the few public acts acknowledging that the two languages coexist at the school, and one which also made a real difference for Graciela, who Teresa interviewed. It was a quiet acknowledgment of both languages, one that was missed by most people. The formal structures for language learning in the school are, more than anything, located in having students from Mexico—whether residents or daily commuters—learn English. Conventional foreign language classes also enable a small number of students to study Spanish, but not with the same, immediate kind of purpose that characterizes English language classes. While "learning English" is the talk one hears all over the school, in general students who are enrolled in Spanish talk instead about "taking Spanish" in the very conventional way most high school students talk about their own limited foreign language preparation. But for the students at HHS, the real language learning environment is far more intricate than this simple, dualistic characterization that is so commonly applied.

Despite the lack of public attention to this full range of language issues and language learning, students at HHS are far from oblivious to the complex language environment in which they attend school and do not reduce it either to "learning English" or "taking Spanish." Many quietly support each other's language needs—sometimes individually depending on personal friendships, other times in classes to help out the teacher—all in the absence of a superimposed educational framework for such a wide range of dual language support. They readily categorize friends and acquaintances according to their language knowledge: "I have a lot of bilingual friends." "She understands some words but can't really talk." "He is Mexican but he doesn't speak any Spanish." "I'm not really friends with any of the kids who only speak Spanish." "His parents speak Spanish, but he doesn't like to." "She's trying really hard to learn English." Maria Cruz ran down the language abilities of her friends this way.

Marisol, she's Hispanic, she can understand Spanish and she can answer me in Spanish kind of, and I correct her from time to time but she understands it more than she can speak it. Alicia, she's the one that's best at it. We speak in Spanish and she's really good at it. She is also Hispanic. And Alma, she can kind of understand it but she really can't speak it well. And Carmina, she doesn't do either, she's just kind of, she's all confused.

And Cathy Roberts, she understands it more than Carmina does. She
learned it from her dad. I think that's all of my friends.

They know that their school is actually quite language rich and that
language capacities vary. In contrast to the discourse of their administrators and teachers, language is more easily talked about and acted on
in the daily lives of students at HHS.

For those who are already bilingual, and for those who are trying to
gain more familiarity—or even fluency—with one or the other language,
it is a topic frequently addressed. But among the students at HHS,
language is often dealt with in that undercurrent of student talk that
dominates all high schools—within the individual and group relationships that ardently engage teenagers no matter what their dominant
language or their cultural background. Or, it occurs quietly in classes,
not really discussed, but directly acted on in hushed—but not hidden—tones, an unobtrusive support, with bilingual students readily
brokering[10] for their newly arrived peers with whom they find themselves in class.

Those who have both languages are often modest in the recognition
of these dual skills, using them without much hesitation—but without much fanfare either. Because these informal language efforts
occur as an almost organic aspect of school, they are mostly hidden
from public view, leading Liliana Sanchez to suggest the launching
of a tutoring/translation club as a means of raising visibility of
bilingual students and providing a real service to the schools, teachers, and students. In Havens, the actions students take in the realm
of language also go beyond conventional notions of brokering, where
students might mediate for teachers and students or for their parents, to include overt support like Liliana had been providing for her
friend Colin to at least develop an appreciation for his mother's native
language, or like the effort Juan Espinosa put out to help make sure
his best buddy Eduardo didn't lose his Spanish. Their efforts seem to
be inspired more by a cultural goal and less by economic motivation,
convenient assistance, or bureaucratic necessity. At the high school
level, there is also an obvious social motivation for students to become
bilingual. Ginny, a senior who comes from a mixed ethnic background
including Mexican and Italian heritage, spoke Spanish as young child
but lost it over the years:

If I did know Spanish fluently, I think it would be better—I would be able
to communicate with people. Like last year, there was this really good-
looking guy. He still goes to school here. But I think the reason why we

never went out is that I didn't know Spanish and he didn't know English. We never even talked. The only thing we did was to say "hi" to one another and pass each other in the hall and smile, and that was it. I remember that my friend who I grew up with, she lives by me and she speaks Spanish really well, when I told her about him, she had talked to him. He felt like it was kind of awkward because I didn't know much Spanish and he didn't know English. I see some girls who want to date a guy who's Mexican, who speaks Spanish, but they're afraid to because of the language.

Ginny does not readily embrace her Mexican side; in fact, she has real disdain for students from Mexico who do not seem to take school seriously. But she understands the gulf that language creates—and so, the bridge it has the potential to be. Juan Espinosa talks about the social language issues this way:

> It's hard for the guy that comes down from Mexico to speak to, you know, an American girl. He'll say, "Oh, she's very beautiful," but they have to have the guts to do it. I have a friend, I've seen him over there in Mexico, and he's the kind who gets out there and talks to any girl. Well, once he's here, I tell him, "You know, go talk to her. I dare you." He won't because he says he doesn't speak English real good, and he's embarrassed of going up there and then being embarrassed and the girl just walking off. That's what he told me. Yeah, language is a problem.

For other students, the social motivation for language learning comes from the fact that one of the partners in a couple is bilingual. This casts a slightly different light on the question of language between them. Tony is Mexican-American; his girlfriend, Sandy, is Anglo. They are seniors; they have been dating for 3 years. They are quiet students who, between classes, spend time engaged in what is everyday conversation for high school seniors. Tony works in the local supermarket and does not take his studies too seriously. Sandy has worked on and off at a video rental store near the supermarket and is an above-average student. They talk openly and sensibly about cultural differences between their families and how they might reconcile them should they decide to get married. They spend time with each other's families. They banter humorously about stereotypes of Mexican and Anglo people and their homes. They also help each other with language. Tony's first language is Spanish.

> *Tony*: When I started school I didn't know any English because all my parents ever spoke was Spanish. They were going to transfer me to Brighton School, which is a bilingual school, but my folks didn't want to do that so my dad would always

speak English to me. He would always try to get us to learn
English. By first grade I basically had it down. I could understand, but I had trouble speaking it. At home it's all Spanish.

Sandy: In seventh grade we had to take a class in Spanish. It was
required. We learned the colors, the pledge, and everything.
I got what I do know when I started hanging around with
Tony. They would talk behind my back so I just started
learning.

Tony: I didn't know that she knew Spanish and I said something
about her one time. What I said to my friends was that it
doesn't matter how quick or how slow you speak it, she doesn't
understand what I'm saying as long as it's in Spanish. And
she said, "Oh, yes, I do understand. You'd better stop talking
about me behind my back!"

Sandy: I learned the bad words first. And then a lot of terms that were
said in the classroom. You start associating things with words
and you just pick up on it. When I first started working at the
video store, there were a lot of Spanish movies and when
people came in, I couldn't speak it. I can understand it now.

Tony: I can speak both languages with no problem. I may have
some problems whenever I try and say a sentence in English and say it exactly the way you would in Spanish. A lot
of times there's a word in Spanish and I know what it is,
but I don't know exactly how to say it in English. I don't
know what the word is and the I tell Sandy, I describe it to
her and she tells me the words. I've learned a few words
like that.

Fine tuning his English and building her Spanish are the informal
language goals that Tony and Sandy work toward, but it is not a
conscious part of their time together. Rather, any language growth that
does occur is a natural development of their relationship.

For other students, "learning English" is also more multidimensional
than a first glance would reveal. Clearly, new immigrants and daily
commuters from Mexico hold the learning of English as primary; that
is why they make the commute in the first place and students who are
learning English often characterize their future roles as bilingual individuals, as a brokering role between countries, as cultural mediators
who in the future will be able to foster an appreciation of both cultures.
But embedded in their personal goals regarding language learning is an

informal community of learners in which those who know more English help those who know less—even if the more knowledgeable one is not totally comfortable with the new language yet. It is in this way that Linda, a daily commuter, could help her friend Patricia.

Linda is a U.S. citizen, but her father farms in one of the small local villages near Frontera in Mexico. Her spoken English is still developing; she is still self-conscious about speaking it. Linda is tall and thin and carries herself with the confidence of an actress or a movie star. She is dressed impeccably, she is always smiling or laughing, and by all of her teachers' reports, she is making great progress in learning English. Linda entered school in Havens in junior high. Several of her cousins also go to school in Havens; some live in Frontera, some live right across the border in the United States. "I wanted to come to school here since I was little. I wanted to learn to speak English. My parents wanted me to learn to speak English. Also, my uncle worked in a ranch near Frontera and they put their children in the schools here, and my dad wanted to do that, too." Linda and Patricia are in the same seventh period English class, a class filled with students who are learning English, but a class that is part of the regular HHS English curriculum. She prefers choosing classes where at least one other person speaks Spanish—to assure a comfort level, and so that there will be someone with whom she can talk. Linda described it this way:

> Patricia's in my seventh period class. She's always asking me, "Hey, Linda, why don't you help me with my English?" and how I can show her and learn for her, no, I mean teach her. She wants to learn English, but when the teacher asks her something, she's so embarrassed and I wouldn't like to be in her case, because I was like her when my English was not as good, and I would like to help her.

> I also have a friend named Becky—I don't know her last name. Well, she doesn't speak Spanish, but she hangs with all of my friends that don't, they don't speak English. So we are always speaking Spanish, and she is just like, she doesn't know anything and she wants to learn Spanish. All the time I speak to her in Spanish and she doesn't understand, she says, "What did you say?" So I talk with her.

Publicly acknowledging the language resources students bring to school and strategically marshaling their natural interest in language learning are both missing parts of the backdrop that might eventually lead to an even greater appreciation for—and action on—two-way bilingual education. In some cases, these resources include students who are completely fluent in both languages, like Liliana Sanchez or Luis Estrada, who spoke at graduation. Other resources include students' sheer willingness to work on language, to press its learning in informal ways, to underscore the belief that whatever language students bring as their first, it is valued and, at least in Havens, is a natural complement to the other language. Students make sense of their language environment based on practical, social, and cultural considerations. How their teachers make sense of it is not necessarily the same.

... and Their Teachers

The majority of the 70 teachers at HHS are not Mexican-American, and the majority also are not bilingual. In the 1993–1994 school year, 26% were Mexican-American, and 14 of these teachers were bilingual. An additional four Anglo teachers were also bilingual; one of these was the librarian and former Spanish teacher, Mrs. Manning. The counseling staff included two Mexican-American counselors; neither was bilingual. Four of the teachers who were bilingual taught sheltered content classes and work primarily—but not only—with limited English-speaking students. The 10 other Mexican-American teachers who were also bilingual taught either special education or vocational education classes; the school's in-house suspension room monitor, not a licensed teacher, was also Mexican-American and bilingual. Among the staff at large, two of the school's three secretaries were Mexican-American and both were bilingual. Higher level academic classes were almost always taught by teachers whose only language was English. Instructional aides are Mexican-American and with one exception were Mexican-American and bilingual. The attendance clerk, who often is the first line of communication with parents, was, of course, bilingual.

Teacher talk in the school is almost uniformly in English; that same undercurrent of student talk in English and Spanish in the hallways and between students in the backs of classrooms is not audible among the teachers and it is more rare to hear teachers slipping into an informal discussion in Spanish. Although teachers who are monolingual English speakers in Havens have acquired some words and phrases in Spanish by virtue of having lived in the southwest—for many years or for a lifetime—few have voluntarily achieved fluency. More like their student counterparts, no teacher in the school is immune from the issue of language; everyone, at some time or another, works with students whose English language skills are limited. New teachers to the school in 1993 were encouraged during their interviews to put learning Spanish on their professional development agendas. Amanda Strom, a new mathematics teacher, recalled:

They asked me what future training I would like. And I said, "Well, my first goal is to get my math classes, obviously." And they agreed with that. But beyond that, I told them I wanted to learn Spanish. It's true, and I think we all should, over time, be required to take classes in Spanish—all the teachers, all the staff.

It's hard right now because I'm new at teaching, let alone can't speak Spanish. So, I find that I go ahead and do my class like normal because I really don't have much choice. I don't have as much experience to whip out things or to communicate with my students in a different way. What I do is to teach it normally, in English. They I try to help my kids on the side, the ones I know are sitting there and they don't know what I'm saying. I try to sit down and actually show them. So I sit there and just write out the problem, and you know, we point to it and I go, "See, this here is this and..." And I think they kind of get a better grasp that way.

The students work so hard. When they're talking to each other in Spanish while they're working, it doesn't bother me at all. You know, sure, if anybody is goofing off and saying things and it looks like they're making jokes, sure, it makes anybody feel nervous if you don't know what they're saying or who they are talking about. But as far as work goes, I know the numbers. I can always hear the numbers that they're saying, so I know they're talking math.

In my other classes I have a lot of Spanish speakers, but they are bilingual. They often converse in class with each other, before and after, you know, telling stories in Spanish. But they do all the work in English. They talk, they tell stories. I think they'd love it someday if I came in and tried to speak to them, and they'd laugh. But they'd correct me. And I think they'd really kind of respect that I was trying.

But it really affects me when I'm up there talking and look at the students who don't speak English. I hate it. I have a girl who gets A's all the time, but I know when she's looking at me she doesn't know one word that I'm saying. As I do problems, I think she knows because she's following what I'm doing, obviously, since she's doing real well in class. But I just feel bad that what I'm saying is going right by them. By now I've already learned how to write "add," "subtract," "multiply," and "divide" and the numbers, so I've learned a little bit. But I really wish I really knew Spanish.

For Amanda, the need to learn Spanish will have an immediate payoff in her classes and the reality of teaching along the border dictates that most teachers will find themselves in a situation similar to hers. Students like Maria Cruz readily put themselves into their teachers' shoes:

I've been in some classes where there's mostly just Spanish-speaking students and it makes it really hard when the teacher doesn't speak

Spanish and they have all of these Spanish-speaking students and it's kind of hard on them. It's just that it's hard to communicate, to get your point across whenever the language difference is there. It would be a little easier if the teachers did speak Spanish, and a lot of times I find myself helping out, just trying to translate and stuff like that.

Despite Amanda's aspirations to learn Spanish, mathematics teaching seems to be the least frustrating for teachers because students from Mexico typically come well prepared in this subject—and even far advanced in comparison to their American peers. Her position on learning Spanish is consistent with the position Richard Logan takes, but it is not universally held. Although several of the monolingual teachers have attempted unsuccessfully to learn Spanish over the years and believe that knowing both would be a definite benefit, they often dismiss their own unsuccessful language learning efforts, in the same way that Jack Sullivan did:

Seriously, I would love to know more Spanish, but I've never been good at languages. I tried my best to learn and I can understand it more, I can read it fairly well, and I can, if people are speaking slowly enough, I can understand. If I know about what the conversation is about, I can usually tell what the drift is, but to speak it, I've never been good at speaking it. I'm trying to deal with parents who only speak Spanish. Most of the time we have a translator who takes care of it, but I find it a real handicap not to speak it.

Valuing two languages and actually being able to speak them are not one and the same, and as adults the possibility of becoming bilingual seems like a distant reality to many of Havens' monolingual (and Anglo) teachers. The district still offers free conversational classes to district employees and encourages their participation. A mandate that all teachers will become bilingual, handed down from the previous superintendent, was abandoned when that superintendent left—but the force of mandate did not sit well with some teachers. How teachers might actually achieve bilingualism seems far from reach—and whether they would need to is also a contested question.

Teachers' Interlude ...

Coach Miller is Anglo; he is married to a Mexican-American woman from the area and her family lives on both sides of the border. They have two small daughters.

I have a lot of students who speak to me only in Spanish because they know I like to learn it and they really enjoy having me converse with them in Spanish. I can carry on a conversation on a very basic level. It means a lot to them, particularly when an Anglo teacher makes the effort to communicate with them. It breaks down any feeling of, you know, whether it's a racial difference of whatever you'd call it, I think making the environment comfortable is very important.

I don't think that it's necessarily important that teachers are fluent, but I think it's very important that they are willing to try to converse and when kids come up and speak to them in Spanish, I think it's very important that they not lash out like "speak to me in English" or something of this nature. That teachers would approach it in a way that the student would feel comfortable, and maybe let the student know that they find their language interesting, and that they would like to at least learn. I think that if a kid, a non-English-speaking student coming in can just get the feeling from you as an instructor that you think their language is important, then it's not necessarily important that you're fluent. Obviously, it's a tremendous advantage for you if you are completely fluent in Spanish. But in terms of the relationship and the atmosphere you are creating, a learning atmosphere where students feel comfortable and that you accept where they are is extremely important.

Sam Jackson is an English teacher; he works with a group of students from the TESOL program and also works with the most academically talented students at the school, preparing them for academic decathalon competitions (in which the district has an accomplished record in the state).

I speak just a few words of Spanish, but not enough really to communicate fluently. I've tried to learn on and off in various jobs that I've had, and people, coworkers, have tried to teach me and I've learned a little bit, but not enough to carry on more than about a three-sentence conversation.

I think it's important for Anglo students to learn Spanish from a couple of angles. One, if you're going to live here, 65% of the school is Hispanic and I think it gives the ability to communicate with every student, not just excluding those who can't speak it. I think that would be one angle. Again, I think just the cultural appreciation notion. It's tied to the history of this region, it's tied to the background of so many people. So, I think when you learn someone's language it seems like you gain an appreciation for their culture.

I'm not sure I know if it's important for teachers here to know Spanish. But it would be sort of hypocritical of me to say yes and not have shown any inclination to learn. I guess probably no. I think some of the next generation needs to be able to pick up the things we haven't been able to.

Bill Williams is a mathematics teacher who came to teach in Havens about 5 years ago. A native of New Mexico, he has spent most of his life in the northern part of the state.

I know surprisingly very little Spanish, although I can get the gist of the conversation. When I was growing up, kids were punished for speaking Spanish and where I was growing up, and it could get rather severe. So you get a negative feeling about learning a language. And I wouldn't say there has been any conscious effort on my part to overcome that or to work on that as I go through life. In my own opinion, it's not that important for teachers here to know Spanish, anyway. I don't think it's real important, but I may be trying to buttress my own set of biases. The fact of the matter is, whether you want to agree with it or not, the dominant culture is an English-speaking culture, and I think we do the kids a disservice if we don't teach them to communicate in that language. And I think that many of the efforts, you know, are well intentioned but ill-advised in the sense that a certain amount of help is okay, but wean them so that they are truly bilingual, not nonlingual—which is what I think the outcome generally is. But in terms of everyday nuts and bolts, it would be helpful to know Spanish. I just don't think it's a necessity.

Eva Ortiz is a special education teacher, a native of Havens, and bilingual. Her first language was Spanish; she attended elementary school when speaking Spanish was forbidden.

Well, I usually keep it a secret that I can speak or understand Spanish. Then whenever there is a problem, I can often step in and since I can intervene and since they do not know that I do speak Spanish, it's less intimidating. Because for a teacher who cannot speak Spanish, and even if the kids are just whispering among themselves about what they eat for breakfast, the teacher feels very intimidated. I see it as an advantage because the kids know that I speak Spanish. It just keeps the general problems down in the classroom because they know, "Hey, Ms. Ortiz, she knows what you're saying so cut it out." Sometimes it helps you because you can give a simple instruction in Spanish even though you've given it in English and it reinforces what you're trying to teach.

Even when I taught elementary, it was great because if you speak Spanish, even if it's halting and grammatically incorrect, because mine isn't always correct, the parents see that you're interested in communicating with them. They don't care if you've said, "I wanted your child to come to school" or "I want your child to come to school." You still want their child to be there, and that's what's important, even if the grammar isn't right.

Well, I figure whether you need to know Spanish really depends on what you teach. I think teachers at the lower elementary levels, they really need to speak, to be bilingual. I know when I went to school nobody spoke Spanish.

Coach Diaz is a special education teacher and a baseball coach. His parents spoke Spanish, but forced their children to speak English to protect them from problems in school. It was his grandfather who encouraged him to learn Spanish.

I do think it's important for teachers here to know how to speak Spanish. I think if you're interviewing for a job and they tell you the percentage of kids who don't speak English, I think you're doing yourself an injustice—and the kids—if you don't. But by the same token, I don't think it's wrong for somebody to be hired that doesn't speak Spanish. I mean, you can learn.

I think teachers have a responsibility to learn it because you know if you have a kid who doesn't speak English in your class, you're not doing him any good. But it's easy for me to say this because I know the language. I mean, gee, if I was somewhere in Maine or something and I had to learn French, I might think differently.

Finally, we again hear from Carmen Mendoza, who today administers a school-based bilingual education program in an outlying Havens school located 3 miles from the border.

Ideally, I think it is important for all of the teachers in Havens to speak Spanish, because all of them are going to have to work with students that have a language deficit. It might not be a whole classroom, but there are some students in every classroom that need to have some kind of instruction in their language. And maybe you're going to start being involved more with the parents. I think the teachers should be able to communicate with the parents.

It is not that the teachers are not aware of the benefits of being bilingual in Havens; they just seem, on the whole, less able to imagine achieving this goal themselves if they are not already there and thus, ascribe less urgency to the task. Their sense of urgency is well developed, on the other hand, for students who do not speak English—mostly because among teachers at HHS this is the way language is talked about and the only real language expectation school-wide is that students from Mexico should learn English. The irony seems lost on the teachers that although it is difficult for they themselves to achieve bilingualism, they expect newly arriving students to learn English, and learn it in relatively short order compared to what scholars of language learning would suggest it takes to learn a new language for purposes of conversation and academic progress.[11]

Students are also less certain that all teachers need to know both languages. Linda, for example, prefers teachers who do not speak Spanish so that she is pressured to use her English. But she is well advanced in her quest to become an English speaker. Practically speaking, many students agree with Bill Williams; it is better if a teachers know both languages because then they can understand what their students are saying. It is also important for teachers to encourage students to speak English, to disallow students from too easily reverting to Spanish.

There are many ways to create sound two way bilingual education programs without all teachers becoming bilingual. Team teaching and the skilled use of paraprofessionals can support its development.[12] It is not the case that teachers in Havens are angry about language learning, but rather frustrated. They wish that the TESOL program was more effective more quickly and they struggle to find effective ways of meeting the students' needs even when they do not have the ability to clarify a concept in both languages or when they cannot welcome a student because they cannot communicate adequately. In contrast, students, already in a learning mode seem, at least on the surface, less daunted by the possibility of learning a second language, be it English or Spanish. But their opportunities are limited by what the school offers to them.

* * *

"Grow your own bilingual teachers. All of your students ought to be graduating with both languages." These were the words of a visiting consultant, Cecelia Baca, who met with a small group of principals and district administrators in Winter 1993, and her comments were warmly welcomed. "This is what will make your students unique," she continued passionately. She talked about it less as a choice and more as a district-wide obligation, as what would be the imprimateur of a Havens graduate. If you care about your students' futures, Cecelia implied, then there really is no other option but dual language instruction.

The current school and community-wide focus on students who do not speak English conceals the emerging, long-term language goal that both Cecelia Baca and teachers, administrators, and parents in Havens are starting to become more comfortable with, namely, building bilingual schools for everyone. Today, in reality, this means creating that "other side" of bilingual education that Jack Sullivan described: a program of Spanish language learning for the 400 Mexican-American and Anglo students at HHS whose dominant language is English. For the time being Havens has opted for a limited program of bilingual education only for its newcomers. It has in many ways been conceptualized as a practical choice to meet an immediate need. The thinking goes, "If students are coming here to learn English, then English is what the school ought to be teaching." At the high school level, where new students only have a few years to "make it," teachers are anxious to guarantee that everyone graduates with their English skills intact.

But the limitations of this singular conception of language learning are apparent. Along with what are fundamentally good intentions, TESOL programming at HHS also has come to serve a marginalizing function: Students are isolated in classes and have restricted opportunities in the structured, academic portion of their day to interact with local Havens' students who are not newcomers—which translates into restricted opportunities in the other, unstructured parts of the day as well. There is too little common ground. When students graduate and continue to live on the border as adults—and this is the most common pattern—they are likely to be unnecessarily isolated by virtue of language.

Teachers and students at HHS already recognize the dual language environment in which they teach and learn—they just do not talk about it publicly. Like the border itself, Spanish and English are part of the backdrop, a condition of life in Havens, and, in the schools, a naturally occurring one. Students may or may not let their teachers know they are bilingual, and teachers may or may not choose to use the resources their bilingual students represent. This lack of dialogue is precisely what would enable several months to pass before a teacher like Janet Otero recognizes the fact that Juan Dominguez is bilingual. Beyond a basic awareness of language issues, much about language learning is left to chance. Teachers at HHS have not had the benefit of formal knowledge to guide their actions relative to language and lack a well-grounded way of discussing the issue. Basic principles of teaching ESL are not part of their early or continuing preparation. In the short run, developing a more sophisticated consciousness of language on the part of Havens' teachers is perhaps more realistic—and necessary—than the goal of having all teachers speak both languages.

The shift from a narrow view of bilingual education as "learning English" to a broad view that can, through the teaching of both languages, build mutual understanding, communication, and most important, respect—as well as the real possibility of expanded job opportunities on graduation—will require a deep understanding of what resources already exist. Dual language capacity is almost a natural resource in Havens, but it is a resource that is restricted as long as the schools only speak to its "first side." In contrast, in the midst of a community that seems to understand the economic pull of bilingualism, and where the students have already developed an informal network for language awareness and initial learning, a two-way program would not be launched in a vacuum. The first harvesting of natural language resources might simply be raising the credibility of those students who already are bilingual, ascribing to them real, visible value in the school. Student and teacher creativity alike can be tapped into only if language is a permissible topic for daily conversation, and it will be successful only to the extent that the discussion of language goes beyond the current worry over "learning English" and teachers begin to view language from a valued, binational perspective.

"He who know two languages is worth two persons." There is a significant distance between this *dicho* as ideal and the language reality along the border. But in many ways the *dicho* is the appropriate guide. Language is the thing that gets you ahead—that is, if you know two of them. If you have one, and it happens to be Spanish, you are seen as being "behind," and language is the thing that can keep you down. To push the community ahead through the students who complete its schools, the only option seems to be the first. One recent HHS graduate put it this way: "A lot of kids didn't know English and we didn't know Spanish. That was a big barrier. We never talked to or got to know one another."

5

Getting Along at Havens High

In the long run, we're kind of in this together. These are the bonds that will make the countries go. You have to think 20 or 30 years into the future. You're raising a group of people in this school. If you do it right, you're raising a group who have a chance to make the relationships between the countries relatively trouble free, and profitable for all. We need to value the talent to do this, no matter where the kids are born.

I see groups that hang out together, like the academic group, the football group, the people who come up from Mexico group.

Friday night is basketball night at Havens High. In these winter months, the gym is usually about three fourths full. Just inside the west entrance of the building, in the hallway, is the ticket booth. Food is sold by the junior class and large jars are on the counter to collect money to support various students who are trying to go on special trips—an international cheerleaders event in England or a chance to play basketball in Australia as part of a special international team are among the options. High school students crowd around the entrance and line up at the stand to buy Snickers, popcorn, or Cokes. The superintendent, principal, vice principal and counselors are all wearing their HHS shirts or sweatshirts, newly purchased for the season.

Like high school gymnasiums all over, the walls are draped with banners proclaiming periodic past successes in sports: state championships in basketball, volleyball, cross country—both boys and girls. By force of habit, high school students mostly sit on the east side; the balcony is perched above it. Parents and younger siblings sit on the west with the announcer, manager, and scorekeepers. The pep band, in which Liliana Sanchez plays the saxophone (and her close friends play trumpet and keyboards) keep the momentum of spirit up from the east side of the gym, too. The Havens High cheerleaders—which include both Anglo and Mexican-American girls, are applauded wildly by their schoolmates. The dance team, which is made up of Anglo and Mexican-American girls and includes Gabriela, Liliana's friend who was reeled into the band the day she came to register for school and who will return to Mexico for college, is a new feature on the spirit agenda this year. By the volume of applause they collect, their initiation is a well-received addition. There is nothing much else going on in town on these Friday nights in winter.

One player, Juan Carlos, a sophomore, began his career in Havens as a daily border crosser. Recently, his mother, brother, and sister moved to Havens to live. This move, from all reports, was to enable the children to attend school here. His father continues to live and work about an hour's drive south into Mexico. His family, like the families of all of the other players, is here to cheer the team on tonight, his father having made the drive north just as many other parents have made the drive south or east or west—depending on which farm or ranch they live. A forward, an Anglo boy, lives in town with his mother, but his father lives 90 miles south in a Mexican community founded in the last century by the followers of the Mormon faith. Both parents are there to support him and his team.

On one of these evenings, I arrived at the gym early and walked over to the cafeteria to watch a newly formed folklorico dance group. Most of the students in this group commute to school each day from Mexico; a few had studied folklorico from a former teacher who was also the principal of the local primaria in one of the communities that is home to students who come to Havens to school. One student at practice was a long-time Havens resident whose parents had immigrated in their teens. She was also on the dance team, and had brought along a friend. Under the direction of Selena Knight, their TESOL teacher, who spoke no Spanish but had ample background in theater and musical productions, the students were practicing for a Cinco de Mayo presentation that would take place several months from now. Because the students had no personal transportation, they were spending the night in town at the homes of friends or relatives. Some would be driven back to Mexico the next day by their teacher. The cafeteria, where they were rehearsing, was a minute's walk down the corridor from where the basketball crowd was beginning to gather.

I had been attending basketball games for several weeks now. I noticed that some of the local students who were in the TESOL classes had been attending and cheered Juan Carlos every time he made an important shot—and this was often. But the students in the folklorico group, especially those from Mexico, typically had no transportation and once they returned home on Friday afternoons they rarely traveled back up to Havens. When folklorico practice was nearing an end, I made my way from the cafeteria to the gymnasium to take a seat. About 20 minutes into the game, amidst all the cheering, shouting, and pep band's music, three of the girls from the folklorico group and two other local students from the TESOL classes—none of whom ever had attended a school basketball game before in Havens—walked up quietly to the balcony, made their way across the front, and took seats in the uppermost corner in the back row. The group included Maria Vasquez, who lives with her aunt in Havens, goes home to her small farming community in Mexico most weekends, and is planning to go into the U.S. military—and her cousin Magdalena, who planned to go to computer school in Juarez on graduation. Yvonne Ramirez was there too—at 22 one of the oldest students in the school, and also one of the quietest and most serious in her classes. Next came Ana and her sister Angela, who lived in a tiny home in a colonia near one of the large chile and onion farms on the outskirts of town; their parents are migrant workers. The girls cheered when the team did well and were engrossed by the game and the energy in the gym. During the last quarter of the game, they all left together. Yvonne, much to my surprise given her prim, almost grave demeanor during the week—was dancing on the way out with a relaxed, happy look on her face.

*   *   *

Activities like Friday night basketball games are in many ways the embodiment of high school social activity, especially in a small town where sports are among the only real outlets students have. Students appear in the gym because of familiarity with the habit and because of friendships, and if those habits are not part of one's routine, it is unlikely that one would attend. It is not easy for Maria Vasquez, Magdalena, Yvonne, and their friends to cross over into the social network high school athletic events represent. On a daily basis, these five girls wait together outside of the east door of the building before school and eat lunch together in the cafeteria. Magdalena rides home with Yvonne on the bus to Mexico each day. The others all live legally in Havens but identify themselves with Mexico (and are so identified by others) and hang out almost exclusively with the students who are learning English—whether they are from Mexico or the United States.

And where are the cultural mediators? At the basketball game, Liliana Sanchez is busy playing saxophone in the pep band, Maria Cruz is busy managing the team[1] and making sure the players have everything they need to play at their best, and Richard Logan is taking photographs for the school paper. Unlike their informal day-to-day interactions in school, at this event they have a specific, structured role to play, one that does not include the informal social networking that might be needed to bring students like Yvonne or Magdalena directly into the fold. On this particular evening, they were in the building anyway to practice their dancing and found a way to enter the social network, but had the folklorico not existed, the chances of their coming to the game were slim. As it is, they appeared in the stands only on the fringes, at the margins of the activity.

* * *

By most standards HHS is very much an American high school. Entering its main front doors, you see a school much like any other. Pennants from academic team wins adorn the foyer, along with advertisements encouraging students to purchase class rings, handmade posters by junior class members reminding everyone about the winter dance coming up in the next few weeks, notices about the upcoming pizza sales, and recruitment posters from the military—all these are visible. At the start of the day, announcements on the PA system also let you know this is a high school like any other. Team scores are read from the previous weekend's athletic exploits, along with announcements of class meetings, clubs, activities, and last minute schedule changes. Students cluster in the hallways, around teachers' doors, and outside near the parking lot in social groupings that define who they are and who they seek out at lunch and in between classes. If there is a bake sale, the lines at the tables are long. Couples linger for a few seconds after the bell rings, then rush off to their separate classes. Girls fix one last dab of lipstick in the small mirrors hanging on the doors of their lockers. Football players, in their jerseys if it is a game day, talk with each other about the evening's opposing team, or exchange words with a short-skirted cheerleader. In the school office, to the right of the main entryway, student assistants are busily helping the secretaries.

One thousand students enter the doors of HHS each day at 8 a.m. Without seeing them, one would be hard-pressed to figure out that in this school, 70% of the students are of Mexican descent and the other 30% are Anglo. Not a single sign indicates the population—no art, no banners of welcome, no language clues. There is no tangible reminder at all, save when the first bell rings and the students flood the halls. Then, their looks and language choices and music define the demographics and it is unmistakably a school on the border. Approximately 100 students commute from Mexico daily, and of these, about 80% hold dual U.S. and Mexican citizenship. The rest of the daily commuters hold student visas.

The question of how opportunity is created for each of these students to integrate into the life of the school, whether they are newcomers to the community from Mexico, longtime local Anglos or Mexican-Americans, or currently residents of Mexico, is in many ways at the heart of the challenge to develop a binational school community. How students are valued, how they perceive their place in school, and how they are enabled to prepare for successful lives are all related to how the school creates its identity as a school on the border. Liliana and Maria, like many others, observed that the real divisions exist between Mexican students and the rest of the school—Mexican-Americans and Anglo students. In reality, the situation is more complex and multilayered. Binationalism is not merely a case of creating a welcoming environment for students who come from Mexico daily; this may be, in fact, only a small part of the challenge. On the contrary, creating a binational consciousness means developing a place where language is shared, where cultures are understood, where the benefits and limitations on both sides of the border are appropriate topics for discussion and debate and, finally, where opportunity itself is widely and publicly accessible to Anglo and Mexican origin students alike. Language itself, as powerful an equalizer as it has the potential to be, is not an exact stand-in for cultural acceptance and understanding or for creating access to all the opportunities the school has to offer.

What Counts as Success?

For the secondary school to continue to be meaningful, the faculty must be perceptive to the needs of a rapidly changing society and must constantly communicate with students through various forms. In this way, the curriculum and methods of instruction can be assessed and revised to fulfill the fundamental purpose of preparing the student for effective living in an ever changing world. So states the philosophy of HHS. It is clear that the world in and around Havens is changing rapidly. And it is in the act of defining those changes that a school decides how to move ahead in preparing its students.

At HHS, success is defined multidimensionally. As a high school in an economically depressed part of the southwest, it is not a place that only serves a single goal, for example, preparing students for college careers. In 1993, only about 20% of Havens' students went on to post-secondary education. Each year a few choose successfully from among some of the more prestigious schools in the country: Georgetown, Harvard, Stanford, West Point, Cornell. Most college-bound students, however, attend school locally at the University of New Mexico, New Mexico State University, Eastern or Western New Mexico State, or at schools just across the state line in Texas. Economics is always a concern for those considering college. Some may attend community colleges in the area. The goal, according to the principal, is to reach toward 60% college attendance—but admittedly that may not be realistic. Others select the military, a traditional choice for many Mexican-American students, whereas many others work either in town or move elsewhere to secure jobs. Vocational education is an important part of the school's offerings, and includes woodshop, metals, cosmetology, mechanics (both agricultural and standard), and health occupations, to name a few. For many years the school owned a farm, now sold, which served as a agricultural/vocational training site. At the same time, a handful of high achieving students, and an increasing number of students of Mexican origin do attend college. Other students, namely, those from Mexico, come to HHS for the instrumental reason of learning English. Some of these students will continue in postsecondary institutions (either in the United States or in Mexico) and others will go on straight to jobs. If they are lucky, most of those jobs will require bilingual skills and they will compete well.

It is a mixed bag and Havens is bound, like so many small rural high schools, to meet a wide range of student interests and needs. It has to provide college counseling and vocational counseling. It has to provide a welcoming environment for military recruiters. It has to encourage students to see beyond Havens for their life opportunities but also be careful not to disengage them from where they have grown up. All of this occurs with many of the same pressures that challenge schools everywhere as they struggle to serve students from multiple cultures and different socioeconomic classes well: how to provide real opportunity, how to avoid the traps of academic tracking,[2] how to help students use culture as a strong base for their own growth and achievement, and how to build confidence among all students—not just those who traditionally have benefited from the school's opportunities—that the school's activities are as much for them as they are for everyone else. These are the same kinds of problems my students at the university in Milwaukee are facing as they begin to take jobs with the Milwaukee public schools—with their array of African-American, Mexican, Puerto Rican, Lao, Hmong, Vietnamese, Polish, and Russian students. So what made the challenge in Havens any different? Why, or how is the situation different because Havens is located near the border?

At one level the answer is, "It is not different." Schools typically need to take heroic measures to transform how they work with students for whom school seems remote in purpose. In Havens, large numbers of first and second generation Mexican-American students move through school unaffiliated and disengaged, and as a result many tend not to finish. Some have to take jobs to support their families; for others, school just seems like a poor use of their time. Like stories of marginalized students everywhere, many students in Havens have to go to great efforts to gain access to the often hidden dynamics of their school's social and academic structure and many have checked out already. And, most of these students are Mexican in origin and have lived in Havens a generation or two.

On another level, the border is what defines the future work environment for many of the students—whether they stay in Havens to farm, ranch, work a regular job, join the border patrol, move to one of the surrounding communities, or move to Arizona (Phoenix is a favorite destination) or Texas. Border culture *is* the local culture. It is a fluid mix of Mexican and American practices and it takes an understanding of both to shape and strengthen a binational community. Students will inevitably conduct their lives on both sides of the border, as they already do and as do many of their families. So for the school, it is not just a question of figuring out how to welcome students who come from Mexico and how they fit in. Instead, the presence of daily border crossers is emblematic of the larger, more fundamental need to attend both to culture and language in building a healthy life on the border. The students from Mexico are often in the conversational spotlight, and with good cause. But their needs exist within a much broader conversation about how all students who attend the school are valued, how the school provides opportunity for all of its students, how to support students in constructing strong personal identities, and where questions of culture enter into that conversation.

The administrators—both at the school and district level—view new immigrants or students from Mexico and first or second generation Mexican-American students as two distinctly different populations with distinct subcultures. As true as this might be, the tie that binds these groups is that for different reasons they do not see the fit between much of what the school is about and their own lives. Some of this is an issue of culture, some is an issue of language, and some is an issue of social class and economics. But for everyone, it is a question of how to locate oneself in a community on the border, of how the various pieces of the American and Mexican cultures—and the regional culture that has come to be known as the border culture—fit together.[3]

Inevitably, it is the more advantaged students, and usually this means a majority of Anglo students who are achieving, whose needs the school is already meeting—those who usually already know what to do and how to gain access to the things they want. Building a more secure educational base for students whose families immigrated in previous generations—who may or may not be economically advantaged—means sanctioning their cultural backgrounds and current practices. This includes students who never go back to Mexico and those who go back to see their aunts, uncles, cousins, and grandparents on a regular basis. It includes students who believe they are not valued in school because they are "Mexican" but rarely talk about it, and those who are willing to take on any one of their peers who use the word *mojado.* It includes Anglo students who have misconceptions about their Mexican and Mexican-American peers and Mexican-American students who think speaking Spanish is another way of marginalizing themselves.

To increase the chances for success on the border, people who live in this area require an awareness of cultural difference, the ability to speak both languages, and a sense of commitment to making the border region work. Preparing students for the cross-border nature of their lives, for the local context in which their work is likely to be carried out, however, is more an incidental rather than an active goal at HHS. Where the border fits into the way the school views itself is still emerging. Much like the dynamics of dual language use, it is students who are taking a quiet but persistent role in this regard. And a few of their teachers are following suit.

Luis and Jose: Promoting Leadership

Luis Estrada, who chose to correct the pronunciation of his name at the graduation ceremonies in May, was a senior the year I arrived, and well on his way to making the important decisions about his college years. Medium height, medium build, he had a quiet but very determined demeanor and seemed more mature than his 18 years. He had lived in many places in the United States, but has been in Havens for the last 4 years; his father's work in construction took them on the road. Luis's father's family lived in the United States but eventually returned to Mexico to raise cattle. His mother is from the area south of the Frontera checkpoint. Spanish is the language they speak at home; Luis speaks accentless English and often people at the school are surprised he is also fluent in Spanish. His father and siblings also speak English fluently; his mother is taking English classes through the LVA program at the Methodist church. She is also part of the fledgling service and action women's group made up of immigrants devoted to increasing cross-cultural understanding in the community and community leadership and advocacy on the part of Mexican-immigrant women. After school Luis

---

*Wetback (highly perjorative term).

works at the local supermarket bagging groceries and translating for customers who cannot speak English.

Both of Luis' parents stress the importance of education, but his father is less convinced that college is a necessity than is his mother. A good job with a good starting salary would suffice. When Luis was growing up, making sure he had a solid work ethic was his father's goal.

> Ever since I was in sixth or seventh grade and he was working in California, he'd come down here for 3 or 4 days and he'd take me out into the chile fields and we'd pick chile, so I knew, so I could establish a work ethic. When he was working in California, he was making $28 an hour—he was general foreman up there. When he was home he'd take me to go pick chile with him here and it was kind of awkward. And afterwards I got paid, like, $20 for a whole day's work. What I learned from that was that it was tough in comparison to my dad's work, and you'd see all the people who had to make a living off of it. And you see how hard they had to work in comparison to yourself. I think my dad did that so that I wouldn't ever look down on these people and say, "Now, look at them," in a manner that is not proper. A lot of the chile pickers come into the store and I think if I didn't have some of those experiences I might do like a lot of people do, I mean, they look down on them.

Throughout my conversations with Mexican origin students in the school, Luis' name would come up as someone who could be counted on to provide accurate information about taking ACT exams, about running for the class executive committee, about showing that Hispanic students could take leadership roles in the school. As time went on, I also learned that he was recruiting students to attend special activities sponsored by the National Hispanic Institute (NHI), an organization "founded with the belief that the Hispanic community can best contribute to the American experience by insuring that its more capable young people achieve the expertise, exposure, and self-confidence to become respected and contributing members of society." The specific aims of NHI are twofold: to support students in pursuing admissions to selective colleges and to foster students' participation in their local Hispanic communities. Luis and a friend of his had attended one of the NHI summer programs a few years earlier and were now working to get more students involved both in the school and in other NHI activities. He actively sought out promising students from the eighth grade on to attend these pro-grams—students who were new immigrants as well as students whose families had been in Havens for a few generations. His concern, more than anything else, was to make sure that his Hispanic peers had access to the opportunies the NHI provided and that they participated in the life of the school. As part of his commitment to these goals, he also visited his mother's service club and talked to the women about the importance of their children getting an education, learning how to use the "system" in the U.S. schools, and taking advantage of opportunities like NHI. In 1993, material about the NHI appeared in the school's guide to preparing for college, a local school handbook to help students plan their full secondary careers with college in mind. He himself planned to attend a small private school in the lower midwest. He advised:

> Take charge whenever you possibly can. Hold any leadership position that's available at any time and get a group of people together to get stuff done. Hispanics have a tendency to always have an opinion on something, but they don't always get in and do something. Politics and stuff like that here in the school, I don't think they really get that much involved in it. I was talking to some people about this, some juniors, about executive committee next year. I told them if they wanted to get stuff done that they wanted, to get in there and, I mean, they never realized that.

In the same way he encouraged Yolanda Ybarra, a first generation Mexican-American, to find out about the tests she needed for college admission; Tony Valenzuela, the child of migrant workers, an honors student who immigrated during his elementary school years and who helps his peers retain their Spanish, to attend a leadership institute; and Jose Ruiz, a former daily commuter and now immigrant, to work with the principal to bring Spanish culture into the school so the Mexican students might be encouraged to participate more, especially during pep rallies.

Like Luis, Jose Ruiz was concerned about leadership among the Mexican-origin students. He himself identified mainly with the newly immigrated students and those who crossed daily. His peers at school saw him as someone who was "more Mexican than American" because he favored using Spanish and wore clothes that were characteristically associated with a contemporary Mexican style of dress. He explained this concern for leadership as serving two purposes: to contribute to the good of the school while also providing credible role models for other Mexican students.

> I wanted to be in those activities [sports, clubs, etc.] not to become popular, but to help out the school in any way. If you have an ability that you can use to help out the school, that's what I would like to do. That way the other people, the other Hispanics, can see that if we can do it, so can they. Because their idea of getting into activities like sports or decathlon is that these are for White people in this school, and that almost all of those other things, like leadership conferences, are for White people, they kind of feel

left out because they think to themselves that they can't do it, like be on the executive committee. They think that they won't stand a chance. The people that come down from Mexico and the Hispanic ones from here, they think that it's not for them, it wasn't meant for them, that they can't do it. But if we've shown through the school that we can do it, that we can get up there on the executive committee or those other activities, we can show them that they can do it too. Because they come from a foreign country it doesn't mean that they can't put the school in a good position.

From Jose's perspective, the issue of contributing to the school community is at least as important as giving Mexican students a chance to participate. It is not a problem of the teachers being unwelcoming, but rather some of the students. "The principal and the teachers told me that because I am keeping my GPA at a high level, they've told me to go into Academic Decathlon, to show some of these other Mexican guys that we can do it."

Old-timers and graduates from the previous one or two generations readily agree that more and more students of Mexican origin are participating in the life of the school compared to when they attended. Historically, there have always been a few Mexican-American students in leadership positions over the years, but they were usually children of economically stable farming or ranching families who had lived in the area for generations. Their presence in these positions was not a vindication of discrimination; they were clearly the exceptions. At a time when, according to the annual HHS yearbooks, the student body of the senior classes was between one third and one half students of Mexican origin, one class officer might be Mexican-American (on the 1946–1947 student council, the only Mexican students of the 20 council members were Beatrice and Alma Herrera, the teacher Ana Herrera's relatives), or one of the representatives to Boys or Girls State might be, or one or two students in the NHS (which included upward of 30 students each year). This was during the 1950s and 1960s.

By 1993 the change in how Mexican-American students were involved in school was perhaps most apparent in activities like the NHS, where nearly 32% of the approximately 150 members and new inductees were Mexican of origin. The Academic Decathlon team included three Mexican-American students. In cheerleading, 6 of the 10 girls are Mexican-American, and on the newly constituted dance team, several Mexican-American and one Mexican student participate. Of the two drum majorettes, one is Liliana Sanchez; the other is one of her good Anglo friends. Mexican-American students always play a leadership role in the preparation of the school's yearbook; Richard Logan is the sponsor. The band seems to be a place where students of varied ethnic backgrounds mix very easily; their music is the point of interaction.

But also in 1993–1994, all student council officers were Anglo, as were all officers for the senior and junior classes. Two officers of the sophomore class were local Mexican-American students. Honors and AP classes regularly have more Anglo students than Mexican-origin ones, but there are always a few Mexican-American students in them. In lower level English classes, the ones Richard Logan is likely to teach, the opposite is true. The school also circulates a periodic list of students who are ineligible for extra curricular activities, notably sports, due to low achievement; it is virtually filled with Spanish names. A new chapter of a service organization, the Key Club, attracted many of the same students on the student council and class executive committees; one or two Mexican-American students finally agreed to join through the direct intervention of the sponsor, Janet Otero. Janet recognized the problem but was not quite sure what to do about it.

> I don't want to beat anybody over the head. I've spoken to a number of my [Hispanic] students about coming and being a part of the Key Club, and they look at the roster and a couple of the Hispanic kids have just said, "No, I don't belong there, I don't ..." That kind of thing. I honestly believe that the opportunity is there for everyone, but that the walls are already up, the walls are already built, and they bring some of that with them to school, and some of it we perpetuate here. I think we could do a lot more.

Eva Ortiz, the special education teacher who chooses not to advertise her knowledge of Spanish and who is a habitual and astute observer of social interactions in the school agrees. Feeling that there was no choice and that it would be highly unlikely that a large group of Mexican-American or Mexican students would participate in the Key Club that Janet sponsors, she has been considering starting a second Key Club.

> There's potential for leadership. And there's some where you wouldn't expect to find it, you know. Like with Key Club. Janet has a second group of Hispanic and low income White kids who want to join the Key Club but no way do they want to have anything to do with the Cindy Dalton's of the school. [Cindy is active in the Future Farmers of America club and in adolescent parlance is viewed as a sort of "snob."] Yet they want the prestige of having Janet be their leader. And they trust her.

In contrast, the Spanish Club is dominated by Mexican students or new immigrants; it is an active club but is not highly visible nor particularly prestigious. The sponsor, who is Mexican-American, takes advantage of leadership training opportunities for the club's members.

In the past, its visibility has been much higher, especially when Susan Hartman, the district administrator who has been fostering better understanding of the power of bilingual education, was its sponsor and was committed to increasing the appreciation of language. The place where Anglo and Mexican-American students seem to stand in equal terms is in sports—both boys and girls. Seeking a sense of where in school things approach equality, I was told that sports was the equalizer. But it stands alone as such, and sports do not regularly include students who commute to Mexico.

These academic and social inequities are regularly noted by some of the school's other Mexican-American teachers as well, who are also looking for signs of progress and seeing some—but not enough. It is slowly being noted as well by some of the Anglo teachers. Individual teachers and the principal regularly encourage promising students like Luis, Jose, and Tony, or cultural mediators like Liliana, to push ahead, to achieve, to take on leadership roles. They remind them how important it is to show that Mexican and Mexican-American students can make it at HHS. Myrna Jimenez, a bilingual business teacher, believes more Mexican-origin students are taking advantage of the opportunities the school has to offer, but that the direct guidance of a teacher is sometimes responsible.

> The coaches will go hunting for kids with talent and pull them in. In this department, if we find a really sharp student we definitely try. "Why don't you take Keyboarding I and II?" Or we just put them straight into computers or the right math class. So I feel that every department probably does that if they see a good student.

But when she arrived in Havens in the mid-1960s to take her first teaching job, this was not the case.

> When I arrived here, I was shocked to find that cheerleaders, student body president, were non-existent—not for the Hispanics, anyway. And to me, with such a great majority and being so near the border, I found myself saying, "Wow! What's going on here?" But now I think we're coming around to the leadership roles.

Capable students who identify with or are from Mexico seem to need an especially personal push to participate in groups like NHS. Although they qualify, it can be difficult for them to decide to actually attend the meetings and to take an active role. They get this push from an individual teacher who knows their academic record. Once a student like a Tony or a Jose is in NHS, it is far more likely that others will consider coming along. But even at this high end of the achievement scale, an imbalance of knowledge and belonging exists—like it did for Yolanda regarding the tests she was to take and some of the internship opportunities that Anglo students had taken advantage of during their junior and senior years—that she had never heard of. She viewed this as an example of inequities within the school.

The most active Mexican-American people in the school, those who are high achievers and who are themselves leaders, all point to instances where they have felt uncomfortable socially because of their ethnicity despite their achievements. Luis felt it when he was no longer accepted by the "football crowd" the year he decided not to go out for the team, or getting into a fight with an Anglo student who called Mexicans "dirty Mexicans." Amber Martinez, an "A" student with a full scholarship to the University of New Mexico, a basketball and volleyball player, and a very popular girl, felt uncomfortable at a party at the home of one of her Anglo teammates from basketball and at a dance where she and her partner were the only Hispanic couple. There is a nagging uncertainly for them, a question, ever present, of being totally accepted.

"It's getting better." Despite the problems, this is the way progress is described by nearly every individual of Mexican origin who has lived in Havens for decades. This recognition of progress in matters of participation and leadership on the part of Mexican-American and Mexican students is noted with a sense of modest optimism for the future. Both at school and in the community, the shift away from the "old days," when discrimination was everywhere and it was virtually impossible for visible numbers of Mexican-origin people to get ahead, is greeted quietly, as a long awaited incremental step toward a more just division of power and authority. At HHS, as in the community, militancy in demanding equity for students of Mexican origin—on the part of the administration, teachers, or students—is considered inappropriate. Over and over again, people in this community and in its schools, with few exceptions, have chosen to work through the existing system to make changes. As the principal of HHS, Daniel Martinez sees the progress but not the eradication of the problem.

> As a general rule we all get along well. Both Anglos and Mexicans have been very supportive of me in my job. As a general rule people are good and kind here in Sonora County. I love my community. I love the people I work for and I love the kids I work with. But there will always be some discrimination.

It is a slow kind of progress, to be sure. And the philosophy that it is the responsibility of individual teachers or students to take the initiative for building a more balanced school community in terms of ethnicity means that some important things are left to chance.

Jose: Welcoming Mexican Students

While together Luis and Jose pressed the leadership agenda, Jose was also thinking long and hard about ways the school could be made more welcoming and inviting to students who either were from Mexico or who were new enough in town that they still identified—or were identified—mainly with Mexico. Only when students feel personally welcomed in the school, according to Jose, are they likely to take advantage of the opportunity to participate more widely in its activities—and when their English had developed to the point that they were no longer self-conscious.

Jose himself was part of the group who lives in the United States but whose primary reference point was still Mexico and Mexican culture. He had lived in town for some time, had met Anglo students, and by now had some Anglo friends. In addition to suggesting to the principal that he and a few others form a mariachi band for pep rallies, an activity that had been successful in the prior school year, another way he thought people might feel more comfortable at pep rallies would be to put up signs in Spanish. "When they put up a sign like that, I thought, 'Well, they're really thinking about these other people.' They could put in a little Spanish culture, a little Spanish music." Along with his desire to introduce "Spanish" culture into the school, he believed that formally arranging meetings between Anglo and Mexican students would also foster cross-cultural communication.

> It would help if the school had like a special session where Anglos could meet Mexican students. They could arrange a time, maybe not like a date, but a time to go out, you know, like to eat. If they would arrange it and would tell them, probably at school, "Go to this restaurant and you'll meet these people," or set up a special program in which Anglos meet Hispanics.

Jose understood well that students are looking for confirmation—of their language, the music they prefer, their characteristic dress, the things that make them stand out in the Havens High crowd. They are looking for signs of interest in who they are.

> Maybe if the people from here, you know, Anglos, if they begin to talk to the students from Mexico, like if they were to talk to me or to anybody else, I guess they would feel different about them, they would appreciate them more. Because some of these guys that come down from Mexico, some of these people that come from over there, they're pretty smart and dedicated. I know lots of them who are on the honor roll.

The feeling of being rejected is something many of the students Jose is concerned about carry around with them and have internalized—even if they themselves have not been the direct recipients of this kind of negativity. His friend Susana saw it this way:

> I felt like I didn't belong here in the beginning. And still now some people look at me like, "You're different." Because I come from Frontera. I just get a feeling. I don't know if they're really thinking something or not. I just get this feeling that they think that I'm not like them. I think it's because we ourselves feel that they won't like us. It's within well, me. Some just don't like us coming here. The language is not stopping me anymore, because I can talk. But my feeling that I don't belong, sometimes it's what stops me from talking to them.

Of the students who do cross daily, Susana is among the most integrated and least isolated. She is in honors classes, she has Anglo friends, but she still carries around a sense of being marginalized. Intentional or not on the part of their American and Mexican-American peers, students from Mexico and their immigrant counterparts carry around feelings of isolation even as they are trying to fit into the mainstream of the school.[4]

Some opportunities are not available simply because of the practical question of having no after school activity bus. A few teachers are quick to point out defensively that this is a problem for students who live on outlying ranches and farms too—students from the United States who are mostly Anglo. But the children of ranchers and farmers typically come to school with their status intact, so the effect of being unable to play sports or participate on the dance team does not have the same consequences as it does for students who already sit on the sideline of the school's activities by virtue of their ethnicity, language, or place of residence. Only those with the means for personal transportation (there is no public transportation between Frontera and Havens) stay after school—and this totals maybe one or two a year. When they do, their visibility is a point of pride for all of the students from Mexico, and they all know one of "theirs" is contributing to the school's sports successes.

In spite of these feelings of isolation on the part of students, the teachers at HHS actually view students who cross daily and those who have newly immigrated in an almost uniformly positive light. Teachers believe they set a standard that for many of the local students would be difficult to reach. They are seen as hardworking and respectful, they wake up at 5 a.m. just to get to school, they appreciate the opportunity coming to school in Havens offers, and they understand their parents' financial sacrifice in sending them to school here. (Although parents of students from Mexico are not required to pay tuition—the appropriate-

ness of this stance on the part of the state is a source of much debate—they sacrifice in terms of paying for the daily bus ride and making
sure their children have the supplies and materials they need to be
successful in an American school.) Bill Williams, the math teacher, saw
it this way:

> Most, I would say, over 90% of the students from Mexico, are maybe really
> more interested in an education than some of those from the U.S. that are
> here. We get those once in a while who are just here to experiment, but
> they usually don't last. But I think a lot of them who are here are very,
> very serious students. So in some ways, I think some are better students
> than some of our U.S. students. They're more ambitious, anyway.

This is not an uncommon opinion about new Mexican immigrants in
schools elsewhere in the country.[5] At HHS it also derives partly from the
way students who are coming from Mexico, as well as those new
residents of Havens, view their own acknowledged status as guests of
the school district. Jose's friend Susana talked about this issue as a case
of right versus privilege.

> It can't be my school, because I'm not American. See, if I had been going
> to school in Frontera or somewhere else in Mexico, I would feel more like
> I had the right to be here. Here if someone says you don't belong here, I
> mean, OK, I don't belong, you know. Because it's a privilege to be here. It's
> not a right. I can't say it's my school.

Even though he feels some of the same isolation and absorbs some of
the same feelings of being a "guest" as do his peers who ride the bus each
day across the border, it *is* Jose's school: He is a U.S. resident. And it *is*
Tony Valenzuela's school and Laura Aguilar's school. In Havens this
sense of transition has a more immediate public and political face; if
students have immigrated formally, they still easily (and not inappro-
priately) associate with students who are not residents and empathize
with their feelings.

At the same time, students from Mexico who violate the high expectations their teachers and peers set and who are not working hard are
judged harshly not only by their teachers, but by their peers as well. It
is from these negative cases that generalizations are, unfortunately,
often made. Spotlighting the Mexican students who can provide leadership, as Jose and Luis wish to do, diverts attention away from the
smaller number of daily crossers who are seen as taking advantage, as
playing around, as using U.S. tax dollars unfairly, as creating a bad
image of all students from Mexico. Richard Logan observed:

I think the ones who aspire to do well and become something see it as a privilege. I think the ones who don't, see it as their right: "How dare you? I'm just as good as you, I'm better. I'm here because I want to be and because I can be. You owe me this." That's the dividing element.

Tony saw the situation similarly:

> I think we're offered the same opportunities as everyone else, but there are some people who don't use those opportunities. I think a lot of students from Frontera don't want to study. They just come here to mess around. But there's also people who want to learn. It's no use to send them if you're a troublemaker down here, because a lot of people don't want us down here. It's a privilege to come here. I don't think it's a right. They have a responsibility to show they are willing to learn.

Myrna Jimenez, the business education teacher, tied it to the general population of the school, implicitly recognizing the fact that it certainly is not just students from Mexico who "cut up" and are not serious about school:

> The students from Mexico, granted that we're the ones paying for their education, I think they should be aware that it is a privilege and an honor to be in school here and if they don't like it, just stay back in Frontera. And know that if you're going to come over here and fool around, maybe be disobedient, if you're going to be here just 3 days a week and then out, that's not going to work out. But if you're going to be in school, be in school. But I think also that all the other students need to have the discipline set straight, too, not only the students from Mexico.

Another aspect of harsh judgment, leveled mostly by other students, has to do with the commitment to learning English. Liliana Sanchez saw it in relationship to obligation:

> I want them to try harder because a lot of kids start saying, "Well, if those Mexicans weren't over here you know, we wouldn't have to do this and we wouldn't have to do that, and it's not right." I want them to show that they can do it, that they can speak English. But for them to come over here and not try hard ... they really owe it to themselves. It's hard when you're a Mexican yourself. I am very proud of my heritage and I love Mexico, but for them to get here and not apply themselves through talking English, then it is sort of a setback for us because they're not improving themselves.

Richard Logan continued:

> Some are not putting out in class like they could be. I had two or three kids last year who could speak English. They shouldn't have even been in

TESOL. But they just sort of refused to do it. It was like, "Well, if I speak good English in this class, then I'm a school boy, so I'm not going to do it." If two or three of those guys started speaking English to everybody in class all of the time, that class would have just gone through the roof. I had to tell them, "I defend you." Every time somebody says we ought to send these kids back to Mexico I say, "These are some of my best students." But when some students don't try, I can't always say that anymore.

Despite these problems, many students from Mexico clearly break the stereotypes that have evolved about immigrants. The most strong-willed plow right in and get involved—as soon as their language skills give them the confidence to do so. Others would like to, but they feel tentative because of their uncertain status.

There is almost a communal responsibility to set a good example, and this is the view that Daniel Martinez makes clear to all of the Mexican students in his role as principal. But at the same time he treads lightly with the students who come across the border each day because of their insecure status position.

When I have to meet with the Frontera kids, if they are cutting up on the bus, let's say, I have to be careful not to single them out too much. They feel singled out already; they're already carrying a stigma. I know their parents are making a sacrifice—much more than I have to.

No matter what side of the border they come from, there is a genuine appreciation here for hardworking students. And likewise, students—including those from Mexico—generally believe their teachers care about them and take the time to work with them. But on a school-wide basis, welcoming the group Jose is concerned about means publicly sanctioning culture and language both, which spills over into bringing questions of culture and language into the open arena of the school, into its public places. How much this kind of overt activity would be supported is not totally clear. Janet Otero, the Key Club advisor, sees it this way:

If someone, if there was the right leadership, some motivation to do it, and he or she found ways to celebrate that culture, I think it would be welcome. It wouldn't be vetoed by the office or ignored by the student body. It would depend on what it is. You know, you could have a whole week of celebrating the culture, and every class could contribute. So it is just a matter of someone taking the leadership, and I don't see that happening in this school. We don't do enough overtly. I think the students from Mexico feel safe, and I think they're happy and for the most part they feel really lucky to be able to go to school after the sixth or seventh grade. But it's not that we go out of our way. It's just, I think it's more by default.

Randy Weston agreed:

I don't really see anything that's done to promote Hispanic culture here. They've tried some, like Mr. Martinez has tried to have some of the people that are musicians play in the lunchroom. That seemed to go over really well last year. On three or four occasions Tomas and his band played there at lunchtime and packed the cafeteria until the bell rang. It was real popular. But other than that, I would say very little. I really think there is a kind of wall there because they are from Mexico and they are in the TESOL program. They are not really part of the school as much as everyone who is mainstreamed.

Everyone seemed to know the mariachi band story—from teachers to district administrators—but few seemed to realize what a small instance it was, that it was only *one* instance. It became a sort of legacy of what is being done, but it seemed more to reflect how much more cultural activity could be done—and that it would be well received. This, in a way, is the same posture that the principal takes. "If anything happens [to promote Hispanic culture], it needs to happen because of the aggressiveness of the sponsor who runs with it." In this way, he believes, activities to promote cultural knowledge and interchange will stand the best opportunity of being accepted within the natural rhythms of the school's extracurricular activities. This is the way the folklorico group was started: Selena Knight, then a new TESOL teacher with a strong background in the arts and performance, learned that some of her students had been in a folklorico group in their school in a small farming village south of Frontera and began to build the group and prepare them for a school-wide performance. She arranged for students to say in town so they could practice on the weekends, she enlisted the support of a bilingual paraprofessional in the school (because she was not bilingual), and she made sure students got back and forth when practice was over on Saturdays. At HHS, taking such individual initiative also extends to the students. It was in this way that the mariachi band had its debut during lunchtime in the previous school year.

One other indicator of cultural border crossing is a guitar class offered through the music department. This class, which was initiated and taught by the band instructor, Mr. Gustavo, who is Mexican-American, included several new immigrants and students from Mexico. Each year they presented their work in the district wide Christmas concert to great applause, and their participation meant that their parents and families also came to the concert, which was held in Havens' performance auditorium in the community's secondary school complex. Because many of the students already played guitar, the class was a direct support to their prior experiences. How to strike an acceptable balance among what is encouraged, allowed, tolerated, or permitted in terms of public welcoming and cultural learning still seems to be a challenge. Privately, in friendships with other students, teachers, and administrators, students can find individuals who welcome them and who are interested in their lives outside of school and their native language. For the students, any public sign that they are in fact welcome in the school would be seen as an act of reconciliation for the political fallout that exists because some students who are not U.S. citizens do in fact cross the border temporarily (daily), instead of permanently.

Learning Culture:
Randy Weston's Hispanic Writers Class

The social and academic border, in addition to the language and the political border, keeps many Mexican and Mexican-American students from enjoying complete membership in their school. It is a border that exists at all levels for students who are Mexican in origin. Through their efforts, students like Luis are attempting to help the Mexican and Mexican-American students push the border back at HHS. But they are also sensitive to the need for Mexican-American, Mexican, and Anglo students to talk with each other, to discuss their differences, to come away from their schooling with a good sense of what each other's culture is really like. Luis and Jose are dealing with two aspects of this issue. The first is access and power; building internal leadership capacity is at the core of their efforts. The second is the basic sharing of cultural knowledge across ethnic groups and creating a place where students who are less secure in their language and social status begin to feel more secure. But in addition to this overt cultural example, Randy Weston was also concerned about a third aspect—cultural self-knowledge on the part of the native Mexican-American population.

Over a 3-year period in the 1970s, during the time when the current superintendent, Eduardo Rios, was a social studies teacher at the high school, he offered a course called "Ethnic Studies." The course included the study of African-American and Hispanic history in the United States. From that point on until the year I arrived in Havens in the fall of 1993, no other course focused specifically on Hispanic issues had been offered. That fall, Randy Weston, the English teacher from Kansas, began to teach a one semester course he had developed called "Hispanic Writers." It is a course that Jose planned to take in the second semester of the year. "Next semester," Jose said, "I'm going to take that class. That class, Hispanic Writers, is probably one of the ways the school has tried to make the students fit in."

Randy's decision to develop the course was an individual one. Among others, the reading list included the classic New Mexican novel by Rudolfo Anaya, *Bless Me, Última,* plays by Luis Valdez, *Pocho* by Jose Antonio Villareal, and the family epic *Rain of Gold* by Victor Villaseñor. Additional authors included Denise Chavez, Sandra Cisneros, Jimmie Santiago Baca, Lionel Garcia, and Ana Castillo. This is the class Liliana talked about when she said it was not until the fall semester that she really began to think about her culture more and how she balances her Mexican heritage with her life as an American. The class was also a sort of awakening for Randy himself.

This last hour I was talking to a couple of the kids now that we're kind of winding down in our first go-round in the Hispanic Writers class, and they were kind of kidding me. I said, "Well, especially this first semester trying to teach this class, I've learned far more than you." And they were asking me why I wanted to do this class, why I wanted to teach this class. And they were kidding me about that really *I* wanted to learn all that stuff, but they already knew it all. They were talking about the cultural things. They were pretty familiar with most of the stuff, and to me it was still kind of a revelation, but to them it wasn't. We've done some really good projects. We're doing two projects right now. One is the oral history, and several of the students seem to be interested in doing that, partly because it's a cultural thing, too, that tradition of stories is a big part of their culture. The other project we're doing is to show an aspect of Hispanic culture. Some of the students are going to make some traditional Mexican foods and bring them to class and talk about where they came from and how they developed, some are going to do the *quinceañera*, some are going to do a project on the development of Mexican music, and a couple are going to do Mexican mural art. But there were a lot of things they didn't know about.

The literature part was pretty much a revelation to all those kids. They just have not ... very, very few of them had ever read anything by Hispanic writers. Luis is one of the few that had. One of the first journal entries that I asked them to do was to tell me who their favorite Hispanic writer was. And the majority of the students said, "We don't know any." And that just flabbergasted me to think that you have Hispanic students who have gone through the school system here in an area that's over 50% Hispanic and have no role models as far as Hispanic authors. They've just never been introduced to any of them. As the class continues on, I've been lending out books at a pretty good rate. I've had some people in my other classes who have to do outside reading and some of those students are starting to choose some of the Hispanic authors to read. I think that it will be a thing that will gradually catch on and grow.

You know, a lot of resentment is passed down from generations and there are a lot of conceptions and misconceptions about what the other culture thinks. When we've talked about these stereotypes in the class, and you say "What are some of the stereotypes that you think the Anglo society has of you?" one of the first things most people say is, "We're all *mojados*, wetbacks, we're all migrant workers." Usually the second thing is, "We're all lazy and we're all dumb." And you know, there's a reason why they say that over and over again. Yesterday we just read one of the Luis Valdez' early works, which were the plays that he put on with the migrant workers in the different striking places with Cesar Chavez in the 1960s, and the kids very much pointed out that the owner of the farm talks to the farm worker like he has no intelligence whatsoever, that because he is the owner he could talk this guy into believing anything, and he tries to get him to believe that because he gives him a free place to stay, free meals, free rides in his truck, this guy has nothing to complain about, that he wished his life was that simple for himself. You know, it doesn't take a class filled with Hispanic students very long to see what Luis Valdez was trying to bring out in those plays.

I have two or three objectives that I really wanted to see—or I hope to see—happen over the next few years. One is that I was hoping to show through the Hispanic authors some good positive role models for some of the Hispanic students, that writing is a viable alternative and it's not something that is closed to Hispanic people, that there is an ever-growing number of successful Hispanic writers. The other thing was to try to insure that some of the Hispanic students not lose their cultural background. There's a real myriad of cultural values. You have some Hispanic families that have come from Mexico and they no longer want to be connected with it and so they insist that their children speak English all the time, they try to discourage speaking or reading Spanish, and in doing that, they lose a lot of their background and their culture. At the other end of the spectrum, there are other families who really insure that their children are bilingual and really stress the continuation of Spanish in the home and really maintain their culture and teach their kids to be proud of that culture.

To be honest with you, since I got the idea last year to put this class together, I have paid a lot more attention to the two separate cultures. Before that, I really, I just never thought about whether a kid was Hispanic or he was Anglo. He was just a kid. The problem with that is that no matter whether you have a cultural mix in our school or not, it's not good to treat everybody equally because everyone doesn't have the same background, everybody doesn't have the same abilities, everybody doesn't learn the same way. So if you say, "I just teach kids," that's a poor educational goal, or at least, a poor educational strategy.

The irony of his being the one to teach the class was not lost on Randy.

My unique experience this year is teaching the new course, which is having a non-Spanish-speaking Anglo teacher teaching Hispanic Writers. What I've really found out is that even though I can't speak Spanish as far as the Hispanic literature is concerned, I'm a whole lot more knowledgeable than anybody else I've run into.

But despite this level of content knowledge, teaching the class did have implications for Randy on the question of language. He continued:

> I really feel at a disadvantage personally because, right now with this class, if I could speak Spanish, I'd have a lot more resources to draw from that I'm just cut out of because I'm not bilingual. I've off and on tried to learn some vocabulary and things, and one of the students had a bunch of stuff written in a notebook the other day in Spanish, and she was showing it to me and I was surprised how much of it I could read, and that kind of encouraged me to get back into it again, to try and learn more.

Randy's class is really the only formal opportunity for students at HHS to learn about their culture directly—and for their Anglo peers to learn about it as well. But between the two sections he taught during the fall semester, only three Anglo students were enrolled. Other teachers, notably Janet Otero, whose own three children fall along a wide continuum in recognizing and accepting their father's Mexican heritage, also informally encourages her students to explore their cultural roots, mostly through topics for written assignments. "How do you keep pride in your own ethnic and family culture and still participate and share in the culture of the community and the nation?" "Have you ever had to make hard choices between your ethnic culture and a national culture?" Essay topics like these, which were assigned in some of the lower track classes where the predominant student population was Mexican and Mexican-American, provided a departure point for class-wide discussions about the school and the students' school experiences. "My parents have German, Spanish, Italian, and Aztec Indian blood in them," wrote Alice Torres. "I am mainly Spanish and Aztec. For me, being so White, automatically everyone expected something different. I was ashamed of being White complected and still speaking Spanish. I finally learned that I had nothing to be ashamed of." Students used this writing opportunity to share some of their pivotal experiences regarding ethnicity and social interaction in the school.

But in general, the reading of literature, the overt confirmation of their own life experiences through study, class-wide discussions of issues of ethnicity and prejudice, which all have the power to contribute to the direct preparation of Mexican-origin students for building self-awareness, self-transformation, and the confidence to take on leadership roles, is more uncommon than common here. Similarly, Anglo students are not encouraged to explore the rich culture that surrounds them and that, for many, is a part of their own family history through traditions of intermarriage that have long existed along the border. But public dialogue about culture and language is largely absent at HHS. What has been introduced—the NHI, Jose's discussions with the principal about the band and the banners, Hispanic Writers, guitar classes, the folklorico—all represent purposes of varying kinds depending on who did the introducing. Some represent the most basic level of cultural awareness—like the folklorico or the mariachi band.[6] As a by-product, they may also bring students closer to the mainstream of the school, as folklorico practice does. Others—like the NHI activities—have both a personal and a political purpose and a clear leadership goal. Personal growth through deeper cultural and political awareness—and a better understanding of the contributions of Mexican and other Latino writers—is the goal of Hispanic Writers. These activities stand in for the wide-ranging ways in which multicultural education—or in the case of Havens, bicultural education—can be practiced. But to be maximally effective, to rethink what it is that leads to education failure in the first place,[7] school teachers and administrators need to view it in a much broader way. Each of these activities is important, and collectively they represent a set of important opportunities across the school. If there is an institutional commitment to developing graduates who are prepared for life on the border at HHS, it is to let most activities come to the surface through individual effort; real structural changes related to leadership, cultural knowledge, and educational achievement across cultures are less apparent.

While Luis and Jose worked hard, from the bottom up, to make new opportunities available, and while Randy and a few others tried actively to raise the issue of cultural knowledge and experience directly, another major educational issue looms large in this border town. What about the students who are not academically motivated, who do not know how to "work the system," and who do not seem particularly interested in doing so? What does going to school on the border mean to them?

New Futures on the Border—For Whom?

As we continued to talk about the Hispanic Writers class, Randy Weston observed:

> My personal opinion is that we spend too much time on the above average student, whether they are Hispanic *or* Anglo. We're too concerned about all the college-bound students and people who really do well and probably need us less than any of the rest of the students. I don't really know if that's true or not, but I think about that myself a lot. We cater too much to the really good students. And when we really need to put a lot of our effort is raising a lot of those average students and below average students up.

In this school, the majority of the students who are average and below average—the ones Randy is talking about— are of Mexican origin. They are also usually the students whose SES is low and whose families have immigrated themselves and have been in Havens for at least one generation. Although they probably could benefit from a course like Hispanic Writers, their needs, as a group, are far greater than this alone. They are the group who, on the whole, seem uncertain of their identity and of where their Mexican heritage fits into their life in Havens and their futures. During any given quarter, nearly 250 of these students might be on the list signifying a GPA below 2.0, and nearly all the names on the list are Spanish. According to the state formula by which dropout rates are calculated, statistics hover just below 10%. According to the raw numbers, nearly 50% of the freshman who enter do not walk across the platform to receive their diplomas at graduation 4 years later. Another sobering factor is that the teenage pregnancy rate in Havens is among the highest in New Mexico. It is usually local Havens' students, rather than those from Mexico, who fall into this category.

At the same time, it is important not to generalize too quickly. Not every student of Mexican origin whose family has lived in Havens for one or two generations is having problems in school. Increasingly students are succeeding academically and doing it quite well. Some excel in sports and are thinking about sports in relationship to college and scholarships. Some, like Ricardo Herrera, want to join the Border Patrol and other want to join the military. In an economically depressed community, the military is a means of opening doors to other educational opportunities and as a postsecondary choice is wisely supported by the school's administration. But it is no longer seen as one of the only options for Mexican-American students, as it was when Eduardo Rios, the superintendent, was in school.

> A couple of us (Mexican-American students) had graduated in the upper 20%, but when we went into the counselor, the counselor wanted to know what branch of the service we were going into without even asking. "We're going to college," we said. So I didn't go to the counselor. My friend and I did everything about going to school ourselves.

Now college coexists as an option alongside others, but structural inequalities still mean that some students may still make the choice to enter the military without having considered or ever being informed about other opportunities. Others plan to attend community college, enter the trades, or take service positions at the hospital in town. For some, these are carefully considered choices made with their family's support. For others, like Maria Cruz, it is apparent that the decision to attend college is a goal despite her father's traditional set of expectations for the role a Mexican woman should play.

In spite of these optimistic developments, the overall statistics are still exceedingly troublesome and the trends are widely acknowledged. The students who are not making it are the ones who seems to have the fewest internal advocates. No Luis' or Jose's or Liliana's or Maria's readily emerge among these students. They are not high visibility individuals—as are the jocks or the academics or the "band kids" or the kids from Mexico. They do not appear in Jose's list of groups in the opening quote of this chapter. They are visible on the eligibility list, in the suspension room, and on the roster of dropouts. Or they are just invisible. It is these kinds of problems that make teaching at HHS much like teaching in any other high school in an economically depressed community.

And Randy Weston is certainly far from the only one worrying about this group of students. These are the same students the superintendent worries do not have either the Mexican or Anglo culture to hold on to and are not well-grounded in terms of their identities. Several other teachers and high school staff members, the principal of HHS, and a temporary youth activity coordinator in town worry as well. In the eyes of these people, most of whom themselves are multigenerational Mexican-American, the answer is helping students and their families understand the value of education. When teachers or others in the community raise this issue, they often do so by contrasting the students from Mexico.

Janet Otero says:

I really think our problems are the Hispanic kids from Havens. My problems are not the kids from Mexico and they're not the White kids who are, you know, who have parents who have a little more money and are a little more affluent and all that. Our problems are the Hispanic kids who live in Havens, which I think it a whole different thing. The little bit that I know I think is just the tip of the iceberg. I think that's really a bigger problem. If you look at the daily announcements, they're dominated with Hispanic kids who are coming from Havens, maybe they walk to school and they're not on the football team and they're not cheerleaders and they're not in the Student Council and they feel like they're being forced to come to school. I wonder sometimes if they are even jealous—or somehow if they're more affected—by the kids who come from Mexico. Because they're all Hispanic, but the kids who come from Mexico are doing better and they're nicer, they're more polite, they're more respectful.

Andy Muñoz is the director of the fledgling youth center:

> We get these kids from Mexico. They travel this far because they want to
> learn. They really want to learn. And then we get the ones from here who
> don't even want to go to school. They'll drop out. One day I recall a couple
> of years ago, at the Youth Center, on report card day, these kids from
> Mexico used to hang around there. The showed me their report
> cards—these were high school kids—and the lowest grade point average
> I saw was a 3.1. All of them from Mexico. Then I asked the ones from here,
> "Let me see your report cards." They didn't have them or they didn't get
> it or they haven't gotten it. So I started thinking, "Why is it that you
> Hispanic guys from here, who have this free school ..." Here they get free
> school and they don't even want to learn, they don't even want to go to
> school, they're flunking. And yet these kids from Mexico, coming here, they
> want to learn and they're on the honor rolls. What's the difference? They're
> Hispanic. You're Mexican. We're the same. So why is there a difference in
> how they view their education?

In Havens, both groups, Mexican and Mexican American students,
fail to see their culture held in high status as a regular feature of their
schooling. But the cumulative effect of multigenerational low SES along
with absence of cultural valuing in school can combine to result in the
educational disengagement of the students Andy is describing.

From Daniel's perspective in the principal's office, it is, more than
anything else, a matter of educating parents:

> This isn't a priority for their parents, and their parents don't feel comfort-
> able in those conversations in school. Chicanos live inside a little bubble,
> right here, and we never burst that bubble. We need to show them what's
> available, and we need to use Hispanic people as examples. Finances are
> a problem in this community since it's so poor.

Information about, for example, financial aid for postsecondary education is not readily available in the Hispanic community, he said, but
needs to be. Without this information, families may inadvertently close
off the possibility of college prematurely.

Daniel's unswerving faith in education accounts for those quiet but
consistent discussions with promising students who are Mexican or
Mexican-American, his encouragement of their success. "If they just get
a taste of it [education]," Daniel continued, "they won't be able to stop."
To this end, the school holds informational sessions on postsecondary
education and has career days where representatives of various postsecondary institutions come to provide information. It also publishes simple
guidelines for students who wish to continue on. But these opportunities

are best utilized by students who are already motivated and who are looking for answers to questions they may already have formulated. Some bring their parents, some translate for them and explain the system of college selection to them. But Daniel also sees a larger political purpose to the education agenda, a purpose that is related to gaining self-confidence and self-esteem in a community where Mexican people are still struggling to climb the socioeconomic ladder: "Whatever action you pursue, you do it through the doors of education," he said. "Then you can walk and talk their language. We have to get rid of this stigma of looking down with our eyes in the presence of Anglos. We need to see people in their eyes."

* * *

Richard Logan teaches several sections of basic English classes, so he comes into contact with many Hispanic students who are not among the school's high achievers. He mandates daily reading, which seems to have a very positive effect on his students. He pushes his classes hard, he does anything reasonable he can think of to motivate his students:

> The kids who are going to college have motivation. A lot of it they get from their parents. The kids who are not, you know, it's just like any other high school in the nation, I think. We graduate kids who have no idea of what they are capable of doing or what they can do after they graduate. They graduate and they say, "Yea, I graduated! But what am I going to do? I don't have any measurable skills, I don't have the money to go to college, I don't want to go to college, so what am I going to do?" Or they don't realize what they need to do during high school to be able to get to college.

Myrna Jimenez, the business education teacher, agrees:

> If the kids aren't into it and the friends aren't into it, why should they be interested? And the parents don't know about it. They're seniors and they're filling out the scholarship forms—Cindy Pacheco is a perfect example. Very nice young lady. She has worked since 10th grade at McDonald's, and she even went up to shift manager and all, and now she's filling out all these applications. She's good in math and thinks she wants to be a civil engineer. But she doesn't belong to anything in school. What's she going to put down? She spent her time working, not because she had to, but because she wanted to buy herself a vehicle. Now she turns around and sees, "Ah, all of this has passed me by. And what do I put down for the activities?" And she being a shift manager, has a real sense of responsibility, but no student activities per se.

The process of educating local Mexican-American families to support their children's education, Daniel Martinez continued, is not a short-term proposition. It is also not just an individual need; it is a responsibility in terms of the entire Mexican-American community in Havens. This also explains his belief that Mexicans and Mexican-Americans are scrutinized more carefully than their Anglo peers and have to hold themselves to a higher standard—for the good of the Mexican community in Havens.

Like his principal, Luis also believes that specific action needs to be taken to educate the parents:

> If people are lower class, here people will say, "These people, they work all the time, they never get anywhere, they must not be ... very proficient or never try," and so forth. They say, "Oh, well, they have all the opportunities that everybody else has and they're not trying. They're just lazy," which is on the contrary. Many of the opportunities are never shown to them. People that live here don't know what opportunities and programs there are. They have this thing that they should be out helping themselves—that nobody should help them, but I don't think that's true. That's not true because everybody who says this someday has had somebody helping them.

How broadly "help" is defined seems to be the key to how much it will be possible to pull in students who are not engaged in life at HHS by creating a school they want to be in—a school whose meaning they can hold on to and one where they come away with a well-developed sense of who they are—as individuals, as learners, and as border dwellers. As critical as educating parents is, it can only take a school so far, only help so much. What goes on in school itself—in classes, in activities, in the hallways, between students and teachers—is the other side of that help, and potentially the more powerful factor.[8] Precisely because educating parents is a long-term proposition, what the school does complements that development along the way and has the potential to give students a reason to stay in school in the short term—rather than to leave it.

For some students, the answer seems to be an alternative form of schooling, for example, night school (which was being developed at the time I left Havens in 1994). At HHS, vocational programs offer another in-school alternative, and depending on their specialization, students can gain much practical experience to help them in their chosen field. Students in clubs associated with the vocational programs also regularly compete in state and national competitions; these experiences provide another level of leadership training, another window into "the system" for students who might otherwise not understand it. If they are in the health occupations option, students have practical experiences in the local hospital as part of their classes. This is also a reality check of their English language skills for those who are just learning English, and their teacher is well aware of this need and builds that awareness into her program.

Strong vocational education programs are extremely important in a community like Havens. Whether they function in a manner consistent with pushing students to the outside limits of their potential is one important test of their strength. When they constitute a low academic track from which there is no detour, opportunity is limited.[9] Students need to be afforded the opportunity to switch from the vocational to the academic track if college is to become a possibility for them—especially if they have never before seen college as an alternative. As their families—or they—learn about other possibilities, students need to be encouraged to make the changes in their educational programs so other paths become realistic options.

And along with these two goals for vocational programs is the very fundamental issue of making school meaningful, a place more students want to be—no matter what program they are involved in. Getting students engaged in their academic subjects as well as their vocational classes, assuring that vocational classes draw seriously on academic skills, building a more stimulating curriculum, providing an education that does not ignore students' cultural origins, these kinds of changes are at the root of how a school needs to transform to increase the chances that its students will stick around and "make it" in the future. And every graduate who "makes it" strengthens the border area that much more. It is a general educational goal; the outcome, if it is achieved, would be to capture this large number of students who do not see school as important. Students who are dropping out are not involved in school. Keeping them there, and keeping them geniunely interested is not a goal that can be reached by individual teachers alone, no matter how committed and creative they are—and many at HHS fit this mold. It is a goal that takes the force of the whole school—at an institutional level. It is also the way many high schools—no matter where they are located—will need to be transformed,[10] especially if they are to capture the interests of an increasingly alienated student body—one that is usually filled with students of color.

It is in this way that HHS is like so many other high schools. Schooling at HHS seems to do little strategically to help students imagine what other possibilities might exist. Especially for this large group of students who do not feel at home in school, the fact that they attend school on the border may not be the defining factor. But what is defining is that, as Mexican-Americans, failure rates are unacceptably high. Their success or failure is bound up with questions of culture, language, and economic status. The border provides a reason for bringing these issues into focus, a potential for enhancing the school's identity overall, a means of sanctioning the family experience of Mexican-American students who by themselves may not know how to value it. This is one way to redefine opportunities, to create new pictures of what might be possible for students who are not engaged. Now, their images seem to be too circumscribed.

Creating Meaning From the Border

According to its philosophy, HHS is preparing its students for "an ever changing world." But what is the new and changing world for which HHS is readying its graduates? In many ways, it is the same world on the border that it has always been. Adults cross, students cross, both languages are heard and used, trade across the border whether for farming, ranching, or commerical business goes on. It is a regular feature of life in Havens and its companion communities across the southwest. Expectations have changed, though; jobs take people across the border, or businesses for which graduates may work will require not only an understanding of language, but of culture on both sides of the line. The advantages will accrue to students who are prepared for these roles. A school like HHS can be instrumental in developing these kinds of advantages for their students; once developed, they become a lifelong resource.

Its identity as a school on the border is literally spilling over at the seams at HHS. Students carry out their social lives on both sides. Students may begin their lives on one side and continue them on the other. The same goes for their educational experiences. Two languages are everywhere. Students are creating friendships, social relationships, and for some, marriages and families that cross the border and cross ethnic groups. They go on vacation in Guadalajara or Chihuahua City. They may come to school in Havens and attend college in Albuquerque, or they may get a job in Juarez or in Nogales, Arizona.

As a result, informal binational knowledge of culture and language is rich here; students like Jose and teachers like Selena Knight are trying to bring that knowledge to the surface. There are many places where students and teachers make deliberate efforts to build relationships across language and cultural groups. But these are individually constructed efforts on the part of a series of individuals. They make school a comfortable place for the students, but these efforts still exist at the edges of the school's main activities. Meaning is created by individuals for individuals. No "regular" clubs have as their goal cross-border activities, no cross-border sports contests are played in the schools, no binational field trips take place, no teacher exchanges, save at Jefferson Elementary directly located across from Frontera. The border is generally downplayed at the same time that the internal, informal resources it offers are utilized daily by the students and teachers. It is regularly acknowledged in that same undercurrent of student talk that enables HHS students to help each other with language learning. But as a formal focal point for academic or social activity, as a reason to address questions of culture openly, it is not often acknowledged. As a result, questions of language and culture are unnecessarily obscured for all of the school's students: Anglo, Mexican-American, and Mexican alike. Those who have the least inclination to explore questions like these, namely, students who are not engaged in school, probably are affected the most by its absence.

This reluctance to publicly acknowledge its identity as a school along the border stands in contrast to the community itself, where cross-border activities are a more regular and more public part of people's lives. At HHS, the border is an opportunity to recreate the school as a more vibrant educational institution for the changing world that is Havens.

6

The Limits of Being Neighborly

I don't think of it as being essentially a border world. Instead of being maybe one line it's like thirty or forty miles on either side. It's the area on both sides. I'm not sure there really is a border.

Border Metaphors

I prefer to live near the mountains or the ocean. To make do in the midwest, where I now live and where there are no mountains or ocean, I reside by a very large lake—an ocean-sized one whose eastern shore I cannot see from the vantage point I have access to a short walk from my home. It is a lake whose southern border is 90 miles away near Chicago, and whose opposite shore is a several hours drive in the wilds of the north. These are geographic interruptions, these mountains, oceans, or great lakes. Should my thinking or my actions ever get complacent, these interruptions remind me that my world is not tightly circumscribed, that it does not end at the end of my street, at the end of my town, or at the end of my city. They create for me the possibility of lives lived differently—mine and others. On the other side of the mountains, on the other side of the ocean, on the other shores of the lake, things are likely to be different. That is solace; the possibility for difference and for expansion fuels me.

My inclination, then, is to see the world as bordered, and to see borders as places to be crossed—or at the least, approached. In my own life I create borders as symbols of potential. They are not political borders, like the border in Havens, but they are borders nevertheless. I welcome the interruptions as borders and the border as an interruption. I want to cross, I want to know the other side, I want to see how life is or is not like mine when I get there, or at least I want to think about it. Seeing the world this way, I was eager to move to Havens, where the border was ever present.

142

This image of the border that I have is related to the vision Gloria Anzaldúa[1] or Renato Rosaldo[2] claim—it is a metaphor for forging new individual identities, for blending discordant parts of one's life, for cultural crossing, and for personal and cultural creativity. Especially for Alzaldúa, borders can be found everywhere; this is a view that is meant to transcend place, one that enables us to take the concept of border with us no matter where we are located. Borders are psychological frontiers to be crossed, different interior locations that persuade us to work on our own evolution[3] and that create discomfort as the edges of different parts of our personal and cultural characteristics clash. On these borders we seek to have others cross over into our own personal territory too—however that is defined—as a way of growing, thinking, expanding. The border can also foster personal instability, or at least insecurity, about personal identity. Borders can be dark or shadowed,[4] they are filled with tension. But despite the tensions such instability might foster, this particular border metaphor is mostly cast in the positive light of the struggle for personal growth and development. As a metaphor for individual possibility, for pushing one's own limits, the term "border" has been well explored—and appropriately so.

It is with remarkable ease that this personal metaphor bumps up against the political border to the south. We see it when Anzaldúa, in her book *Borderlands / La Frontera*, moves from her physical life on the Tex-Mex border to her figurative life on the border of the straight and gay worlds or Latino and Anglo worlds. When we first meet Alejandro Juarez, the protagonist of Chris Carger's book *Of Borders and Dreams*,[5] in one breath in the introduction we move from his crossing the Rio Grande to the struggles he has crossing the borders of literacy. In her autobiographical last chapter in the book *Translated Woman*, Ruth Behar tells us,

> I was crossing borders without knowing it long before I met Esperanza—but through knowing her, I've reflected on how I've had to cross a lot of borders to get to a position where I could cross the Mexican border to bring back her story to put into a book. We cross borders, but we don't erase them; we take our borders with us.[6]

These very real political borders, the lines drawn in the sand or the rivers that stand in for fences, are readily absorbed into how we think about the personal struggles and challenges that have come to be powerful, searching visions of borders. We are comfortable moving seamlessly between the two, seeing the physical crossing of a national line as emblematic of all the symbolic crossing we have had to do, or will do, in our lives. It is a commanding connection, one that has emerged as a happy consequence of the growing body of contemporary writing of Latina and Latino writers who are Mexican and who often move between personal, cultural, and political borders as they frame their writing and explore their experiences.

It seems natural to want to venture deep into what happens on the borders, to explore the dimensions that take us to where we differ—among or within ourselves. We do it almost automatically. Borders create interest because it is on the margins that we are forced to see ourselves from more than one perspective. At some level, it is a question of reconciliation no matter what is on either side. It is in the extremes that we are not insulated from the possibilities outside of ourselves; there is always a big "other" out there that stretches our conceptions of who we are. It is on the borders that we question who we are and what we value.

But in the United States, the political border to the south has spawned its own set of metaphors that are not so easily mingled with the idea of private, inner borders. It is, fundamentally, an international line designed to separate people. There have been similar political borders that I have not been permitted to cross. I visited Jerusalem before the Six Day War, in 1964. For me, because I am Jewish, the border was defined as the gates of the Old City. Guards stood atop the wall and would not let me cross—their guns kept me out and kept me from seeing the possibilities. I was stunned at their friendliness; as they waved their weapons, they smiled and waved their hands. But I could not enter. It was forbidden, and I left curious about the other side. I came back several years later at a time when I could, after the Six Day War, freely cross into the Old City, to confront the differences, to wonder about the limits of my life.

In a more emotional tone, some see the border between Mexico and the United States as a wound.[7] "A 1,950 mile long open wound," says Gloria Anzaldúa in her poem "El otro México," "*una herida abierta* where the Third World grates against the first and bleeds,"[8] and thus is a continuous cause of pain. This raw quality is said to attract those far out on the margins of life, creating a zone that is perpetually unstable for those who are already misplaced. It is a vision without the hope that other metaphors might generate. A second metaphor for the political line, one that is unfortunately too well known, creates a vision of a sea of Mexican people rushing over the political line in huge, never-ending waves. There is no low tide, the waves are always high, and there is never a chance to come up for air, for the political line to surface under the pressure of the water. This powerful vision has little to do with personal growth or forging an identity from multiple personal experiences. Instead, it is the metaphor that is used by politicians to argue for restrictions that tread on the most basic rights of citizens and visitors alike, or to garner support for English-only initiatives. It is a metaphor for keeping people in, or keeping them out, depending on the side from which one is looking. It is a one-sided concept, a vision designed deliberately to create a negative image, a view of Mexican immigrants as takers. In popular practice in the United States, the term *border* has systematically been diminished as a possible metaphor for anything positive, enriching, or worthwhile to the south. In contrast, on the Canadian border to the north, experiments are being conducted with unguarded electronic border crossings in remote areas to enable local citizens to participate in regular cross-border family functions, such as weddings, in the absence of a formal 24-hour border checkpoint.[9]

In Havens, the image of the border that surfaced most often was not the personal struggle of an Anzaldúa or a Behar, nor was it border-as-raw or border-as-teeming-waves-of-humanity. To be sure, personal exploration may drive individuals like Liliana Sanchez, and the economic realities of an increased stream of Mexican immigrants from low SES groups clearly do result in strain on the local social and educational system. But for the most part, the metaphor that has guided the understanding of the border over the years in Havens—and the one that was commonly expressed during the many hours of conversation in which I participated—was the simple notion of the border as an informal line between neighbors. It is a benign image that suggests the expectation of being friendly, of helping out in a time of need, of doing reasonable favors. Finding themselves together, neighbors attempt to do the right thing as a means of coexisting peacefully; such neighborliness is practiced often in the realm of rural life. It is a metaphor of happenstance without intense obligation, and any obligations that do exist do so on a purely personal level between friends or relatives. As neighbors, people can choose to do the neighborly thing or not. Mostly, people elect to help out. As a metaphor for the border, the idea of neighbors is very much grounded in the present. It is a passive image, one of what exists, of what we are faced with on a day-to-day basis. It is expressed in comments reminding us that there is less friction in Havens than in other places, and that it does not have the high tension of other border towns like Nogales, for example. "It's still a friendly town," sums up the metaphor of neighborliness.

* * *

Metaphors create images that help us make sense of what is happening. As the metaphors we use to describe various situations differ, so do our understandings of those situations. We accept these metaphors as stand-ins for reality; when they vary, they remind us that we have the power to think about our current realities differently. If they are limited, we limit the understandings we achieve and the questions we might raise. Conversely, when someone throws a new, alternative metaphor our way, we are pressed to consider the issue from a different vantage point.

Throughout my stay in Havens, I kept bumping into pockets of activity and interest that signaled a growing commitment to a more active agenda for defining life on the border. Although many of these efforts were yet informal and incidental, like Jose Ruiz's incurable desire to revive the mariachi band at lunchtime, others existed within the institutional structure but were still developing their capacity, like the bilingual education programs. Ideas about how to support newcomers were on people's minds. Also, the community seemed to accept its identity as a border town willingly. As I listened, watched, and grew to understand more about the community and its schools, I kept coming back to an image that surfaced early on in my stay. Havens was a source of great opportunity—opportunity that, up to now, had not been taken full advantage of. Well beyond the confines of being good neighbors, there were cultural and linguistic resources in and around Havens, there were broad-based beliefs in the value of bilingual education, there was fundamental agreement that figuring out a way to make relationships work across the border was a worthwhile endeavor. But it remained just that—an opportunity—one that could be cultivated more deliberately and acted on more creatively, or not.

As a question of potential and possibility, the metaphor of "border as opportunity" differs from the intense private journeys so eloquently described by many contemporary Latino and Latina authors—journeys that may begin at political borders but that are quickly routed into interior psychological landscapes and the world of personal possibility. We work things out on the border on multiple levels. For Havens, it is a question of a more practical sort, a matter of civic rather than personal possibility, a challenge to create a more satisfying community identity that embraces the border, rather than an individual one. Just as individuals work to make sense of their own bordered lives, so too can border communities work consciously on theirs.

As yet another metaphor for the border, opportunity signals a recognition of the potential that does exist and presses us to consider using that potential explicitly and creatively to generate a more focused

binational context that draws on both sides of the line. In the borderlands, the impact of the political line is ever present; the border influ-
ences lives on a daily basis. It is a genuine force to be reckoned with in
a real context; there are real pressures that, left to chance, leave only
the nagging negative metaphors that popularly—and often inappropri-
ately—define life on the border. Havens provided me with a way of
thinking about the role schools can realistically play in reconciling life
on the border, in building on and then transcending those time-honored,
neighborly commitments, creating a sense of opportunity that embraces
the cultural and linguistic capital that has always characterized the
borderlands.

Because the southern border of the United States is economically poor
and isolated from sophisticated centers of political and social activity,[10]
defining the border as a site of opportunity also demands an understanding of the limits of opportunity, of the kind of assistance that might
be needed to shore up the community or the school's efforts to support
the development of a binational life. Havens is a poor rural town. From
an outsider's perspective, Havens is a community saddled with the
enormous responsibility to build international relationships, and because of the political line its decisions and moves always stand the
chance of being scrutinized internationally. Frontera is even poorer.
These are regional relationships to be forged first in the borderland,
where questions of interdependence are not academic, but have daily
consequences—for Havens' students, shopkeepers, ranchers, farmers,
teachers, migrant workers, and for families struggling to figure out how
best to educate their children for a life on both sides of the border. It is
both a tremendous international responsibility and nothing more than
a local responsibility. There is local talent to generate solutions, and
there is a need for external conversation and ideas to provide a wider
perspective on local conversations. The interplay is constant, but the
motivation for finding solutions is primarily a regional affair. In the
region that includes Havens, there is less animosity about the border
than there is local frustration. The border is anything but a wound; it is
a natural feature, it is a challenge, it is a situation that requires careful
attention. But it is not a source of widespread community hostility—although an occasional individual in the community may be hostile. There
is a deliberate effort not to create a hostile environment, but rather to
coexist. This attribute, perhaps more than any other, makes opportunity
possible.

For me, the image of opportunity is an image filled with restrained
hope, with the belief that border communities like Havens are best
poised to take hold of the local capacity they know exists and grow from

there. The potential is obvious; despite economic obstacles, fledgling efforts can be identified and can turn into full scale ones, and much, much more is possible. These efforts and values are the markers, the threads of opportunity that promise the possibility of weaving whole cloth on the border.

Markers of Opportunity

Marker 1: The Value of Two Languages

They're still offering free Spanish classes, but how much can you learn in a class once a week? If they really wanted to do something, they should pick 30 teachers and send them down to a university in Chihuahua or something for a month. You know, that's how they'd learn something. They probably have 30 or 40 teachers who would go though a language school. They could bring in somebody who does intensive foreign language training here and have a 3 or 4 week semi-institute and teach people so much more than they could learn in one of those weekly classes. And you know, it would cost more, but if you look at all the piecemeal efforts they've had, it probably wouldn't cost much more than all those put together. (Richard Logan)

Markers define a kind of starting point for what might be achieved in the future. Three markers of opportunity bear consideration when it comes to language. Richard's concern is with increasing the number of teachers who, like himself, are bilingual. While not all teachers believe they must be bilingual to be effective, nearly all acknowledge how much easier life would be on a practical level if they were able to speak both languages. The reality of life on the border dictates it. For teachers, this is not just a matter of acquiring language skills. The majority of teachers who are bilingual at HHS and in the schools in general are of Mexican origin. Many are natives of Havens and the surrounding area. This creates a natural division among teachers. Mexican-American teachers are massed in vocational and special education; Anglo teachers are not. With few core academic teachers being bilingual (one biology teacher and Richard in the English department), students who do speak Spanish—especially those higher achievers—have few outlets during face-to-face class time. For example, a rookie English teacher, himself a monolingual English speaker, was interested in letting his students write in both languages for poetry and creative writing, but had no way to make such a move possible from a teacher's standpoint. In recognition of the general problem, free Spanish classes for district employees have been a standard fixture for some years, but they were not conceptualized to be an intensive language learning experience and so have not resulted in increased numbers of teachers becoming bilingual. The idea of having teachers learn Spanish is also a marker; it is valued to the degree that these classes continue to be offered, but it has never been presented in terms of a real opportunity for intensive language learning. Instead, the job of translating, and in most cases brokering, falls to students or to instructional aides, and to the small number of teachers who are already bilingual.

A second marker of language opportunity is students' natural motivation to learn Spanish or English, stemming from a desire to communicate more broadly with other students in school and from a realistic view of what it means for employment in the future. The informal sharing of language that goes on among the students signals their widespread interest. They play with language, they surprise each other with their second language knowledge, they use it to build a more friendly school community. But it is an unstructured practice that results in primarily surface rather than deep language learning—although ironically it is also the way many students whose first language is Spanish claim they learned English. It is not a practice that is so widespread or acknowledged that it buffers the social divisions that have developed between students who are just learning English and those who participate in the school's mainstream activities and classes. Nor have the structured opportunities for language learning at HHS been designed to capitalize on this natural interest in language among the students. The ESL/sheltered content bilingual education program separates students (conversation is not its strong point), and the traditional foreign language program is one in which conversation is also not a strong component—as is the case in many traditional high school foreign language programs. This means that whatever institutionalized opportunities do exist for language learning do not combine to offer consistent enough opportunities for spoken language, which is the one feature that has an immediate wide-ranging benefit in school. Only the unusual interview that Teresa Allen conducted with Gabriela indicated for her Spanish class assignment encouraged student interaction around language.

Clubs, language tutoring, or other structured activities that acknowledge students' language resources are not part of the instructional landscape. Yvette, a high profile, very popular Mexican-American student whose dominant language was English but who was trying to recapture her Spanish (none too successfully yet, by her own admission), saw the school's tradition of senior students serving as teaching assistants as an opportunity to provide support in the area of language. She was concerned about the time teachers spend explaining a concept to a student who has a language barrier and she understood the need for interpreters as a matter of efficiency of teaching. "You know how we have assistant teachers?" she said.[11] "I think it would be a really good idea to bring in at least one who could speak Spanish and English. I think it would help a lot. It would help the kids [who can't speak English]." The concept of a cadre of bilingual teaching assistants or formal language mentors, which could elevate the whole value of being bilingual, is one that has not been explored within the school. The Spanish Club's members are primarily students from Mexico, so a two-way interchange is less likely to emerge from this group alone. Nowhere in the school is status associated with being bilingual; it is a tacit resource valued in such an understated—or unstated—way as to render it invisible in any public activity in the school. Yet it persists as a resource, just under the surface, and teachers could not function without it. This marker, located within the students themselves, will need to be drawn out into the mainstream of the school.

The third marker of language opportunity is the simple fact that people who speak both Spanish and English on the border are better poised to compete for many available jobs, and the power of this as motivation to foster language learning cannot be understated. It is a different, more practical kind of marker, one that holds the irresistible allure of greater economic opportunity on a personal level. As a pragmatic means of launching dual language instruction in HHS and graduating students who speak both languages, the economic stimulus for knowing both Spanish and English seems to represent the potential for cultural and political crossover for any such efforts. It raises the possibility of creating a unified base of support in a way that benefits the whole community and at the same time levels the language playing field. As an opportunity, then, dual language learning has great power to crystallize some of the disparity that exists with respect to how language is treated and learned.

In political terms, the practical move toward dual language instruction that this marker represents exists alongside other critical arguments linking language and culture for Mexican-origin people, or at least language and individual identity as a source of personal stability and self-worth. It also exists alongside the belief that dual language learning has important implications for creating healthy personal interactions between Anglo and Mexican people. These last two arguments for language learning locate the primary benefit within the Mexican and Mexican-American community in Havens. This is the part of the community that still lacks sufficient economic and political power and for which any benefit is a small step toward rectifying the long-standing, historical inequities in Havens. The current political reality is that many Anglo,

Mexican-American, and Mexican parents all value dual language learning, but the distance between the valuing and creating programs that will satisfy all community stakeholders—and be feasible—is still great. And while some see dual language learning as an opportunity, others see it more pointedly as an obligation, or at least, an opportunity not to be squandered, one that could potentially distinguish Havens on the border.

Although these particular markers converge on dual language learning, the limitations on this opportunity also bear consideration and the magnitude of the task cannot be underestimated. As Jack Sullivan observed, there is still much work to be done on improving the quality of the existing, transitional bilingual programming. How to build more consistent opportunities for oral language use in these programs is one challenge. It is perhaps one of the biggest challenges in a community where Spanish is so prevalent; despite their motivation for learning it, students who are studying English can go for long periods without using it. At the same time, school is likely to be the only place that provides a consistent structure for speaking English, so the opportunities there have to be maximized if legitimate progress is to be made. In Havens it is only two languages that are at issue. If developing a cadre of bilingual teachers is a valued overall goal, is it also important to hire TESOL teachers who themselves speak Spanish? Is it equally important to provide all teachers, bilingual or not, with basic ESL methods because invariably students are in their classes who will require such accommodations?

This same kind of consistent structure will need to be in place in any program of Spanish as a Second Language (as opposed to a traditional U.S. high school foreign language program). Alternatively, language learning could be arranged as a cross-border enterprise with language teachers from Frontera's schools providing Spanish instruction for HHS students and HHS English and ESL teachers providing—as they do now—English instruction for students from Frontera. A cross-border arrangement would enable the fiscal question of whether it is more costly to move the students or the teachers, and which is more worthwhile, to be considered. It would also provide another perspective on teacher recruitment and retention for Havens, whose salary scale is low even by New Mexico's standards and as a result suffers from turnover and difficulty in attracting teachers from other parts of the state or country who may have precisely the language education skills to support dual language learning. Importing high numbers of teachers who are bilingual is not likely given Havens' isolated location and salary structure; working binationally or growing their own bilingual teachers is a far more realistic possibility—whether these are teachers in regular subject areas who happen to be bilingual or teachers prepared to teach using bilingual methods.

Right now, the official use of both Spanish and English at HHS is limited to parent conferences or telephone conversations in which translators are often required for administrators and teachers to confer, and dual language preparation of most official documents that go home, including the annual school calendar. It is unclear whether a dual language goal for students would result in a more accepting environment for both languages in other "official" situations—assemblies, pep rallies, banners in the school, and the like. The first goal, it seems, is to develop a healthy, respectful dual language environment, one in which language might be the foundation of greater commitment to creating a bicultural school, one that is responsive both to the local Havens community and its neighbors across the border in Frontera. Accurate knowledge regarding what the schools and their bilingual programs actually look like and sound like is also important public information. A prominent businessman in town, one who was active in some important school decisions over the years, explained to me rather heatedly one day that at Jefferson Elementary only Spanish is spoken. This is an inaccurate portrayal of the program at Jefferson, where both ESL and bilingual education methods are used to promote dual language facility and where English is regularly used.

Havens exists, however, within a national context that seems to shun the possibility of Spanish and English coexisting. It is unlikely, for instance, that signs along the southernmost interstate highways would be posted in Spanish and English—this despite the fact that one can see French and English signs on the U.S. side close to the Canadian border in New Hampshire and Vermont. As a country, we simply do not seem to like our southern neighbor. Whether Havens chooses to buck this pressure and see dual language as an expression of its own brand of life on the border—taking pride in its singular potential to create a greater sense of binationalism—is yet unknown. It is a matter of taking on primarily a regional role, recognizing the peculiar blend of culture that better characterizes Havens than does the picture of any other small town elsewhere in the United States.

Marker 2: Educating Students From Mexico

After all, it is a foreign country with its own government and that country should be responsible for its own citizens. However, we accept those citizens in our homes, they clean them, they tend our crops, they attend our schools, they work in our businesses, and eventually many of them become full-time American citizens. A great many already are American citizens. Some have dual citizenship and some don't. It's a real complicated thing, to define where responsibility lies. On a moral plain it's easier to answer. People are people and if they're here you work with it. We really are family in many cases, cousins of cousins of cousins, and sisters of aunts and uncles and whatever. On an economic plain you have to be realistic. I suppose you have to say if that if our schools are filled then we cannot overburden the taxpayers of Sonora County just because we have these students coming across. Morally, it's not the same. (Susan Hartman)

The long-standing practice of educating students from Mexico rather than keeping them out is one of the most salient markers of binational opportunity in Havens. Students who live in Mexico and cross the border daily to attend HHS have come to be emblematic of Havens' relationship with Frontera and the moral ties to which Susan Hartman—and many others—regularly refer. The longstanding agreement that Mexican students attend school in Havens is an historic recognition of that complexity and of the ease with which the border can be ignored as anything more than another direction from which kids come to school. Crossing for school is a practice that is contested in intent only by a small number of outsiders whose reservations have mostly to do with holding down the protectionist political line: "They don't live here and they don't pay taxes, so they shouldn't attend our schools." But most longtime residents reject this unidimensional argument, recognizing instead the complicated nature of the situation, and expressing the frustrating moral dilemma that they do not want to prevent anyone from getting an education—they just do not want anyone taking unfair advantage of the community's limited resources. This is particularly true of the community's Mexican-American population,who less than a generation ago were often in the same situation. Further, many of the students who cross daily are U.S. citizens, having been born on the Havens side of the border. It is a very real frustration. While there is cynical local speculation that the only reason the cross-border schooling ever started was to keep open the lone Havens elementary school directly on the border (which did not have enough U.S. students at various times in its history), it is hard for anyone to remember a time when students from Mexico did not come to Havens for their education. More than anything else, HHS serves as a regional high school, and that region happens to include students from Mexico as well as those from ranches and farms on the U.S. side to the north, west, and east—and south as well.

There are less lofty, more immediate economic repercussions to taking a protectionist stance as well; someone has to drive the school bus from Frontera to Havens; if the route ends, so do those jobs. The interdependence is obvious; it is hard to get away from when the conversation turns to the daily crossers. But the recent increase in the number of students from Mexico has shifted the basic question from whether HHS has enough space to absorb all the students who wish to go to school to how Havens and Frontera as a binational region are going to address education as a whole and what kind of binational conversations and subsequent decisions need to occur to help address the situation. At the secondary level, it is a question of meeting the needs of students who wish to learn English and whose families see coming to Havens as the closest, most expedient, least complicated choice. It is also a question of expense; secondary education is not free in Mexico as it is in Havens. Many families whose teenage children come to Havens struggle to pay for the interior bus in Mexico that takes their children to the border to meet the Havens bus each day. Others do not face such a struggle; they can afford to pay, but Havens is free and English is better taught in Havens than in either the *secundaria** or the *prepa*** in Frontera.

As a marker of opportunity, the relationship with Frontera on educational issues is not one to be taken lightly, but nor can it realistically remain a question of only whether Mexican students will be allowed to attend school in Havens. If preserving a working relationship with Frontera is valued, then the question of schooling is worth working on together. Given the long-standing commitment to having some Mexican students attend its schools, it seems critical to continue bringing Mexican students to Havens, but perhaps in some kind of focused, more purposeful binational manner—rather than dealing with it only from the perspective of filling vacant seats available in a given school. When the question of the community's obligation to students from Mexico came up, one frequent response was couched more from the perspective of foreign policy than of moral responsibility. "I'd rather spend my tax dollars on the schools here than send them to some godforsaken country on the other side of the world," the argument went. In other words, If we are going to spend tax dollars on foreign countries, they might as well be countries we have some kind of local relationship with, money spent on people we know. Once again, the pull of the region, of being neighbors, was strong—stronger, it seemed—and more persuasive than the arguments against supporting the education of students from Frontera. This is the side to getting along that argues for educating students

---

*Middle or junior high school level.
**High school level.

from Mexico as a good investment, a kind of banking on the future and providing a stronger backbone for Mexico and increased goodwill toward the United States. Manuel Porras, a vocational education teacher, said:

> See, the ones who go back are the most important ones to me. Those are the ones that are really worth the time, the effort, whatever we can give them because then they're going back there and making that place better and taking back what they've got. They get themselves educated, go back over there, offer it to their communities. Those are the ones we should concentrate on. A lot of students from Mexico can function in both worlds here, you know, in both countries. My having treated them with respect and dignity, I don't think that's going to be bad for foreign affairs, to be honest with you.

This approach means that great faith and responsibility are placed on the "ones who go back," and might argue for more of a student exchange program structure for making decisions about who does and does not come to school in Havens at the secondary level, for purposefully creating a cadre of Mexican students who might eventually live on either side, but who, should they live on the Mexican side of this integrated region, would take back with them the benefit of having had a well-structured, well-supported experience in Havens. Such an approach would suggest the need to figure out in some kind of systematic fashion who would and would not be permitted to attend and what the expectations would be both for the students and for HHS. As incidental guests, students from Mexico now are constantly placed in a position of doubting their own worth and having others do so as well. As welcomed guests, they could be publicly identified as persons who bring important language, cultural, and personal resources to HHS and who require access to the same high levels of educational experiences extended to residents of Havens. They might even have a place to speak on the graduation program.

It would also be useful internally for teachers to be clear about where students reside, in recognition of the fact that not every student who "seems" to be from Mexico, whose primary cultural identity is with Mexico, actually lives there. This is not to be confused with formal checking for residency, a practice that the superintendent is dead set against. He will not stand in for immigration officials in school and will not check students individually for citizenship, opting instead for a fundamental level of respect that must be accorded all students. Havens, like so many communities on the border, is in a constant state of transition with a regular flow of newcomers. Any assistance that newcomers might require is usually found in a highly committed ESL teacher or in the cadre of ESL paraprofessionals who support these programs—whether students are from Mexico or from Havens. But at this point in time there is no sense of a structured transition for newcomers, no orientation per se, no real conversation about U.S. high schools and what might be expected in them, or specifically in HHS. The marker of opportunity for this kind of action—which can benefit students from Mexico and new immigrants alike—is found in students like Jose Ruiz or Maria Cruz, who regularly interact with students who identify with Mexico and also have strong feelings about what it will take to "make it" at HHS. This marker might also be thought of in teachers like Janet Otero and Eva Ortiz who are ready to provide greater leadership in extracurricular activities and who are supportive of Mexican and Mexican-origin students, but who have not yet taken a proactive stance in making those activities especially available to newcomers.

Even if Havens did not educate students who cross the border daily, it still would have to address the question of how students are welcomed. A healthy tension between "guests" from Mexico and newly arrived Mexican residents in Havens provides a way to open up a more public conversation about these issues, issues that heretofore have been treated silently. If daily commuters stopped today, there would still be immigration, still be students who live in Havens whose past educational experiences are not well understood by their receiving teachers, and who would still need English language education. Families would still go back and forth, and students would still choose to reside with aunts, uncles, sisters, and brothers and return to Frontera and other towns south for the weekend. The issue is not just one of students coming from Mexico, but their presence raises all sorts of important issues that Havens has not yet addressed directly.

What is the marker of opportunity for the other side of the border, for defining the role of Frontera and Chihuahua in this binational conversation? What is the role Frontera might play, especially in the all-important challenge of language learning on the part of local Havens students and teachers? It is a marker that for the time being is located in the relationship between the Jefferson Elementary School, which sits directly across the border from Frontera within the Havens school district, and the schools in Frontera. A new teacher exchange program has been launched, one that brings a public face to the regional commitments that have always existed. This is a more serious view of mutual responsibility, one that might serve as a model for all the schools in the future.

This marker also represents the opportunity to extend knowledge of Mexican schools to the teachers at all of the schools in Havens. Teachers at HHS will always receive students whose prior education has taken place in the Mexican educational system, whether those students today live in Mexico or in Havens. When teachers receive students from other U.S. schools, they already have a fairly accurate blueprint for what that student's education was likely to include. While the specifics might vary, and the texts and materials might differ, teachers have a pretty good sense of what a U.S. school is like. But when a student arrives from Mexico, most U.S. teachers have little understanding of the system of Mexican schooling, of the expectations, the curriculum, and the methods that are typically used.[12] It is not considered important information; much like students are to conform in terms of language and learn English, they are also expected to adjust to the American system of schooling without a bridge from their prior experiences. Teachers may not be aware of students' near universal belief that schooling in Mexico is much more demanding, that the expectations are higher, that they work harder and learn at more advanced levels, especially in mathematics. They are likely to have little understanding of the social structure of schooling in Mexico. In Havens it is a systematic part of the dynamics of schooling that students regularly arrive from Mexico. But it is not a part of the current structure that receiving teachers on the U.S. side need to know something—anything—about Mexican schools. Most bilingual education teachers in Havens learn something about schooling in Mexico by virtue of their regular interactions with students from Mexico, whether those students are residents of Mexico or newly arrived residents of Havens. Viewing information about Mexican schooling as important knowledge for all HHS teachers is a check, a way of assuring that educational efforts in this region are taking place from a more balanced binational perspective, and not just from the perspective of the U.S. educational system. As the Jefferson Elementary teachers establish relationships with teachers from Frontera in their own exchange program, their experiences can pave the way for a similar exchange at the secondary levels.

There is no marker at present, however, for the kind of exchange that might place Anglo students or Mexican-American students who do not speak Spanish in schools in Frontera for purposes of language and cultural learning. Frontera is not a community of high economic means, neither is Havens but comparatively speaking the schools in Havens are better supported. This is the place where the third world, as Anzaldúa says, meets the first,[13] although the corner of the first in which Havens is located is economically depressed. To have the regional government in Mexico pay better attention to the quality of the schools in Frontera, one idea is to place pressure on regional governmental agencies to improve local schools by reducing the availability of schooling in Havens.

If the number of places available for Mexican students is limited, this means that the only other alternative are the schools in Mexico—and parents in Frontera believe they need to be improved. But local Frontera parents who send their children to Havens are not optimistic: "They forget us. We are so far away from Chihuahua City. And I want my children to learn English." The language-based motivation is strong, suggesting that however English is taught now on the Mexican side is not as effective as parents would like it to be.

These are the kinds of issues that bear serious discussion in meetings of school administrators and teachers from both sides of the border. How do you take the value of both sides and build structured educational experiences? It is, as are most things on the border, a complicated scenario in which language, culture, economic levels, educational resources, teaching priorities, and knowledge about schools are all inextricably linked. Identifying what the strength and capacity is on both sides of the border is not business as usual when it comes to education. Clearly there are important resources—although they are not economic at least in the local sense—south of the border. The conversation has to be binational because the situation already *is* binational—although it has been thought of alternatively as Havens' tradition or Havens' problem. These are conversations that need to go far beyond simply trying to straighten out a particular student's visa situation for purposes of schooling, or making sure that the border patrol allows parents whose children come over the border to school—and who may not have appropriate papers—be able to attend parent meetings or school performances with relative ease. Such friendly accommodations that provide immediate relief from specific personal difficulties arise from a loose cross-border, neighborly agreement about education. They are problem-specific interactions. Shifting the focus to what will be mutually beneficial, or agreeing to operate under what Stoddard has identified as a "doctrine of mutual necessity,"[14] changes the whole style of the conversation, signifying an end to a view of the border as a place that Mexican people leave, bringing little of value with them.

Marker 3: The Importance of Preserving What Is Special About Havens

A third marker of binational opportunity is the connection longtime residents—Anglo and Mexican-American alike—feel to their border community. Despite its shortcomings, despite its problems, despite the day-to-day absence of enough for the children to do and the shifting demographics, most people who live in Havens like it and want to make the community work better. They want to believe their children will come back to Havens after college or the military and will be able to find a secure job; they want their families to be together; they like the air, the water, the mountains, the schools, the close-knit feeling for which this community has traditionally been known. They like the uniqueness the border offers. It is a genuine feeling. But it is a tentative marker indeed until the question "what is worth preserving?" is asked—and what is worth strengthening—that could best lead to a stronger binational community. And once again, these are issues that involve dynamics both within Havens itself and between Havens and Frontera.

Within Havens, this third community marker raises the question of how to preserve the amicable tenor of life in Havens while paying close attention to the real quality of the relationships between Anglo and Mexican-origin people. It is within the community that relationships in school are embedded, and the whole idea of a serious binational goal hinges on how well Anglo and Mexican origin people get along on a deep—rather than only on a neighborly—level. From the perspective of families, it is already the case that marriage between Anglo and Mexican-origin people take place in Havens on a regular basis and are a strong foundation for building solid relationships between the cultures. It is an accepted part of life in Havens: a basketball coach, a state senator, a secretary in the school district, a principal, a social studies teacher, a bilingual education teacher, a store clerk, a prominent physician, the grandson of one of the area's most successful early Mexican ranchers, now Liliana Sanchez, and in the future perhaps Tony and Sandy, are all part of a large and growing group of Havens residents whose families are blended culturally. It is within these families that one or another member is likely to have relatives in Mexico, to visit them regularly, to recognize on a new level the meaning of the border as a region—in the simple terms of family. Families become the most solid basis for people learning to get along across cultures on a personal level, for heightening an understanding of the ethnic and cultural tensions that exist and demand action in Havens.

Closed circles exist, however, and what has become emblematic of the border as an entity that excludes is the small local country club, where several Mexican-American people whose families have been in Havens for generations regularly feel shut out even as they have begun to hold membership and participate in activities there. In other words, in Havens, as elsewhere, families are one thing and power relationships are another. Mexican-American residents of Havens are just beginning to participate in the community's power structure, to find the means to start more businesses, to become more active in the political process and in the schools. Relatively speaking it is a late awakening; it is a community that shies away from confrontation. So when some people in Havens talk about wanting to preserve a sense of community, what they really may be talking about is preserving the past, a past in which the founding Anglo power structure was not jeopardized. I am convinced that among Havens' longtime residents this is a minority, a small but stalwart group, as Richard Logan noted, that puts up borders as a matter of routine and that finds some support in newly arrived retirees. But when most old-timers and their children talk about preserving community in Havens, they are instead talking about preserving the sense that people know each other, that they are responsible to one another, and that—unlike other border communities—they do get along and support one another regardless which side of the line they reside. They are also talking about preserving the town in a physical sense—preserving the buildings, the neighborhoods, the sense of safety. It is out of genuine desire that these wishes emerge; there is a sense that something tangible is being lost.

Some of this is simple reminiscence, a yearning for keeping the town small in size when demographic shifts suggest otherwise. For others it is in direct response to an ongoing crisis in migrant housing that has forced the overcrowding of local buildings, especially in the downtown area, and the spilling over into the streets of poor transient workers. With the help of a nearby private agency, the community has finally—after much deliberation—responded to the migrant housing crisis, a marker in itself that is it possible to respond to local dilemmas creatively. In a town like Havens, though, each problem, each situation has the potential either to build or weaken cross-cultural community strength. If anticipating these repercussions is not a conscious part of the process, the results are always likely to have negative consequences for Havens' Mexican-origin citizens. For example, failing to respond more quickly to the migrant housing issue created a new language of bias against Mexican immigration, a continuing sense that the town is "going downhill."

There is an uncomfortable public silence about the reality that as a community, Havens is deeply affected by its location on the border. Save for the eventual willingness to develop a plan for migrant worker housing, little other structured activity exists in terms of welcoming newcomers to the community or considering whether this might be a good service to provide. New residents come and they make it or do not make it on their own or with the help of their families. There is no central location to provide information, to orient newcomers to life in Havens or in the United States in particular, to support a transition in anything other than a haphazard way. Locally, the club that Luis Estrada's mother belongs to is the one effort to take some action—ironically, on the part of newcomers who themselves are just learning English or becoming acclimatized. The schools and the community reflect each other in this regard: with the exception of one-way bilingual education classes, assistance is incidental and events happen informally, when an individual decides to take the initiative to act.

Proximity to the border, its citizens readily argue, is also exactly what makes Havens unique, what adds a cultural dimension that other small rural communities lack. Without the border, Havens is just another small town. But as a border community, it has a unique identity that is only partly encouraged to surface. The real test of commitment to community lies, it seems, in its willingness to acknowledge both legitimate threats to community (which more often than not are economic rather than cultural) as well as legitimate strengths, and then build on its strengths as a bulwark against a realistic assessment of the problems and challenges that do and will inevitably arise. It is not just a question of what Havens worries about losing, then, but what it consciously needs to build to be a viable border community. Biculturalism and bilingualism are community strengths, but they are now taken for granted in Havens and are not perceived as real resources in any kind of deep legitimate way.

And what is the role Mexico plays in building this concept of community? What kind of partner is Mexico, and what kind can it be? Actually, cross-border relationships are more publicly and more commonly recognized in terms of the community at large than they are in the schools. The relationship is probably best defined by what the local paper reports: the social relationships, the service club relationships, the charitable acts, and periodic cultural exchanges. But there are also reports of binational meetings to discuss issues like a cross-border tourist loop or specific highway needs that affect the region. These kinds of meetings provide a reality check that the border is a regional concern and not a series of problems left to the United States alone to solve. In actuality such meetings have taken place periodically for decades, but they have rarely focused on education. They also exist outside of any expectation that Havens might consciously work toward a more purposeful sense of its own bicultural character.

In the same way that paving highways or creating tourism are cross-border concerns, education needs to be understood and acted on as a cross-border concern as well and not just as a "problem" for Havens to solve. It is in Havens' schools where the greatest cross-border pressure is felt, not just because of the students who cross daily, but because of the way the border helps, de facto, to define the school population, its needs, and its goals. Addressing education as an ongoing shared concern rather than as an immediate and intractable problem places it among the other important and foundational community issues that already are thought of, or at the least are beginning to be thought of, as cross-border responsibilities.

As a marker of opportunity, the commitment to preserve community is also directly connected to the quality and health of the schools. Schools are a measure of the strength of small communities and they are often the focal point for community-wide activity. If the development of a stronger binational identity is a goal, then efforts that occur at the community and the school levels should be mutually reinforcing. As the schools work on language issues, for example, the question of language as a community-wide resource is an important part of the conversation. If the schools work to build a dual language program, how will the use of language look in Havens outside of the schools? Will the community view such a program as a centerpiece of its educational system, something that Havens can be uniquely proud of, something that extends real and unusual opportunity to its graduates? Will it clash? Can the community be viable if there is no place for acknowledging the cultural celebrations of its Mexican-origin citizens? Is it appropriate for a community like Havens to ignore an event like Cinco de Mayo? Is there a way to cultivate cross-border celebrations for specific major holidays as a means of educating the region's citizens about both sides of the border without expecting dual allegiance in the narrow nationalistic sense of the word? If the schools undertake such celebrations, how will the community react? Likewise, is there a way to elevate both languages on formal occasions so the need for and appreciation of being bilingual is extended into the community at the same time it may be strengthened in the schools?

In both the community and school arenas, there is substantial need to open up dialogue about who the schools are serving well and whose needs are not being met. In this context, school-based activities that are trying to bring cultural awareness and cultural self-understanding to the school, or activities like the NHI that are trying to provide a structure in which Mexican-origin students can reach higher levels of achievement and leadership, are also markers of opportunity. Issues of equity are not isolated concerns only for the schools; they are serious community matters. The last page of the local history of Sonora County perhaps speaks best to the need for this public community dialogue. It is a page dedicated by a prominent Anglo businessman in Havens to a particular Mexican-American individual, Solomon Chavez, who came to Havens from Mexico in the 1870s and lived there until his death at the age of 116. It is a dedication that honestly acknowledges in writing the history of discrimination in the community more than in any other place I could locate and, in a sense, implores the Anglo community to do better. It is a dedication that also portrays the enduring hierarchy in the community as well as in the schools, one in which Mexican-origin people are to be thanked—as guests more than anything else rather than as equals—for their presence:

> Clarence Stevenson knew Solomon Chavez very well and has dedicated this page in honor of him, but not only for him alone. This page is an expression of gratitude from Clarence and Margaret Stevenson for all of the Mexican-American residents of Sonora County who stayed, raised fine children, overcame hardships, forgave discrimination and prejudice, and helped to make the County what it is today, warm, friendly, intelligent, progressive and prosperous. It is their hope that the misunderstandings of the past may be put aside forever and that all Sonora Countians be proud of their heritage, going forward into a future of friendship, freedom of expression, and understanding.

The heritage that the Stevensons are alluding to is still not clear even in this tribute. Their vision of the future is also not clear. But what seems certain is that it will be easier to assume more of the identity of a binational community in the future the more it is permissible to speak about and debate issues of ethnicity, class, achievement, and opportunity—for the community and for the schools. Obviously there are no simple answers, especially when the relationship between ethnicity and social class is considered. But it is a relationship that is not going away soon; most people newly arriving from Mexico are not likely to be economically secure, migrant families in the United States are among the lowest on the economic scale, children continue coming to school without knowing English, high paying jobs are scarce, and students who drop out of school curtail their potential for good employment. The more Havens is a place where, based on the personal friendships and family relationships that exist between Anglo and Mexican people, these issues can at least be discussed, the more likely it is that action can be taken, that new possibilities can be imagined, or that a collective consideration of new social norms might be created.

Opportunity, Civic Creativity, and Constraint: Companions on the Border

Life on the border of the United States and Mexico is filled with contradictions. The border is rich with culture and language, but generally poor in economic resources. It is filled with newcomers whose people in reality are much older, original inhabitants of the region than are their Anglo neighbors. It is rich in its awareness that life does not end in the United States or begin in Mexico, but it is difficult to know exactly how to create an integrated life that is regional and includes both sides. It is dependent on cross-border commerce, but schools on neither side prepare students well in terms of language for this eventual real life necessity. Havens, unlike its larger counterparts like El Paso–Juarez or San Diego–Tijuana, is an isolated, rural western region, more used to the stereotypical cowboy's individualistic, rugged, western way of life than one that may require collective decision making and action to foster progress.

It is these contradictions that can fuel the creative act—whether it is an act of personal creativity, as the new border authors and artists see it, or an act of *civic creativity*, which seems to be the challenge for Havens. The presence of the border forces people in Havens to recognize the complexity of the choices they face; the door to another world, which in fact is their world, is just a short drive away. Contradictions like these create opportunity; they form an inherent invitation to move beyond what is commonplace, regular, and routine, instead taking the stance, "What does it mean to be a viable community on the border in the 21st century and how can we get there?" This civic cultivation of opportunity can lead to a whole raft of questions. Relying on a collective creativity, what is it possible to achieve? How might we distinguish ourselves as a community? What do we have to build on, and what do we need to create? What are we doing well, and what must we recognize we are not doing well? What is reasonable to provide as a border community, and what is it reasonable for our friends on the Frontera side to provide?

Questions like these can take the action out of the realm of "helping Mexico" and shift the conversation into the realm of the regional culture that has always existed, into the unmistakable hemispheric reality that has always been a feature of life in Havens and Frontera. It is a hemispheric reality that bears greater attention today than ever before because the pressures on Havens are greater, and because it will clearly take more than Havens alone can offer to nurture a robust binationalism that works for both sides of the border. Determining what kind of schools figure into this larger community goal is crucial precisely because the schools are such a central, public reflection of the community itself and of its values. The schools are markers of civic creativity; at HHS, it is by weaving the personal creativity of teachers and students into a larger context so that civic or institutional creativity can be bolstered. Ideally, these forms of creativity interact in mutually reinforcing ways.

A place filled with opportunity does not guarantee that opportunity is limitless. In Havens, the human and fiscal resources to act on creative solutions may be limited. Left alone, the schools in Havens have honored their commitment to cross-border responsibility and identity chiefly by their local generosity in educating students from Mexico. It is from an honest desire to acknowledge the realities of a regional border life that this practice has continued. But this is only a small part of the cross-border picture, one that in isolation too easily causes other crucial needs that can more richly promote binational capacity to receive less attention—like developing a strong program of dual language learning. If, in fact, the test of a nation's generosity is its variety, an institutionalized appreciation for linguistic and cultural variety as it naturally occurs in the region that includes Havens and Frontera is the opportunity that already has fledgling roots in Havens. Yet a serious commitment to dual language learning, to creating educational environments that actively honor the bicultural character of the students and their families, or to launching structured teacher and student exchange programs with schools in the Frontera region will require progressively more complex and more costly programmatic efforts. The schools will require many strong leaders for dual language learning, for example, or to bring equity issues to the table. It will take know-how, moxie, and some shaking up in a community that has its own tempo and style of making change, but that is, de facto, already steeped in its own border identity and cross-border commitments.

To be sure, it is easier to be generous when unlimited resources are available to solve complex problems. To venture beyond its own current limits will likely require a confluence of local leadership and external resources that identifies Havens as a target of binational opportunity. Although the activity required to enact a more complex binational consciousness is local, as a small, rural, and relatively poor community, Havens is unlikely to be able to bear all the pressure to build that capacity alone.

The border deserves our attention as a region of serious cultural and economic opportunity. In the southwest today, a community and its schools can either be overwhelmed by the border, or they can grasp hold of the border as the source of opportunity it represents. In Havens, this opportunity is within reach—principally because the community has steadfastly rejected an adversarial view of the border that seems to be the norm in so many other places. But past local and neighborly practice is not likely to be powerful enough to retain this unusual stance as the demographics shift and the world shrinks. Rooted in its bilingual and bicultural past, and limited only by the degree to which it wishes to embrace those roots, Havens is poised to become a fully binational community, one in which its schools develop citizens who embrace the regional character of their lives and who can negotiate life on both sides of the political border in Spanish and English. Its historical insistence on a quiet life on the border provides a departure point that is rare along the 2,000 miles that divide, and yet bring together the United States and Mexico.

Epilogue

I read the daily paper from Havens. It arrives a week late, and I know from the months I lived in Havens that it does not provide the most complete coverage. It is a distant window on life there, but from the distance I nevertheless learn from it. The schools, to no surprise, continue to be the focal point of much of the news. Sports teams are doing well and some former students are accruing scholarships, graduating from college, and taking important positions in local and national companies and institutions. Others are in the armed forces, and yet others are struggling and are involved in local petty crime. Marriages continue to be announced, some between Mexican-Americans, some between Anglos, and some that are bicultural. The local youth center is soundly on its feet and is finally providing a place for after school and weekend activities. A little more Spanish seems to have crept into the *Havens Star* over the years, with more announcements and a periodic translation of an article. I see this as progress. Carmen Mendoza, one of the district's first bilingual education teachers, is retiring. Like her predecessor Ana Herrera, she will undoubtedly claim a well-deserved page in the next volume of the local history of Havens. The schools need more money, as do most schools in New Mexico, and particularly those on the border.

In the meantime, new federal immigration laws mean that the only students from Mexico who can readily attend school in Havens are those who are U.S. citizens or who establish legal residency in Havens. This policy cuts off some of those who to date have been students at HHS—and high schools all along the border—and who now are barred from completing their high school educations because they are Mexican citizens. But it is a small percentage of Mexican students who cross the border each day; the majority of the border-crossing students in Havens have always been U.S. citizens residing in Mexico, and this is not likely to change anytime soon.

So notwithstanding the national furor over immigration, and the extraordinarily antagonistic atmosphere created by recent immigration legislation, many things in Havens have still not changed much on a day-to-day basis. Life on the border here, and for the schools in particular, continues to require attention to the binational, bicultural character of the students who will complete their educations in Havens. Students will continue to come from Mexico to school in Havens and will continue to require some form of bilingual education program to make their transition, and their learning, possible. The gap between Mexican-American and Anglo students, most evident in achievement, will continue to require focused attention and hard work.

And the community will remain essentially what it is: a small, rural town isolated on the border. It is unlikely to garner more than passing attention. The uneven effects of NAFTA, the ever-present question of which crops will dominate and which will be picked by hand or by machine will continue to have implications for sorely needed jobs on both sides of the border. The social impact of its border location in the community and in its schools, the economic levels of its citizens, and the potential shift away from agriculture all indicate that Havens will require a combination of private, state, and federal monies to grow and develop. As other, larger border communities might reap the benefits of cross-border trade and attention to the border, such regard is likely to bypass Havens. Large companies like IBM are not likely to make Havens one of their locations and singlehandedly infuse the resources that are needed. Whatever jobs can be created will not be enough to support the infrastructure that is needed in terms of social services and education.

It will undoubtedly take both local energy and focused political work in Santa Fe, Washington, and Chihuahua City to strengthen this community and its schools and to assist in the development of the region surrounding Havens as a strong binational community. It will also take moving away from a bilateral view of the frontier to a view that is based on enabling people to live together well. Gustavo Esteva promotes the notion of "hospitality" as a way of bypassing the concept of frontiers as divisive or as places where cultural difference is merely tolerated.[1] In Havens, "hospitality" has been at the foundation of what people have been trying to accomplish in their cross-border relationships. Even as the concept of hospitality must be preserved as the foundation of a regional lifestyle, if the border is to be seen as the binational regional entity it is, it will take going beyond hospitality to build a richer, more deliberate cross-border life in Havens and its environs.

* * *

And where does this all fit now? No longer living on the border, what do I do with the refrain I live with each day? Clearly, something clicks in when I am in schools with large groups of immigrants from Mexico and from Central America. Their stories make sense, their lives have a sensual counterpart that smells of sand, mesquite, and the acrid scent of roasting fresh chile. I am invited to a local *quinceañera* and am instantly transported to the church in Frontera where I first attended such an event. These are issues of memory, though; they exist on a personal scale that is embedded within an issue of much higher stakes. How we perceive the border and how we act—whether proximally or distantly—to contribute to the development of a reasonable, tolerant, hospitable, and yes, binational life on the border is the creative act in which we are obliged to participate as the millenium, which is unmistakably global, approaches.

Notes

Chapter 1

1. The Border Research Institute at the University of New Mexico–Las Cruces keeps these statistics. These data are from a February 1993 publication.

2. Gloria Anzaldúa, in her book *Borderlands / La Frontera: The New Mestiza* (1987), makes a distinction between the border as a line and the *borderlands* as an area that results from this unnatural line (p. 3).

3. The Treaty of Guadalupe Hidalgo set the borders between Mexico and the United States until 1853, when the Gadsden Purchase was finalized. This purchase extended the U.S. border to include the territory in which Havens is located.

4. C. L. Sonnichsen, (1961), *The El Paso Salt War*, (p. 4).

5. Carey Mc Williams, (1990), *North from Mexico: The Spanish Speaking People of the United States,* (p. 66).

6. This is a term that is infrequently heard only in the southern part of the state, but is common in the north. *Hispano* is used to distinguish families whose origins were directly with the early Spanish settlers from those whose families came directly from Mexico. A class distinction is often implied with this term.

7. Oscar Martinez, (1988), *Troublesome Border*, (pp. 114–115). Martinez ties the "culture of sin" on the border to the end of the 19th century.

8. According to the 1990 Census, per capita income in the state of New Mexico is slightly over $14,000, ranking 46th among all the states. Statewide, between 16% and 17% of the population lives below the poverty level.

9. The explanation offered by Oscar Martinez (1988) is that the border naturally produces what he called "tension-generating circumstances" (p. 6), and that local people have regularly solved such problems informally without taking into account what is strictly legal.

10. M. Lipsky, (1976), *Toward a Theory of Street Level Bureaucracy*.

11. Goode, Schneider, and Blanc (1992), identified how different school contexts can provide different kinds and levels of support for immigrant

students, and that schools can differentially "help create, reinforce, or transcend boundaries" (p. 209). The quality of various programs in bilingual education and support has also been studied by Robert Dentler and Anne Hafner in their book, *Hosting Newcomers* (1997).

12. This edition of the show was aired on PBS on January 2, 1995.

13. As Carey Mc Williams noted, the *bracero* program enabled farmers on the U.S. side of the border to assure themselves a steady flow of cheap labor that was legally sanctioned and sponsored by the U.S. government. *Braceros* were allowed to come into the United States legally during the harvest season and then often returned to Mexico. Officially, according to Meier and Ribera (1993), the *bracero* program ended in 1964.

Chapter 2

1. The gifted anthropologist and writer, the late Barbara Myerhoff (1979), described this occupational hazard for those who engage in fieldwork in her book, *Number Our Days*:

> The amount and variety of information accumulated in a field study is overwhelming. There is no definite or correct solution to the problem of what to include, how to cut up the pie of social reality, when precisely to leave or stop. Often there is little clarity as to whom to include as "members," what to talk about with those who are. The deliberate avoidance of preconditions is likely to result in the best fieldwork, allowing the group or subject to dictate the form the description ultimately takes. But there is always a high degree of arbitrariness involved. Choices must be made and they are extremely difficult, primarily because of what and who must be omitted. (pp. 28–29)

2. I hesitate to use the common qualitative terminology "informant" to describe the friendship Liliana and I developed over the course of my stay in Havens. On one hand, that is the role Liliana often played; I learned about the school and the community from her. On the other hand, and put more simply, we connected as human beings and our relationship continues, however sporadically, to be a close one. Although she certainly informed my study of Havens, she did so, I hope, as a function of our relationship and the contribution it made (and continues to make) to both of our lives.

3. Matt Meier and Feliciano Ribera, (1993), *Mexican Americans/American Mexicans: From Conquistadors to Chicanos*. The story of discrimination in the schools has been chronicled by Thomas P. Carter (1970) in *Mexican Americans in School: A History of Educational Neglect*.

4. Matute-Bianchi's (1991) study classifies immigrants according to their primary place of identification. Although Gabriela fits closest to

the category of being Mexican-oriented, unlike the students in Matute-Bianchi's group she did not reject her Mexican-American peers.

5. The 1986 Simpson–Rodino Immigration Reform and Control Act (IRCA) provided for these amnesty privileges. Two categories of amnesty were created. One was for multiyear, continuous residents and the other was a special category for farmworkers (the *Special Agricultural Worker [SAW]* category).

6. The citizenship classes to which Maria was referring were classes that were initially taken as part of the amnesty program. In Havens these classes were started by a Mexican-American man, Juan Garcia, a longtime resident who was active in the local labor community. During the year I lived in Havens he was joined in these efforts by Olga Suarez, who at the same time was organizing a culture club/support group of newly immigrated Mexican women in the community.

7. A similar grant proposal was finally approved and funded, and the program was implemented in 1997.

Chapter 3

1. "I salute the flag of New Mexico and the Zia symbol of perfect friendship among united cultures." *Saludo la bandera del estado de Nuevo Méjico, el simbolo Zía de amistad perfecto entre culturas unidas.*

2. McWilliams, *ibid.*; Meier and Ribera, *ibid.*

3. Carter, *ibid.*

4. These requirements appear in Article XII. Section 10 of this article, which includes the language regarding equality, and concludes with the mandate that this particular requirement can never be amended except by a vote of the people of the state.

5. See Castellanos (1983), Gonzalez (1990), San Miguel (1987), and Carter, *ibid.*

6. Mc Williams, *ibid.*, p. 265.

7. Gonzalez, *ibid.*

8. Castellanos, *ibid.*, pp. 28–29.

9. San Miguel, *ibid.*, Moore, (1970).

10. Gonzalez, *ibid.*

11. There is a persistent myth promulgated in the United States that immigrants, and especially Latino immigrants, do not wish to learn English. But Crawford (1991) indicated that Hispanics as well as members of other minority groups already acknowledge the importance of learning English and in fact that Hispanic children regularly do so. Valdés (1996) noted this as well.

12. Meier and Ribera, *ibid.*

Chapter 4

1. Tse (1995) described the prevalence of language brokering on the part of Latino high school students, noting that every student in her sample engaged in brokering. She makes an important distinction between *translating*, where the intention is to preserve the meaning of the original message, and *brokering*, where students regularly change the meaning and thus influence how their families and others for whom they broker make decisions.

2. According to Crawford (1991), the Lau Remedies, which were invoked in 1975, told school districts "how to identify and evaluate children with limited English skills, what instructional treatments would be appropriate, when children would be ready for mainstream classrooms, and what professional standards teachers should meet. Also, they set timetables for meeting these goals" (p. 37).

3. Despite the potential of two-way bilingual education, Crawford notes that it remains only a slowly growing approach—the exception rather than the rule—to the complex issue of language learning in American schools.

4. Crawford, *ibid.*

5. Krashen (1996) identified the critical importance of "comprehensible input" for second language learners, that is, messages that make sense to the listener, but that also stretch the listener just beyond the point of easy understanding in the new language (i.e., English).

6. Macias (1990) documented the lack of knowledge regarding schooling and curriculum in Mexico among receiving U.S. school districts.

7. These three aspects of a strong bilingual education program are identified by Krashen (1996) as essential criteria to high quality programs. The second is weak in Havens.

8. Krashen (1996) noted that one way to deflect exaggerated criticism regarding bilingual education is to insure that programs are above reproach in terms of their quality.

9. Although such an intensive course might solve the immediate problem of interaction in the schools, a well-supported body of research indicates that it typically takes 5 to 7 years in order for students to acquire deep language knowledge that will enable them to participate successfully in higher level academic classes.

10. Tse, *ibid.*

11. Crawford, *ibid.*, Krashen, *ibid.*

12. Krashen, *ibid.*

Chapter 5

1. At HHS it is common for female students to hold the position of managers of the male sports teams.

2. The problems with academic tracking are discussed extensively in Jeannie Oakes (1985) text, *Keeping Track*.

3. The border has long been described as a place characterized more by a regional rather than a national culture. Early border scholars like McWilliams (1990) recognized this and the appropriateness of the concept of a region has been corroborated by more current border scholars like Oscar Martinez (1988) and countless others.

4. Michael Olneck (1995) summarized studies in this regard in a chapter in the *Handbook of Research on Multicultural Education* entitled, "Immigrants and Education."

5. Olneck, *ibid*.

6. James Banks (1997) described 4 levels for the integration of ethnic content, ranging from contributions and discrete cultural elements to social action as a means of transforming society.

7. Sonia Nieto (1992) identified structural, linguistic, and cultural factors that all contribute to school failure because of their capacity to result in unfair treatment of students who are not members of the dominant group in a given school or school district.

8. Nieto, *ibid*.

9. In addition to general studies of the problems of academic tracking (e.g., Oakes), the specific problem of treating vocational education as a "dead end" track and the importance of high quality vocational programs was explicitly addressed by the National Council of La Raza (1993) as an important educational issue that deserves attention.

10. The general question of how to reform and renew secondary schools in America has been the focal point of the work of the Coalition of Essential Schools under the leadership of Theodore Sizer (1984).

Chapter 6

1. Gloria Anzaldúa (1987) explores the border as a personal metaphor in her book *Borderlands / La Frontera*.

2. Renato Rosaldo (1989) explores the complexity of border life and the need to openly study the heterogeneity of its culture in his book *Culture and Truth*.

3. Anzaldúa, *ibid*.

4. Anzaldúa, *ibid*.

5. Carger's (1996) book describes the school experiences of a Mexican-American youth who was a student of Carger's in Chicago.

6. Ruth Behar (1993) in *Translated Woman*, p. 320.

7. This metaphor is used both by Stavans (1993) and Anzaldúa.

8. Anzaldúa, p. 3.

9. As reported in *The New York Times*, February 8, 1996, p. A15.

10. Martinez, ibid.

11. Jose Macias (1990) introduced the concept of "scholastic antecedents" and their importance as information for receiving teachers in American schools.

12. Anzaldúa, *ibid.*

13. Stoddard's (1984) concept speaks to the fundamental interdependence of the area and the need for recognition on multiple levels—local, federal, and international—that working together to build stronger border communities is an essential binational act.

Epilogue

1. In his writing on development, Esteva (1987) identified "hospitality" in opposition to "tolerance," specifically stating that when the ideology of the frontier as an inviolable dividing line dominates, no spaces exist where people are meant to come together collectively as one means of acknowledging and respecting others.

References

Anzaldúa, G. (1987). *Borderlands/La Frontera: The new Mestiza.* San Francisco: Aunt Lute Press.

Banks, J. A. (1997). *Teaching strategies for ethnic studies* (6th ed.). Boston: Allyn & Bacon.

Behar, R. (1993). *Translated woman.* Boston: Beacon.

Border Research Institute. (1993, February). *New Mexico border crossings overview.* Las Cruces: New Mexico State University.

Carger, C. L. (1996). *Of borders and dreams: A Mexican-American experience of urban education.* New York: Teachers College Press.

Carter, T. P. (1970). *Mexican Americans in school: A history of educational neglect.* New York: College Entrance Examination Board.

Castellanos, D. (1983). *The best of two worlds: Bilingual-bicultural education in the U.S.* Trenton: New Jersey State Department of Education.

Crawford, J. (1991). *Bilingual education: History, politics, theory and practice* (2nd ed.). Los Angeles: Bilingual Educational Services, Inc.

Dentler, R. A., & Hafner, A. L. (1997). *Hosting newcomers: Structuring educational opportunities for immigrant children.* New York: Teachers College Press.

Esteva, G. (1987). Regenerating people's space. *Alternatives, 12*(198), 125–163.

Gonzalez, N. L. (1990). *The Spanish-Americans of New Mexico: A heritage of pride.* Albuquerque: The University of New Mexico Press.

Goode, J. G., Schneider, J. A., & Blanc, S. (1992). Transcending boundaries and closing ranks: How schools shape interrelations. In L. Lamphere (ed.), *Structuring diversity: Ethnographic perspectives on the new immigration* (pp. 173–213). Chicago: The University of Chicago Press.

Krashen, S. D. (1996). *Under attack: The case against bilingual education.* Culver City, CA: Language Education Associates.

Lipsky, M. (1976). Toward a theory of street level bureaucracy. In W. Hawley & M. Lipsky (eds.), *Theoretical perspectives on urban politics* (pp. 186–212). Englewood Cliffs, NJ: Prentice-Hall.

Macias, J. (1990). Scholastic antecedents of immigrant students: Schooling in a Mexican immigrant-sending community. *Anthropology and Education Quarterly, 21,* 291–318.

Martinez, O. J. (1988). *Troublesome border* (PROFMEX Monograph Series). Tucson: The University of Arizona Press.

Matute-Bianchi, M. E. (1991). Situational ethnicity and patterns of school performance among immigrant and non immigrant Mexican-descent students. In M. A. Gibson & J. U. Ogbu (Eds.), *Minority status and schooling: A comparative study of immigrant and involuntary minorities* (pp. 205–247). New York: Garland.

McDonnell, L. M., & Hill, P. T. (1993). *Newcomers in American schools: Meeting the educational needs of immigrant youth.* Santa Monica, CA: Rand Center for Research on Immigration Policy.

McWilliams, C. (1990). *North from Mexico: The Spanish speaking people of the United States* [New edition, updated by M. S. Meier]. New York: Praeger.

Meier, M. S., & Ribera, F. (1993). *Mexican Americans / American Mexicans: From conquistadors to Chicanos* (2nd ed. of *The Chicanos*). New York: Hill and Wang.

Moore, J. W., with H. Pachon. (1970). *Mexican Americans.* Englewood Cliffs, NJ: Prentice-Hall.

Myerhoff, B. (1979). *Number our days: Culture and community among elderly Jews in an American ghetto.* New York: Meridian.

National Council of La Raza. (1993). *The forgotten two-thirds: An Hispanic perspective on apprenticeship, European style* (Report of the NCLR Consultation on Apprenticeship). Washington, DC: Author.

Nieto, S. (1992). *Affirming diversity.* New York: Longman.

Oakes, J. (1985). *Keeping track: How schools structure inequality.* New Haven, CT: Yale University Press.

Olneck, M. R. (1995). Immigrants and education. In J. A. Banks (ed.), *Handbook of research on multicultural education* (pp. 310–327). New York: Macmillan.

Open, Sesame. (1996, February 8). *The New York Times*, p. A15.

Rosaldo, R. (1989). *Culture and truth: The remaking of social analysis.* Boston: Beacon.

San Miguel, G. (1987). *"Let all of them take heed." Mexican-Americans and the campaign for educational equality in Texas, 1910-1981.* Austin: University of Texas Press.

Sizer, T. R. (1984). *Horace's compromise: The dilemma of the American high school.* Boston: Houghton Mifflin.

Sonnichsen, C. L. (1961). *The El Paso salt war* (1877). El Paso, TX: Carl Hertzog and the Texas Western Press.

Stavans, I. (1993). Foreword. In H. Augenbraum & I. Stavans (eds.), *Growing up Latino: Memoirs and stories* (pp. xi–xiii). New York: Houghton Mifflin.

Stoddard, E. R. (1984). Northern Mexican migration and the United States border region. *New Scholar, 9*, 51–72.

Tse, L. (1995). Language brokering among Latino adolescents: Prevalence, attitudes, and school performance. *Hispanic Journal of Behavioral Sciences, 17*(2), 180–193.

Valdés, G. (1996). *Con respeto: Bridging the distance between culturally diverse families and schools.* New York: Teachers College Press.

Index

About the Author

Marleen C. Pugach is professor of education in the Department of Curriculum and Instruction at the University of Wisconsin–Milwaukee, where she directs the elementary teacher education program. She completed her doctoral studies in 1983 at the University of Illinois at Urbana–Champaign with a dual emphasis in teacher education and special education.

Most of Dr. Pugach's work focuses on how well-intentioned school programs like special education regularly result in the marginalization of children and youth (and especially minority children and youth), and how teacher preparation can be reconfigured to diminish such practices. With a particular commitment to preparing teachers for urban schools, she is concerned with clarifying the relation between special education and cultural diversity/multicultural education.

Her previous works include *Encouraging Reflective Practice in Education* (1990), *Collaborative Practitioners, Collaborative Schools* (1995), *Curriculum Trends, Special Education, and Reform: Refocusing the Conversation* (1996), and *Teacher Education in Transition: Collaborative Programs to Prepare General and Special Educators* (1997). In 1998, Dr. Pugach received the Margaret Lindsey Award for Distinguished Research in Teacher Education from the American Association of Colleges for Teacher Education.

Dr. Pugach teaches research courses in qualitative methodology in the Urban Education Doctoral Program at the University of Wisconsin–Milwaukee.